Is That All There Is?

What Are You Doing for the Rest of Your Life?

BY

Bruce Turkel

FOREWORD BY CHRIS CROWLEY,
NEW YORK TIMES BESTSELLING AUTHOR OF *YOUNGER NEXT YEAR*

Is That All There Is?

What Are You Doing for
the rest of Your Life?

Copyright 2021, Bruce Turkel
https://bruceturkel.com

ISBN: 978-1-7373790-0-3

*To my wife and love of my life Gloria who has
stood by me and supported me every time I asked
"Is That All There Is?"*

The search for a purpose in our lives is universal and will never change.

— Ferry Porsche

Contents

Foreword

CHRIS CROWLEY, New York Times bestselling author of *Younger Next Year*

Bʀᴜᴄᴇ kindly asked me to write a foreword to this book. I am honored because I have such a warm regard for him and his book. But I am also tickled to pitch in on its merits.

Because I have been thinking and writing about this stuff for a while, I have become a proselytizer for making fundamental change—or at least considering it and *deciding* to change. In my experience it is one of the most important things we can do.

Good old Thoreau was right: Only the "examined life" is worth living. Making the decision to change is part of that. It is much easier to coast—to stick with what we're doing. And plenty of us have to do that for financial and other reasons. But coasting has its costs, too. Like a plant that's kept in a small pot for too long, you can get root-bound. Sometimes the answer is to re-pot yourself, as hard as that may seem. And sometimes it is not. But thinking and deciding about it is a good idea, regardless.

As you'll read later on, I re-potted myself twice in this life: once when I was five years out of college and went off to law school—with a wife and three kids and a dog and a cat in tow. It worked like gangbusters. It turned my small, boring life into a pretty big one, and a beauty. And a second time, at 56, when I retired after 25 years as a litigation partner in a wonderful New York firm to become a ski bum and a writer. Both decisions were scary, against-the-odds, and dangerous; the second one cost me a fortune. But they were the two best thing I ever did. Maybe that gives me some authority to write about the subject and maybe it just makes me dangerously optimistic. But where I come out as far as advice to readers is concerned, is that—if the notion of profound change is on your mind all the time—it makes a ton of sense to think the possibilities through carefully. Really carefully and slowly. And then make the best decision you can. If you're forced to make a change on the run because the ship is going down, think about it while you race for the lifeboats. And then decide, while you're teetering in the davits. Bruce's book of living examples will help inform that process.

Your resource here is Bruce and the stories he has collected. They are going to get you thinking. But to get started, here are a couple of thoughts which may help you frame your consideration of what you're about to read:

First, it takes deep resolve, energy, and determination to make a conscious, profound change. If you haven't been thinking about it a lot already—if you're not deeply uncomfortable where you are or yearning to be somewhere else—then maybe to hell with it. Sounds like your life is pretty good.

Another one: It makes a lot of sense to take an inventory of your gifts. Are you a words or numbers person? Are you a people-person or more comfortable one-on-one? Are you a speaker or does that notion terrify you? Can you write? Can you fight? Can you lead? Some people are natural motivators, natural leaders, others simply are not. Those talents are gifts, and they are parceled out unequally at birth.

Some people love the idea of sticking their face in someone else's face in a cross-examination or a tough negotiation; some are absolutely horrified at that. My daughter came to court once to hear me cross examine a New York City police lieutenant in a major case to promote more Black and Hispanic cops. The blatant confrontation literally made her nauseated; she had to leave the room. One of her daughters went off to law school last fall. She loves the prospect of confrontation, the dear girl, and she's good at it. I so look forward to seeing her in court. Maybe it skips a generation.

Make a long list of your gifts, with the outstanding ones on top, and a short list of stuff you dread. Study it and rearrange it and think about it hard. How come? The great key to happiness in life is using your best gifts at the highest end you can. It just plain feels good and makes you more effective and happier. I had one job for three years that was at war with my gifts. It was agony; I've never been so wretched in my life. I didn't just hate the job; I was starting to hate myself. I've had two jobs since that were a perfect fit, and they took up most of my life, which has been a joy. Using your best gifts is, in a way, like being your true self. If you have a job or a life where you cannot be yourself, oh boy. I've tried it. It's a kind of hell.

Third: Change alone is a virtue. One of the realizations that hit me like a truck when I was in my fifties was that we only have one life to live. I was living a beauty and knew I wouldn't be as good at anything else. But after a bit, I began to want to live more than one life—wanted it with a force that caused me to give up that career and sail off into something entirely differ-ent, at great risk. And it worked. Against great odds. But here's a caveat: by that time I could afford it even if it were a total financial failure.

Don't look down on incremental change. It gives much of the satisfaction of change with less risk and more probability of success. You'll read several stories like that here. One of my personal favorites is about a New York lawyer whom I admired. He'd been the head of a leading firm. When it came time for him to hand over his responsibilities, he offered to go to Moscow with a couple of associates and open a new office in a thoroughly different world. He was doing the same stuff at one level. But it was a trip to the moon, too. He thrived on it.

Key one: be realistic about dough. We may be able to live on less, but we can't live below a certain level. Financial pain can kill you. We can live on less than we are used to, but we can't live on air. You have to figure that out for yourself. But may I also say that living on much less is worth it if you are chasing the dream. Read Michelle Obama's book, the part where they look at the financial risk of his giving up a great, traditional job to run for office. Great stuff. Hilly and I live on some 20% of my old income. We surely notice that, but it's fine. We needed less than we thought, and it was so worth it.

Thinking hard about living with much less is good policy in general. We all tend to assume that our peak earning is the norm and it's always going to be that way. Maybe, but I doubt it, and you should, too. Everyone should have a cut-down plan, maybe a deep one. Shit happens, as we liked to say back in the sixties— divorce, illness, failure of a company or a whole industry, a plague. Have a plan. Or you can just wait and crawl under the bed. See how that works for you.

If finances and other issues dictate that you cannot take chances, by all means stay put. Or limit yourself to careful, incremental changes. They, too, can be deeply satisfying—not quite as romantic as running off and being an elderly ski bum, but stuff like that really has to be fully funded. If we hadn't made a dime in our second life, we'd have been okay.

Some people make fundamental change by conscious decision. Good for them. Others have fundamental change thrust upon them—the guy racing for the life-boat. They retire or get fired or—like one wonderful woman in this book—they get sent to prison. They have to create new lives, on the run. Oddly enough, a lot of people who simply retire and have plenty of time to think and plan do the same thing; they just launch into the next phase without a thought. Hate to be mean, but that's dumb. Maybe it was okay in the old days when you retired at 65, played a few rounds of golf, and died. Fine. But now, the likelihood is that you'll live into your 80s or 90s. Retirement is going to be a huge section of your life. It makes great sense to plan for that every bit as carefully as you planned for your first career. People think of retirement as if it were a vacation or a sabbatical—as if it were a chance to get in more golf. Well, it is. But, unless you're a hell of a golfer, you may get bored after the first ten or twenty years. Better to plan for a *life,* not a vacation.

Fundamental change. Very hard. Very rare, really. But it can be done and it can be wonderful. Read the book. Think about it. Could be pretty good. Could be amazing.

Inspiration

Wʜᴇɴ songwriting duo Jerry Leiber and Mike Stoller played their song "Is That All There Is?" for singer Peggy Lee, her response was, "This is the story of my life! How did you know?"

Although the lyrics to Leiber and Stoller's song might suggest a despondent view of life, Lee didn't see it that way. In her own words: "It's about the experiences you go through in life, necessary for growth.... The attitude has a lot to do with how we survive. If you can love work enough to take the dues you have to pay, it's worth it. If not, there must be something else you can do to make you happy."

Maybe you've reached a stage in your life where your relative level of success doesn't seem to be enough. Perhaps you've felt the that there must be something else out there. Perhaps you, too, believe there's "something else you can do to make you happy."

Perhaps you're feeling that way right now.

If so, this book is for you.

1

The Plumber's House Leaks and the Carpenter's House Creaks

Is THAT all there is?

Surely there must be more to life than this!

If you've built a successful business, achieved a certain station, or attained a certain degree of comfort, you may even feel guilty when these whines of discontent appear in your head. *What's wrong with me? I have everything I fought for! What right do I have to not be happy?*

Whether there's something you'd just rather be doing, or you're not sure what that *something* is but you'd just rather be doing anything but *this*, you're grappling with a normal, uncomfortable aspect of being human. Think of it as a second adolescence—a time ripe with promise and fraught with contradiction.

After about twenty years of running my advertising agency, I noticed an interesting pattern. More and more of my friends were making appointments to visit my office to talk to me about their careers. Many of them were successful lawyers, accountants, doctors, and businesspeople. I even met with a childhood friend from Los Angeles who had built a spectacularly successful career producing movies. His filmography includes famous movies you know and you have probably watched.

Though each of my friends and their situations were different, they all said the same thing: Each was unhappy with what they were doing, unmotivated by the money they were making, and bored with their lives. Many of them had reached enviable levels of success but no longer found their day-to-day activities interesting, fulfilling, or satisfying.

So were they coming to me?

They told me they could see what I was doing and thought it was what they wanted to do, too. They liked the creative nature of my job. They were interested in writing or design or shooting commercials or speaking at industry events or whatever it was they saw me doing that they thought they'd enjoy. And they all concluded that because I was growing my agency, creating great work, and looking like I was having a great time that I had it all figured out.

What they didn't know—and what I was embarrassed to tell them—was that I was just as bored as they were.

Maybe even more.

I started to see a pattern. Once I realized how similar everyone's complaints seemed to be, I started sharing my observations and telling my friends how common their complaints were. Of course, I didn't share any names and I didn't betray any confidences, but I did tell my distraught friends that they weren't alone in their discontent. If misery loved company, it would make my friends feel better to know that more and more of their peers were suffering from the same sense of ennui that they were.

Though I didn't have any good advice for them, I offered a list of ideas I thought they could try. Most consistently, I suggested that there was an opportunity for any one of them to be the voice in the darkness. They could recreate their lives around being a resource for an entire generation of affluent, educated, vital, involved people who seemed to have lost their collective way. Perhaps the zeitgeist itself was their solution.

I also suggested that each of them keep a journal to track their progress as they reinvented themselves and tried to recapture the excitement they had felt when they were younger. Once they emerged on the other side of their life-pivot, they could look back at how they had gotten to where they were and perhaps help others find the pot of gold at the end of their own rainbows.

I heard what I was saying to my friends and then looked back at my own journey.

All those friends who came to me to share their discontent and express their envy of what they thought was my "wonderful career" didn't know it, but they had done me an incredible favor. While I didn't have any transformational advice to give them at the time, I saw my reflection in their frustrated eyes. This not only pushed me to make dramatic changes in my own life, it got me thinking and writing and about this powerful and important question that is so often whispered when what it wants is to scream: "Is that all there is?"

2

All I Ever Wanted

Lots of kids grow up having no idea what they want to do for a living.

I never had that problem.

As a child I was always interested in art and drawing. Even though I didn't take a single art class in high school, most of my time in my other classes was spent drawing pictures of my teachers and the kids around me. My biggest concern was how not to get caught doodling. Few of my teachers would have been flattered by my caricatures of them.

My parents were in the restaurant business. The graphic designer they hired to create their logos, posters, and annual reports was an incredibly talented guy who was a big influence on me. I loved visiting his studio, paging through his stacks of design books, and looking at the projects he was working on.

Because I was interested in art and politics, my first dream was to become a political cartoonist. I drew cartoons for my high school newspaper and for Miami-Dade College's student newspaper. I got an internship at the Miami News and worked for Pulitzer Prize-winning cartoonist Don Wright, one of the top political satirists of all time. I chose my first college because they allowed students to create their own majors; I was going to invent a degree in political cartooning. Of course, I drew the cartoons for their student newspaper, too.

After my first year in college, I decided such a small school wasn't the right place for me and I transferred to the University of Florida. As soon as I got to Gainesville, I dragged my portfolio across the street from the campus to the school newspaper office. Within weeks I was drawing cartoons for *The Florida Gator.*

I tried a bunch of different majors — economics, political science, literature, and business. I wasn't turned on by any of them but thought they would be the *responsible* choices for my studies.

Go Gators

I should have known that planning my future success by studying subjects I had no interest in was not the best strategy. But it wasn't until I registered for *Introduction to Accounting 101* with professor Doug Snowball that I learned just how wrong I was.

A few weeks of accounting passed without incident. I was mostly lost and mostly bored, but I kept attending Accounting 101 because of professor Snowball's funny top-ten lists, and because a big part of his grade was based on mandatory attendance. I might not have had any idea what amortization meant, but I was certainly capable of showing up on time.

But this day was different. After taking attendance, professor Snowball posed this question to the class: "Tell me," he asked with his Australian accent, "is a client deposit an asset or a liability?"

My hand shot up. For the first time I knew the answer to one of Snowball's questions!

Professor Snowball looked stunned as he examined my raised hand. I had never opened my mouth in class before; Snowball had no idea who I was.

"Yes, Mr...." Snowball paused while he scanned his seating chart looking for my name. "...Mr. Turkle?" (people who don't know me pronounce my name "Turkle" instead of "Tur-Kell.) *"You* know the answer?"

"Yes sir" I responded excitedly.

"Okay Mr. Turkle. Tell us. Is a client deposit an asset or a liability?"

"It's an asset!" I said, proud as punch.

Professor Snowball looked crestfallen. He sighed loudly and said, "I'm sorry Mr. Turkle, a client deposit is a liability."

"No sir, it's not; it's an asset."

"I'm sorry to disappoint you, Mr. Turkle, but a client deposit is a liability. It belongs on the right side of the balance sheet. When you receive a deposit, you owe either products or services against the payment. I assure you a deposit is a liability."

"With all due respect sir," I answered, "if I have *your* money then it's an asset. Most small businesses call that working capital … and by the way, my name's Tur-KELL—not Turkle."

Professor Snowball burst out laughing.

"I see your point Mr. … Turkel—and it is very illuminating. What it tells me is that you probably will not be a very good accountant…."

Snowball paused and smiled before continuing, "…but you'll probably make one hell of an entrepreneur."

Father Knows Best

A couple of weeks later, my father came to Gainesville on a business trip and took me out to dinner. My dad asked how I liked the University of Florida.

"I like it fine," I told him. I was in a band, rooming with friends. There was lots to do and lots of cute girls and I was glad I was there.

My dad shook his head. That wasn't what he meant. He wanted to know about my studies. Did I enjoy studying business?

"Actually," I told him "I don't like it very much. I don't understand accounting at all, I can barely stay awake in my finance class, and I'm sure business ethics is an oxymoron."

I told him the Snowball story.

"What do you want to study?" my dad asked.

"Art and design."

"Then why are you studying business?"

"Because I don't want to be a starving artist. I figured that business was the responsible thing to study. If I get a business degree, I can always get a job."

My dad smiled and shook his head. "Look. Even if you study what you're passionate about, when you graduate and get a job there will be days you hate going to work. But if you study something you don't like and get a job you don't enjoy, then what will your workdays be like?"

The very next day I applied to the University of Florida College of Fine Arts. There was sacrifice involved because the design school required classes I hadn't taken. Making up those mandatory classes added a few more semesters to my college career, but once I started to study typography, printmaking, drawing, and graphic design I loved what I was doing and I loved the people I was doing it with.

I Love New York

Graduation came sooner than I expected. I moved to New York and looked for a job in an advertising agency or design firm. Getting a job as a political cartoonist at a major newspaper would be like searching for a needle in a haystack, but I could use my freshly minted Bachelor of Design degree to get a great agency job.

I roomed in a small attic bedroom in my uncle's house on Jewel Avenue in Queens. Each morning I would take the bus to the subway station and then hop the subway into Manhattan. I'd walk from the Times Square station to Rockefeller Plaza because the buildings there had an endless bank of pay phones. Armed with a fresh roll of dimes I'd spend the day in a phone booth calling ad agencies trying to get an interview to show my portfolio. Between interviews, I took an internship with a well-known photographer and learned quite a bit about running a studio and taking commercial-grade tabletop photos. I also learned how to handle clients who were clearly more interested in shots of scotch and lines of agency-purchased cocaine than they were in producing great product photography.

It wasn't too long before I was working as an assistant art director at a large multi-national agency. Reinhold, the creative director was my boss. He had an interesting habit of showing up as late as 11:00 in the morning and leaving for lunch pretty quickly after that. Sometime in the afternoon he'd stumble back to the office and toss a bunch of rumpled bar napkins on my desk. It was my job to interpret the scribbles he had made on the napkins (between cocktails) and turn his doodles into finished ad layouts we could present to the agency's clients.

I would finish translating Reinhold's stack of sketches (most nights I was done by about seven or eight o'clock) and often be the last one to leave the office. With my day's work complete, and no one around to assign me more things to do, I would head down the elevator, out to the subway station, and back to Queens.

You Made it!

You went to school and graduated, landed the job, worked hard, pleased your clients, paid your rent, and attained your goals. You survived a few storms, caught a few lucky breaks, and drove past the big "Welcome to *here*" sign on the great highway of life. How exciting! You did it!

But as they say, "Wanting is everything." *Having* is the difficult part. Maybe as a child you dreamed of owning a puppy. But you probably never dreamed about housebreaking chores, chewed shoes, and unimaginable vet bills. Or maybe you married your dream partner, only to find that the routines of day-to-day living, parenting, and co-managing a household are a lot less exciting than courtship.

This was supposed to be it—everything you wanted—everything you worked for. How could you not be happy?

This Will Be Even Better!

As much as I liked working in a big agency, I missed my hometown. After a year or so I returned to Miami. I worked at a few different ad agencies until I finally decided that I knew more about what they were doing then they did. Of course, you already know just how wrong I was. But you couldn't have told me that back then. And so, at the ripe old age of 25, I set off on my own and opened my own design firm.

I'd set my sights on a goal that aligned with my gifts, got the degree, landed the job, and proven my worth on Madison Avenue. But I wasn't in control of the clients, the production schedule, or how things got done. Going to work for another agency wasn't even an option. I just *knew* things would be so much better—and so much easier—if I could do them my way.

My father laughingly referred to this as "the confidence of ignorance." As you'll see, he knew exactly what he was talking about.

3

The Confidence of Ignorance

My INTERACTIONS with Professor Snowball notwithstanding, I still knew nothing about running a company. Run-ins with dishonest clients combined with my own ignorance of how to manage a business could have turned out much worse than they did. But over time I learned how to hire employees, win accounts, and do all the other things necessary to manage a small design firm.

My company won a lot of advertising and design awards, got published in a lot of advertising books, and did some great work. Plus, I earned a good living for myself and the hundreds of people who worked in my firm over the 33 years I was at the helm. What I'm most proud of is that across all those years—through good times and bad—we never missed a single payroll. Don't get me wrong; that sometimes meant my business partner and I didn't take a paycheck for weeks at a time, but the people who worked in our agency always did.

But despite all our successes, as time passed I grew less and less interested in the business. I remember rushing out to pitch a new piece of business and coming back late at night to report the results to my partner:

"I have good news and bad news."

Roberto's face lit up. "Tell me the good news first."

"We won the account. We're their new agency of record. We've got a lot of work to do and we're going to make a lot of money."

"That's great!" I knew Roberto was already calculating the revenue this new piece of business would add to our bottom line. "So what's the bad news?"

"We won the account. We're their new agency of record. We've got a lot of work to do and we're going to make a lot of money."

It wasn't that I was afraid of doing the work. I *loved* doing the work. What I dreaded was what I already knew would be the mind-numbing series of backs and forths the new relationship would require. We'd not only have to solve our client's market-ing problems, we'd have to deal with their bureaucracy, manage their insecure executive vice-presidents, and deal with some of our own employees' issues simply to meet deadlines, budgets, and expectations.

As much as I enjoyed earning and spending money, I under-stood the drudgery that came along with the cash—the bookkeep-ing, the accounting, the audits, the spreadsheets, the taxes, and so on.

I welcomed my clients' marketing problems. To me, creating the ideas was the sexy part. Implementing the ideas was the part I dreaded.

My friend Mike Tomas' father used to say, "Don't bring me problems; I've got plenty of those. Bring me solutions." That's what I tried to do; I thrived on solutions. What brought me down were the hurdles we had to jump over to provide those solutions—hurdles I thought were bureaucratic, wasteful, and stupid.

The Man in the Mirror

Remember those meetings where my dissatisfied friends would tell me how much they wanted to do what I did for a living? Remember the pat advice I gave them about setting off on their own journeys and keeping a journal of the trip? I started to real-ize that I wasn't actually talking to my friends.

I was talking to *myself.*

Have you ever wondered why *other people's* problems are so easy to figure out?

As Pogo Possum said, "We have met the enemy and he is us."

Physician Heal Thyself

Despite all my pontificating, did I take my own advice? Of course not.

What I was hearing from others was exactly what I was going through myself. Like my troubled friends, I had reached some level of success and then found my time at work to be both uninteresting and unmotivating. But while I had obvious solutions for my friends to try, I felt powerless and trapped with no way to fix my own problems. I had no idea what to do next.

Specifically, I thought there were three things my friends needed to do:

1. Pursue their passions
2. Create new challenges for themselves
3. Try something new

Perhaps I needed to do those things for myself.

It's not like I wasn't trying anything new. I started speaking about branding and creativity at conferences, and I enjoyed those experiences. I wrote and published a few books and worked on promoting them. I became a television talking head, appearing more than 400 times on FOX News and Business, CNN, and CCTV (China's international news network). I loved every minute of it.

But none of that changed how bored I was in the office, sitting behind my desk or listening to clients prattle on about their problems.

While the solution I offered to my friends might have been a good first step, it was neither courageous nor insightful.

It was time — time for a big, scary, bridge-burning, no-turning-back, *Bruce-are-you-freaking-crazy?* seismic change!

I made a deal with my business partner to buy out my share of our advertising agency.

I sold our office building to remove the burdens of maintaining the facility and paying for it and to put some money in my bank account.

I found an agent to help me get more speaking gigs.

I found another agent to secure a publisher for the manuscript I was working on.

I interviewed digital media experts to who could help me monetize my content.

I talked to consultants and speakers to learn how they had built their businesses and lived their lives.

My plan might have sounded well-organized and carefully-thought-through, but it included one major mistake: It was all predicated on the understanding that I was going to keep doing the same thing I had done before, albeit without my firm's infrastructure behind me. I would still be a branding and marketing professional; I would just do it without my ad agency to help with the projects.

Little did I know how significant that single mistake would turn out to be.

4

A Little Help from My Friends

MANY successful people stress the importance of working with mentors. According to Michael Grimme, you have to:

>...just make sure you pick the right people.
>
>You want mentors who are willing to tell you what they did right, and more importantly, what they did wrong. You want to know what they wouldn't do again because that knowledge is so powerful. It can help you so much and give you a much better quality of life than if you think you know it all already.
>
>I have friends I can talk to, guys in their seventies, eighties, nineties. I'll buy them breakfast and I'll ask them questions and then I'll just sip my coffee and shut up

and listen. And that's the cheapest learning I could possibly do.

I wanted and planned to leave my business, but that didn't mean I was able to leave. Knowing what you should do and actually *doing* it are two different things.

My livelihood was tied up in my business and so was my personal identity. For as long as I could remember, I had wanted to be an art director involved in graphic design and advertising. And because my name was on the door of the company I had started, my existence was linked to the business. I had a partner, employees, and clients whom I truly loved. Leaving would be abandoning them!

Deciding what to do next was stressful. When so many people depend on you and what you do, how do you share your concerns without freaking them out? I was certain I was the only one in the world dealing with what I was going through. I had not yet learned that *every single ambitious person who has accomplished something special goes through this every single day.*

Every … single … one.

Every … single … day.

You simply cannot rely on your own counsel. If you spend too much time in your own echo chamber, you start marching in lockstep to your own voice, believing your own hype, getting high on your own supply. It's great to have a singular vision and to follow it despite all evidence to the contrary, but it's a comfort to be able to discuss your ideas and concerns with people who have your back, care about your success, and are honest and concerned enough to tell you the truth—when you want to hear it and especially when you don't.

I knew I wanted to change my day-to-day business life and I knew I needed help doing it. Lucky for me, I had friends who were there to help me.

When the Student Is Ready...

I met Susan Ford Collins back in the early 2000s. Together with a few other business leaders, Susan and I founded a South Florida networking group called The Strategic Forum. This organization of 45 entrepreneurs, business owners, and C-suite professionals meets once a month with the sole purpose of helping one another with our businesses.

When we first met, Susan gave me a copy of her bestseller, *The Joy of Success.*[1] I dove in and polished off the book in a weekend. It was well-written and full of good information, but I can't say it made any great difference in my life or my understanding of my business.

Susan's life took a fascinating change when she went to China to train business leaders on how to move beyond the simple success they'd achieved running their companies. Fortunately, by the time I decided I was ready to move on from my business, Susan had moved back to the states. I called her up to rekindle our friendship and schedule a meeting with her to discuss my impending life change.

A few days later I was sitting in Susan's office. I explained my predicament and what was causing me trouble. I told her I needed insight and good advice.

Susan's response?

"You need to read my book."

She reached behind the couch, plucked a copy of *The Joy of Success* out of a carton, and tossed it to me.

"I already read it," I said. "Back when we first met."

"Well, you need to read it again."

I took *The Joy of Success* home and started reading it that night, expecting to simply review what I had quickly scanned a few years before.

This time I felt as if every word was written especially for me. I read and reread each page because Susan's message was so relevant. I underlined powerful phrases, made notes about things I was going to do, and mind-mapped the book on the inside front cover. It took a lot longer than a weekend to get from cover to cover. In fact, when the weekend was over, I had only completed about 45 pages.

Why did the book matter so much more this time than the first time I read it?

They say, "When the student is ready the teacher appears."

I used to think that was part of some "the Universe will provide" pseudo-spiritual belief system: When you broadcast your intention to the Universe—*poof!*—the teacher will materialize out of thin air.

What I discovered was that the teacher was *always there*. What had changed was my willingness to pay attention and learn.

Addiction doctors and therapists talk about how patients must reach a low point before they're ready to do what's required to fix their situations. Though our willingness or unwillingness to take action doesn't have to be contingent on us reaching such a dramatic nadir, we are much more likely to pay attention and learn what we need to learn when we have a vested interest in the results—skin in the game.

Susan asked me two questions that changed the way I looked at my business and my future. She asked me how I felt when I'd return to my office after a long day of meeting with potential clients.

"Do the people you work with give you presents? Do you feel like they're there to help make your life better?"

I thought about that for a minute and answered with an unwavering "Sometimes."

"My partner Roberto, and our CFO Sara, and my bookkeeper and assistant Zoila and a couple of our art directors do. I always feel like they're doing things that I either can't do, won't do, or couldn't do as well—and they usually do those things without me having to ask them."

"Or," she continued, "does returning to your office make you feel like a mother bird returning to the nest only to look into all of those hungry mouths demanding to be fed?"

When I take notes, I create them half with words and text and half with drawings. When Susan asked me this question, I drew a nest full of open-mouthed, red-throated baby birds.

After Susan stapled that picture firmly in my mind's eye, I knew I had to leave my nest.

THE BABY BIRD WITH ITS MOUTH OPEN GETS THE WORM

Kick Ask!

As with most of life's important challenges and decisions, a little help can go a long way.

Accepting help is not a weakness. George Washington didn't win the Revolutionary War without an army to help. Big, profitable companies are built by well-structured organizations full of people who help. Successful executives work with coaches and participate in mastermind groups. Cleaning house, whether it's the one you live in or the one that lives in you — is always easier with help.

And if you're unsure quite what to ask for help with, you can ask for help figuring that out, too.

The fact that you're reading this book suggests you're already on your way to finding the answers you seek.

Where can you find a mentor? Look for encouraging leaders around your industry — or in the industry you want to pivot to. Join industry associations and connect with likeminded professionals on a similar path.

Still stuck? Just ask. Write a social media post that explains the kind of mentorship you're looking for and what you're willing to exchange for it.

Demonstrate your willingness to "do the homework" and offer value in return. Be the "student who is ready" and your teachers will appear.

And of course, you'll find inspiration and guidance in the fourteen mentors who share their stories in this book.

The Power of the Mastermind

Even with Susan's good counsel helping me figure out my next steps, I still had a daunting job ahead of me. I had to review my options, come up with a plan, and make sure I was doing the right thing. Plus, I had to find a way to make sure I would do what I needed to do, even when it was difficult to do or was easy to put off.

While this particular problem was new—I'd never walked away from a business I'd spent thirty years building before—facing a situation that required a combination of good input, good advice, and a good dose of accountability wasn't. Throughout my career I'd encountered dilemmas that had forced me to look to others for input and assistance.

Gonna Try with a Little Help From my Friends

Here's where I turned to a second group of people—a collection of friends and associates whom I get together with twice a year to discuss our businesses and our lives so we can push each other to do what we need to—because listening to your own counsel can be a dangerous strategy.

While it's great to be self-motivated and self-directed, few of us know enough about everything to be able to look at a problem—or an opportunity—from every important angle.

In *A Boy's Life,* Robert De Niro said "I know a thing or two about a thing or two."[2]

I made a list of business associates and leaders I respected and invited them to lunch in my office. I brought in an accountant, a couple of lawyers, a real estate investor, a tech entrepreneur, a pension fund manager, and a few other professionals. Over coffee and sandwiches, I told them what was bothering me and what I was thinking of doing about it, and I asked them for their input.

Their answers were loving and supportive but also direct and realistic. Of course, they pointed out all the things they thought I would do well but they also listed a number of pitfalls they wanted me to watch out for. Most of those things were not on the lists I had made for myself.

A team like that—whether assembled casually or formally, from friends and business associates or simply from like-minded professionals—is called a mastermind group.

Harvard Business Review says: "A mastermind group can provide honest feedback, help you refine your ideas, and share insights and leads. They can also inspire you with their successes and support you when you face setbacks."

A mastermind group is a collection of people who help you deal with whatever it is that jerks your eyes open at 3 AM. While they may not be there when you're tossing and turning, wondering and worrying about what to do next, and what to do about what you've already done, they are there when you're ready to discuss it.

According to *Forbes Magazine,* "Mastermind groups are relatively new to most people, even though Napoleon Hill created the concept around 75 years ago with his book *Think and Grow Rich.* A mastermind group is designed to help you navigate through challenges using the collective intelligence of others."

Peter Shankman, social media raconteur, founder of HARO, and professional mastermind facilitator puts it this way: "In the 21st century, community doesn't come as easily as it used to… mastermind mind groups are where you can find your professional tribe that can also go deeper to helping you with personal goals."

Mastermind groups provide new ideas, help vet concepts, provide accountability, and expose you to the honest support that can help you and the people around you achieve success.

I participate in two groups and also put together ad hoc masterminds when I have a particularly vexing problem or potentially powerful opportunity to deal with. The strength of their collective thought and concern, together with the varied experiences of the participants, helps me benefit from thinking out loud and exploring different what-if scenarios.

These groups work so well that I've started hosting groups myself—using what I learned writing this book to help people with their own life and business shifts.

When it was time for me to figure out what to do next with my life, it was only natural that I would turn to my mastermind group for input and assistance.

But there's something else: As we've discussed, knowing what to do and actually doing it are two very different things. Yes, I had decided that I was going to leave my business, but I still had to actually *do* it.

Accounting for Accountability

My work with Susan was empowering, but I wanted more — more ideas, more perspectives, more people to challenge me, more people to correct my course or agree that I was heading in the right direction when I wasn't sure. And I wanted the kind of accountability I knew I needed to get the job done. I wished I would be able to find the same accountability partnerships in my professional life that I have with my daughter, Aliana.

When Aliana relocated from Washington DC to Los Angeles, I had free time on my hands. I was booked for a speaking engagement in Anaheim, California at about the same time Ali needed to report to her new job, so I had the good fortune to be able to fly to Washington DC, rent a big SUV, and drive across the country with my 25-year-old daughter and her possessions.

It was the first time I'd ever crossed the continental US by car, and not in a pressurized aluminum cigar tube 36,000 feet high in the sky. And I got to spend a full week of face-to-face (or at least shoulder-to-shoulder) time with my adult daughter. How many dads my age get to do that?

I was sure that at some point on our journey Ali would get sick of listening to me or I'd be driving through Arkansas or Oklahoma or somewhere and wonder *What the hell am I doing?* But neither thing happened. We had a great time chatting, listening to each other's favorite music and podcasts, and visiting out-of-the-way places we had never heard of before.

What a delight!

Somewhere west of Nashville, Ali mentioned that she was having trouble in her yoga class because she didn't have enough upper body strength to do some of the exercises. We decided we would do pushups together when we got to our hotel each night.

Ali started off doing "knee pushups"—that's where you rest some of your weight on your knees instead of your feet to make the pushups easier. Soon she was knocking them out right along with me. And before long she was banging out more pushups than I could.

Since that great journey, we still help each other with our fitness goals. Each evening Ali texts me the word "Yoga," meaning she's

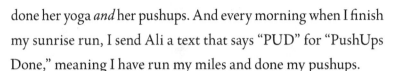

done her yoga *and* her pushups. And every morning when I finish my sunrise run, I send Ali a text that says "PUD" for "PushUps Done," meaning I have run my miles and done my pushups.

Besides helping us stay in touch, these daily notes add *accountability*. On days when I don't want to get out of bed and run, or don't want to do my pushups after my run is complete, I know I need to send Ali a text letting her know that I did what I said I would do. Accountability motivates me to do what I don't want to do.

As much as Ali loves her yoga classes, I'm sure there are times when the only reason she rolls up her mat and goes to the yoga studio is because she knows I'm waiting to hear if she went or not.

It was the same with leaving my business and reporting to my mastermind group. Just talking about my plans wasn't enough. At our June meeting, I promised my group I was going to make a change. I had to *do it*. When I saw them again in January, they would not accept me telling them I hadn't done what I'd said I would. My mastermind group's support made me accountable to achieve something I wanted and needed to accomplish. I was still uncomfortable taking the first step across the chasm, but thanks to my mastermind group, I did what I had to do.

But facing my fears, settling my accounts, and starting my new life, wouldn't be enough.

It Takes a Village

Making big changes happen on your own is difficult, scary, and frankly not that much fun. Seek mentors and guides, and find a mastermind group that will empower you to see more deeply into yourself by helping others with their problems. Don't overlook the value of accountability partnerships. Your partner may be working on goals and challenges that are entirely unrelated to your own, but when you declare an intention out loud, you've made a promise. And when you keep that promise, it feels good to know that your accountability partner is going to applaud your efforts.

5

Time for a You-Turn

Hindsight is 20/20

As strategic as I tried to be, I was changing everything while changing nothing. I simply transformed myself into the same old wine in a different bottle. What I did not do was improve the bottle or the wine.

I was leaving my new home office to have lunch with an old school buddy, a successful attorney who wanted to get together to talk about where his life was going and what he could do now that he no longer wanted to practice law. I left a few minutes early because I wanted to stop by a local video production studio to drop off a digital file I needed converted.

Walking out of the studio to my car, it hit me. In my old life I would have had *someone else* deliver the file to the video company. Now that I'd made this painful shift and gotten rid of my infrastructure, I had to do the delivery work myself. The only thing I'd accomplished in my transformation was to add additional responsibilities to my day. As my friend Randy Gage says, "If you don't hire a personal assistant, you are a personal assistant." I'd gotten rid of the responsibilities and burdens of having employees and a big office, but I'd also gotten rid of the help, camaraderie, and valuable input they'd provided. I was still doing the same things I had been doing before — plus a whole lot of other things I didn't want to do.

I took a deep breath and headed over to meet my friend for lunch. I was looking forward to seeing him but I knew what to expect. He was going to tell me that same old story about how unhappy he was doing what he was trained to do. And I was going to tell him about pursuing his passion and keeping a journal and *blah blah blah*.

Walking to my car, I experienced a road-to-Damascus moment. But it wasn't my first one. That one had happened almost 20 years before.

I had been hard at work growing my branding agency. We were picking up profitable business and doing great work. My family was healthy and happy and my marriage was strong. And my first book had just been published. Before it was even released, I received an invitation to do a book signing at one of the most prestigious design conferences in the country.

Very exciting.

When the day came, we checked into our hotel and then and went to the opening dinner. When we arrived, we were escorted to the front VIP table and seated next to Steff Sagmeister. If you're not a designer you might not know who Steff is but back then, Steff was the designer to the stars—a tall, handsome German guy dressed in all-black who spoke charmingly accented English.

Steff had also released a new book, and he was going to do a book signing with me! Wow.

But it gets better. Sitting on the other side, right next to my wife was the Chief Marketing Officer of one of the most design-forward corporations in the world—a potential client whose account I had lusted after for a long time. I figured that after I did my book signing, I'd get the opportunity to pitch my firm to him.

The next morning, I got up early and went downstairs to arrange my books and Sharpies. Once everything was just the way I liked it, I went for a run, showered, and headed down to breakfast with my family. When it was time for the book signing, my six-year-old daughter, Ali, asked if she could go with me.

The elevator doors opened and we walked out hand in hand, to find a long line of people standing outside the expo hall, waiting for the book signing. Ali turned to me and asked if all these people were waiting in line for my book. Figuring this was a teaching moment—and not wanting to sound quite as full of myself as I felt—I told Ali I was sure that some of them were there for Steff's book, too.

We walked past the line and into the expo center. The line continued all the way to the back of the room and then snaked around to the book signing tables. We finally got to the end of the line and turned the corner only to find—you guessed it—all of the people in line were lined up at Steff's booth. There wasn't a single person lined up at mine. Not one.

I walked behind my table and sat down, being careful not to make eye contact with anyone. Ali busied herself drawing pictures with my exquisitely laid out Sharpies while I tried to magically will people to come up to my side of the booth.

Every so often I would catch someone's eye and they'd either turn away quickly or give me a look of pity. I didn't think I could feel any worse than I did at that moment.

I was wrong.

All of a sudden, Ali decided to take measures into her own hands. She jumped up from her folding chair, darted under the table and popped out on the other side. Then she ran up to people in line and tugged at their hands. "Buy my daddy's book!" she said excitedly. "It's really good!"

Now I was sure I couldn't feel any worse.

But I was wrong again.

Just then, my beautiful wife came walking up and she wasn't alone. Sfter breakfast she'd run into the potential client we'd met the night before. She'd convinced him to come with her to see my triumphant book signing, and promised him a free book and the opportunity to talk to her brilliant designer superstar husband about his company's latest project.

They stood there dumbfounded as I sat behind my piles of books and pens, while my daughter tried to drag reluctant people to my booth.

By this point Steff had sold all of his books. He was now posing for photos with the hordes of grinning people who had gotten one of his precious signed volumes.

Here's the most interesting part: Neither of our books had been released so nobody knew what was in either of them. Steff's books sold while mine did not because Steff was a well-known quantity and I was not.

If I wanted to be successful, I needed to change the way I did things.
What did I do?

I joined the National Speakers Association to learn about the speaking business.

I started speaking at design conferences and corporate events to build my reputation within the industry and with potential clients.

I got myself booked as a marketing expert on TV news programs, eventually doing more than 400 appearances on CNN, MSNBC, CCTV, and Fox Business.

I looked for new openings where I could help rather than compete and build the kinds of relationships that would expose me to new opportunities.

The Success Paradox

If you've ever had a mean boss or a low-paying job, or been in a situation where your ideas and efforts weren't valued or recognized, getting out of the frying pan becomes a much more important concern than whatever fire you might land in. But what if everything's working fine? You're making money, your contributions are being recognized, and you're treated with respect? After all, first-world problems are still problems. If you're unhappy in spite of your success—in spite of feeling like you *should* be happy—trying to force yourself to be grateful will only add fuel to the fire in your heart. Fulfillment is a moving target.

And sometimes, discontent arises when things get too easy. Though few of us admit it, most of us — especially successful people — love a good challenge. Isn't that what drove you to achieve success in the first place?

Heading to lunch nearly twenty years later, I realized it was time to change again.

Why was I giving people advice that I wasn't taking myself?

What if I stopped playing it safe and created real change in my life?

What if I decided to become a change leader — a go-to-guy for people who wanted to reinvent their lives?

What if I stopped talking the talk and tried walking the walk?

6

What the Hell
Are You Going to Do?

Don't Quit Your Day Job!

O<small>NCE</small> I dropped that video file off at the production studio and had that moment of clarity in the parking lot, I never looked back. As soon as lunch with my friend ended, I sat down at my desk and wrote the introduction to *Is That All There Is?* before I went in for dinner. And I edited and rewrote the introduction that very evening. I was so excited that I was wide awake at four o'clock the next morning mapping out next steps and deciding on some of the people I wanted to interview.

I started writing this chapter minutes after that. As excited as I had been about the other books I've written, this had never happened to me before. Writing had always been a pleasure, sure, but it was work. Writing this book was different.

I was ready to give up years of agency work to pursue this new idea!

But on reflection, beside my natural aversion to discomfort, my concern about not being able to pay my bills and—dare I say it?—my bald, quaking fear of the unknown, I wasn't willing to give up everything I was doing. I like solving client problems. I like the travel. I like the rush of coming up with new ideas. I like the "Why-didn't-I-think-of-that?" moment of seeing the solutions the other people in my office came up with. And while I may not have found the goose that laid the golden egg, I liked the goose I did have—even if it had only laid silver or bronze eggs.

I remembered a book by one of my design idols, the late creative director of Hallmark Cards, Gordon McKenzie. It was titled *Orbiting the Giant Hairball* and I remembered it having a big impact on me when I read it all those years ago. I rummaged through my bookshelf to find it and then paged through it until I found my favorite passage where McKenzie explains the space between the excessive poles of doing everything and doing nothing:

"So: Sky diving without a parachute is suicide. Total freedom is suicide.

"And: Holing up in a closet is vegetating. Total security is vegetating.

"Somewhere between the ridiculous extremes of vegetating and suicide is the right place for each of us. That right place is different for you and me — a different place for different times of our lives and different parts of our lives. Generally, though, my suggestion is, if you want to live more fully, start somewhere toward the safe end of the security/freedom continuum and move mindfully, ever so mindfully, toward the free end."[3]

I was too excited to move "ever so mindfully." I wanted to throw myself headlong into this enticing new affair. Yet deep in my consciousness I knew that wasn't such a good idea.

While I desperately wanted to tell my clients "Sorry, I don't do that anymore," my speaking calendar wasn't full enough to cover my expenses. Though I wanted to change quickly, I needed to phase my old job out.

McKenzie was telling me I didn't need to throw everything away at once. Don't throw the baby out with the bath water. Don't quit your day job.

Of course, this is easier said than done. How do you decide where the wheat ends and the chaff begins? How do you choose what's worth keeping and what's worth discarding? Surely some of those decisions are no-brainers—I could follow the hedonist's code and maximize pleasure while I minimized pain. But maturity teaches us that not everything pleasurable is worth hanging on to any more than everything that hurts is worth eliminating.

What did I get rid of first? What I liked the least, of course. Which in my case was implementation. I still enjoyed being creative and solving problems and I was still good at it; I just didn't want to *construct* the solutions and I didn't want to manage the people who were building them.

What I needed to do was hold on to the things I cherished—the things that provided value while I worked towards accomplishing the things I thought would guide me toward future satisfaction.

My morning runs are a case-in-point. Almost every morning I'm in town, I meet my jogging buddies at 5:45 AM for a group run of somewhere between 5 and 15 miles. While I dearly love the camaraderie of the group and enjoy the health benefits running gives me, I can't say I enjoy getting out of bed at zero-dark-thirty in the morning any more than I like pounding the pavement. But would I give up my running habit to minimize the pain it causes? Not on your life. The benefits I get from running with my friends are worth much more to me than the momentary discomfort of sore calves, aching thighs, and gasping lungs.

Deciding what to keep and what to discard is a matter of ranking the different parts of your life and what they provide you.

Rumi said, "Little by little, wean yourself,"[4] which at first read sounds like good and prudent advice. But all that prioritizing can lead to "paralysis by analysis." As with jumping headlong into an icy cold swimming pool, you can't think some things through too carefully or you'll never do them. You just need to hold your nose, count to three, and hurl yourself into the unknown.

If you follow Rumi's sage advice and slowly wean myself away from the life you're used to, you'll never slip the yoke that's oppressing you. On the other hand, the thirteenth-century Persian poet counseled us to, "Let yourself be silently drawn by the stronger pull of what you really love." For me that's thinking, writing, speaking, and teaching. For you, that could be a hobby, travel, a new profession, or making time to serve others.

7

Timing is Everything

It's Been a Long Time Coming.
It's Gonna be a Long Time Gone

In 1900, the average life expectancy for an American was 46 years; today it's 79. Clearly we're living longer—almost twice as long. But have we only added years to our life, or have we also added life to our years? Maybe the answer depends on your perception of age.

As you consider which fork in the road to take on your life's journey, reflect on how old you feel—not chronologically, but energetically, psychologically, and spiritually. Are you "old and tired" or "ready for another run?" Are you "road-weary" or "experienced?" Various people of the same age will answer these questions differently. We all know that life is a terminal condition, but how do you imagine yourself living on the day before the end? In a rocking chair? On a mountain top? Somewhere in-between?

In her book *Elderhood*,[5] Dr. Louise Aronson points out that "owing to improvements in public health, nutrition and medical advances, the percentage of people older than 70 in the United States in 2018 was 15% and climbing…. If you make it to 80, you have a good chance of making it to ninety or beyond."

From *The Wall Street Journal's* review of Aronson's book:[6] "The precise time old age kicks in is not altogether clear. For some 65 … marked the beginning of old age. Of course, many people 65 and well beyond neither looked, nor felt, nor acted old. As Dr. Aronson writes: "There is no set age when we transition from adult to elder, and both the speed and extent of aging vary widely. As geriatricians are fond of saying: 'When you've seen one eighty-year-old, you've seen one eighty-year-old.'"

What kind of 45, or 55, or 65-year-old are you? Does 60-years-old mean how it actually feels to you or the way society *says* it feels?

In his book *Threescore and More*, Alan Weiss wrote, "Life stages are social constructs. What we call them and how we treat them is within our control and informs our behaviors."[7]

The way you choose to define those constructs is completely up to you, no matter how old you are. Your lack of satisfaction, desire for change, or what's commonly referred to as your 'midlife crises' can happen any time. After all, we can't know when 'midlife' is unless we know when 'endlife' will happen. What we *can* know is that there's no good reason for continuing in a situation that makes us unhappy, regardless of how long that time is going to be. And living better can also help you live longer.

From the WSJ article review of *Elderhood:*

> Dr. Aronson cites three of the places whose denizens are longest lived: Okinawa, Sardinia, and Loma Linda, California. Loma Linda is on the list thanks to its large Seventh-day Adventist population, who outlive their neighbors by five to ten years because 'they abstain from alcohol, cigarettes, and other drugs; have strong spiritual lives; a close community; a vegetarian diet—and lower levels of stress hormones.

While choices of what to eat and drink and whether to smoke or not are purely within our control, so is the decision to live a life with greater or lower stress. Exercise, a full sense of community, and an appreciation of our true purpose all have been shown to reduce stress.

Weiss continues, "When we are engaged in activities that have high meaning for us—and (that means) creating meaning for yourself, not searching for it or using someone else's metric for meaning—and they create happiness, we are in a constant success state."

Not only does purpose lead to happiness but, as we'll see, it can help control our evolutionarily developed Threat Response System. In other words, we can better pursue happiness and a longer, more satisfying life by abandoning what doesn't work for us while we replace it with what does.

Are You a Writer or a Waiter?

Maybe you want to write the next great American novel. If that's the case, you need to sit down, write the book, and then go out and sell it. That's all it takes. But if you prefer to sit around and wait for the muse to strike and a publisher to knock on your door looking for her next bestseller, then you're a waiter, not a writer.

Louis L'Amour, author of 89 novels, 14 short-story collections, and two nonfiction books said, "Start writing no matter what. Water does not flow until the faucet is turned on."

Whether you're writing a book or changing your life, you are going to have to make a move. Sooner or later the faucet is going to be turned on and you're going to be swept away from your complacency, whether you like it or not.

Your catalyst might be something great—a profitable liquidity event, say, or a windfall. It might be something subtle like the inevitable passing of time. It could be something disastrous—divorce, disease, incarceration, or a modern-day version of the pogroms my grandfather escaped from in eastern Europe. What's certain is that *something* is going to happen. The only constant we can count on is change. Doesn't it make sense to at least start thinking about your next steps now, when you can still take them thoughtfully and cautiously?

Are You a Dancing Bear?

Dancing bears were commonplace throughout Europe and Asia from the Middle Ages to the nineteenth century and could still be found in the 21st century in some countries. A dancing bear is a wild bear captured when the animal was young or born in captivity, and used to entertain people in the streets for money. Shockingly, they were still present in the streets of Spain as recently as 2007.

Dancing bears were also commonplace on the Indian subcontinent. According to the BBC, the last of them were freed in 2009.[8]

Besides the injustice of taking these animals from their natural habitats and forcing them to perform unnatural acts, the dancing bears' training regimes were cruel. The bears would be chained and caged, muzzled, and beaten into submission. Even standing on their hind legs for long periods of time was an unnaturally painful posture that needed to be coerced.

To train bears to perform acts they wouldn't normally do in the wild, their trainers hopscotched back and forth between pleasure and pain—frightening the animals with whips and rewarding them with sugar cubes. This risk/reward strategy broke the animal's spirit and further coerced it to do what the trainer demanded. Eventually these two extremes became the bear's poles of existence; from pain to pleasure and back again.

But assuming the injustice of trained dancing bears was mostly eliminated nearly a decade ago, what does this have to do with you?

This book can be a great incentive for many of us to think back on where we've been and look forward to where we're going. But rather than simply list the things you're going to do with your new-found freedom ("Now I'll have the time to write my book") and the things you're no longer going to do ("I am not going to practice law anymore") why not dig deeper and look for your motivations for doing these things?

Are you operating from fear or are you accomplishing the things that will make you feel good about yourself and your life? Are you yo-yoing back and forth between pain and pleasure or are you moving positively into the future? And even more importantly, are you making plans that allow you to further express your authentic truth or are you allowing the status quo and your comfort level to force yourself into unnatural behaviors?

Maybe it's time to reflect on whether or not you are using punishments and rewards much like the whips and sugar cubes that coerced dancing bears to get up on their hind legs and hop around when the music played.

It wasn't much fun for the bear. Can't be much fun for you, either.

Mark Twain said, "The two most important days in your life are the day you are born and the day you find out why." Since there's nothing we can do about our first day, why not make it your promise to work on point two? True, you'll probably never actually figure out why you're here (or even whether there actually is a reason) but the exploration will help you decide what to do (and what not do) next. While it is too late to do something about Twain's first day, it's never too late to work on the second.

Instead of just focusing on the things you do, concentrate on identifying who you are and how that persona can resonate with the person you want to be. Then, as you move forward into your new life, you've already got the head start only you can enjoy.

But first you have to stop being a dancing bear. The one thing you can be sure of is you can't keep doing what you've been doing because of the metaphorical whips and sugar cubes that have determined your past.

8

Change is Hard

It is not the strongest or the most intelligent who will survive, but those who can best manage change."

— Charles Darwin

CHANGE IS SCARY, especially when we've found a safe and comfortable place. Many of us would rather be bored and dissatisfied than face the unknown. We think about how far we've come and how hard we've worked, and remind ourselves to be grateful. Why would we start a new life when we already have such a rich one?

And then we think about the unknowns. Do we really want to walk away from the comfort zone and start a new struggle?

What if we fail? What if we succeed and find ourselves dissatisfied with our *new* success?

What if...?

What if...?

What if...?

It's been said that the one universal theme in all of literature and human endeavor is the search for meaning. As you write a new chapter in the book of your life, consider...

What Do You Need to Change?

"The more things change, the more they stay the same"? Do you know where that saying comes from?

Neither do I.

But that saying is many people's pat response to confronting their fear of the unknown. If we're afraid of what we don't know, afraid of what we don't understand, and afraid of what we don't see coming, then our logical defense is to not let things change in the first place.

That's a problem. Because whether or not we *want* things to change, they are going to change anyway. And mankind has never experienced a time of greater change than the time we're living in right now.

And what could bring about a bigger change than your response to the question, *"Is That All There Is?"*

At a minimum, changing your life means trying a new way to make a living. But your change could be much more profound. Once you start on the journey of discovering what you want to be, you might find that it's not just your job that needs to change.

Maybe your new career will require you to move to a new city, state, or country. Maybe the prudent response to your new entrepreneurial opportunity will suggest that you downsize to cut expenses. Maybe your partner won't want to go on this journey with you. Change is an ongoing process and often one change leads to another and another. And that can be scary.

How Do We Deal with Change?

Our Threat Response System (TRS), evolved over hundreds of thousands of years to deal with the situational changes that threatened our lives. Saber-toothed tigers and poisonous mushrooms taught us to fear what we can't control and don't understand.

But today, saber-toothed tigers are much less of a threat to our well-being than middle-of-the night phone calls, online phishing scams, Internet disruption, or even an overwhelming sense of ennui.

You know that and I know that.

Scientists who study change and sociologists and counselors who deal with change know that, too.

Unfortunately, our evolutionarily honed Threat Response System doesn't know that.

Faced with danger, our bodies experience complex physiological responses. Changes occur in our brain, and in our nervous and endocrine systems, all refined by evolution over millennia to keep us safe. Our heart rate, blood pressure, and sweating increase while our digestion and oral secretions decrease. Our senses go on full alert and our pupils dilate. Our brain releases endorphins and our pancreas releases sugar. Our muscles tense, our pulmonary passages engorge, and our breathing rate increases.

Stress avoidance reactions are systemic, unconscious, and powerful.

Today we respond to perceived threats with the same wash of adrenaline, the same flush of cortisol, the same pounding heart and shallow breathing as we did 100,000 years ago. But today's threats do not warrant the same all-hands-on-deck response that fueled our lifesaving fight-or-flight response.

We still freak out over change, but today that change might be the end of our pleasant afternoon, our most recent marketing strategy, or our career path—not the end of the world.

This phenomenon of an overactive threat response is particularly clear when it comes to leading our new lives. A leader's job is to not to know what's coming next, but to prepare the people they lead for dealing with whatever it is that's just around the corner. A leader's job is to crawl a few steps out on the ledge, check that the ledge is solid and secure, and then turn back and say, "Ok, it's safe to come out here with me."

Sometimes leaders can even prepare their followers for what's around the corner even though they can't see that far. It's a matter of becoming comfortable with being uncomfortable.

Of course, it's not just people who lead others who have to deal with venturing into areas that are uncomfortable. It's also something we have to deal with if we're going to lead ourselves into the brave new world of our better future. But ironically, just as we try to make the sincere effort to move ourselves forward, it's often our past that holds us back.

Because our Threat Response System evolved over hundreds of thousands of years, it's not going to adapt to our new normal within our own relatively short lifetimes. We have to learn to accept that we can't know what's around the corner but become confident that we're going to be able to deal with whatever it is effectively. We have to understand the difference between danger and discomfort and accept that while the discomfort of "not knowing" might be discombobulating, it is not the end of the world.

What Do You Value?

Some people value money above all else. Some people value experiences. Some people value the time to pursue passions or provide community service or spend time with their loved ones. Some people value being left alone. Some people value doing as much as time will allow. Some people value doing as little as possible.

What do you value? What do you care about? How do you decide what's worth doing and what's worth turning down?

Regardless of whether or not you've set your own personal price, you're always going to make the decision to do something in return for something else. You're going to say "yes" or "no" to most every opportunity you're offered based on some personal interpretation of value.

It's important to understand that the real question is not whether you're going to say "yes" or "no." It's whether you're going to say "yes" or "no" based on a life strategy that you've thought through and planned. Or, will you make the decision based on your momentary situation or emotional state?

There's nothing wrong with making the choice based on momentary needs. Money is at least one of the reasons most of us work. Sometimes we need the cash regardless of how little it is or what we're giving up. Sometimes we need something the deal provides even if it's not congruent with our longer-term strategies. Being honest with yourself about your true motivations is the first step to properly evaluating the offers and opportunities you receive. The real trick is to know exactly what you're getting and what you're giving up. Then make the decision based on *what you want*.

Know What You Want

Troy Hazard was showing his audience of public speakers how to price their services and successfully negotiate their professional fees. He drew an XY coordinate diagram on a flip-chart in bold, black marker. He pointed to the lines as he explained the concept of value exchange.

"You can do all this," the keynote speaker said in his Australian accent, "or you can simply decide what matters most to you."

Troy switched to a personal story to explain what he meant.

"Here's my equation: If I'm out of town working with clients, I'm not on the beach. And if I'm not on the beach, I'm not building sandcastles with my three girls."

"Each time a client wants to negotiate my fee down from my initial proposal, my wife and I simply ask ourselves, 'Is the amount we're going to earn from the gig worth a sandcastle?' If it's not, I don't do the job. Simple as that."

Besides having the world's greatest crime-fighting superhero brand name (especially when said with his charming Aussie pronunciation: "Hazard. Troy Hazard.") Troy has created the perfect Rosetta Stone you can use for translating value. Simply put: Figure out exactly what your time and effort is worth to you.

And here's a hint: it doesn't have to be money.

Know What You *Don't* Want

In 2017 the AARP reported that the members of Generation X (the demographic cohort born between 1965 and 1980) were no longer interested in the same things their Baby Boomer (the earlier demographic cohort born between 1946 and 1964) parents wanted. According to Patty David, director of consumer insights at AARP, Gen Xers' idea of the American Dream was to focus on "well-being, to be healthy, and not necessarily worry about the big expensive things and having all the money."

From *The Wall Street Journal:*[9]

> Susan Patil Swearingen was 48, living in Chicago, and was 25 years into a corporate career when she fell into a depression. 'I had a very full, successful life. I burned out,' she says. Ms. Swearingen went to therapy and took a hard look at her life and what she wanted for its second half.
>
> Clearly the successful career, and the things that came with it, no longer gave Swearingen the same fulfillment or pleasure she had thought it would all those years before. Instead, she says she wanted the rest of her life to be "… much more focused on meaning."

Why did Swearingen find such a big difference between knowing what she wanted and what she didn't want? My guess is that you wonder the very same thing about your own life.

If you want a specific car or a home in a certain neighborhood, you know all the facts—how much it will cost, what the monthly payments will be, what interest rate you're likely to get, etc.

But when you *don't* want something, it's often because of a feeling, a sense, a certain something. And while you can't always put your finger on that certain something, it's a real problem just the same. It seems as if our desires can be measured intellectually while our dislikes tend to be more emotional—and that can cause lapses in judgement.

Raymond Chandler's noir detective novel *The Little Sister,* provides a sound explanation for this.

In the story, Detective Philip Marlowe, is offered money for an envelope full of incriminating photographs by Sheridan Ballou, a high-powered LA theatrical agent who thinks Marlowe is trying to extort his client for murder.

> "You can't buy anything, Mr. Ballou. I could have had a positive made from the negative and another negative from the positive. If that snapshot is evidence of something, you could never know you had suppressed it."
>
> "Not much of a sales talk for a blackmailer," Ballou said, still smiling.
>
> "I always wonder why people pay blackmailers. They can't buy anything. Yet they do pay them, sometimes over and over and over again. And in the end are just where they started."
>
> "The fear of today," Ballou said, "always overrides the fear of tomorrow. It's a basic fact of the dramatic emotions

…. If you see a glamour star on the screen in a position of great danger, you fear for her with one part of your mind, the emotional part. Notwithstanding that your reasoning mind knows that she is the star of the picture and nothing very bad is going to happen to her …."

When we're trying to decide what's next, it's not uncommon to see the future of a wonderful dream of opportunity. But that fantasy can be quickly overcome by doubt of the unfamiliar and the fear of what could if we untether ourselves from the comfortable and head off into the unknown. If the question of what's just around the corner defeats our understanding of the good we might yet accomplish, there is very little reason not to change.

Marlowe's last line sums up our dilemma succinctly: "If suspense and menace didn't defeat reason, there would be very little drama."

As you consider your next steps, figure out what you want and be specific about what you don't want. Often, it's the don't-wants that are easier to visualize. If you're single, you may want to meet someone who has blue eyes, though a brown-eyed someone might surprise you and turn your head. But if you're a non-smoker, you may not want to date a smoker. Take inventory of your don't-wants as these can offer valuable channel markers that will keep you from running aground in the shallows on your journey toward bigger and better.

Being Comfortable Being Uncomfortable

An easy way to think and act differently is to simply replace the word *change* with *growth*. While *change* acts as a threat response in our brains, *growth* helps us manage our journey into the unknown.

Change encourages the development of new neurons needed to deal with new situations. Trying new things and learning new skills force your brain to bypass your Threat Response System and deal with the *new*. There is no change without growth.

Change is inevitable whether you welcome it or not. You don't have to embrace change or encourage change or even *like* change, but you can't stop it. Just look around you.

Retail purchases used to be made in bricks and mortar stores. Today, more and more of them are made online.

Politicians and celebrities used to communicate with voters through press secretaries, publicists, and multi-level public relations outreach. Today, more and more of them Tweet directly to their audiences.

Big organizations used to control the conversation with their customers. Today, more and more customers have larger social media footprints than some Fortune 500 companies.

Currencies used to be valued based on the strength of their securitization, be it precious metals or the good faith of their issuing governments. Today, cryptocurrencies are changing the way people buy, sell, and invest with no clear country of origin or backing collateral.

People used to go the theaters to watch movies and to arenas to watch sporting events. Today consumers have high-definition digital screens. Cable, satellite, and Internet connections bring worldwide entertainment right to them.

Children used to be seen and not heard. Today, more and more of them are still not heard, but only because they're too busy texting on their cellphones to bother to talk to their elders.

You've experienced most or all of the recent phenomena I've just listed. Yet while you've seen all this change around you, you've still stood still, doing many things the same way you did before any of these changes created successes and failures around the world.

Change can be uncomfortable and stressful, but change is where opportunities can be found. In the world of *The Old Way of Doing Things,* most of the ripe fruit has already been harvested. In the world of *What Happens Next,* you'll have to find new ways to survive and thrive, but you get to plant the new crop. Get comfortable being uncomfortable. Substitute the word *growth* for the word *change* and make it happen.

The Courage to Change

What makes the elephant charge his tusk
In the misty mist or the dusky dusk?
What makes the muskrat guard his musk?
Courage!

—The Cowardly Lion, from *The Wizard of Oz*

Acceptance is all well and good, but beside having the willingness to change and understanding that the key to change is growth, crossing the chasm to enjoy your new life takes one more thing:

Courage.

Throughout history, plenty of great thinkers have written about courage:

Winston Churchill said, "Success is not final, failure is not fatal: it is the courage to continue that counts."

William Faulkner wrote, "You cannot swim for new horizons until you have courage to lose sight of the shore."

Anais Nin wrote, "Life shrinks or expands in proportion to one's courage."

Courage can manifest itself in lots of different ways, from silent, stoic acceptance to boisterous "damn the torpedoes" bluster. But regardless of how it works for you, experiencing the opportunities that lie out there in the great unknown is the answer to the things that are bothering you now. You already understand the risks of staying where you are. What you don't know is what will happen if you exchange the ordinary with the potential of a brighter future.

Courage is *not* the same thing as fearlessness. When you make big changes, it's a given that *you will be afraid.* You'll worry, doubt yourself, and wonder if you made the right decisions. The big question, then: Will you let your fear paralyze you or motivate you?

Could it even be that one of the reasons you no longer feel excited about whatever it is you've been doing is that it's too easy and there's just nothing left to be afraid of?

Change is Hard. Not Changing Might Be Harder.

What will happen if you decide not to change but instead choose to stay right where you are? It wouldn't be that bad, would it? It's not like your life depends on it, is it?

When my great grandparents uprooted their families and fled Eastern Europe, their lives did depend on it. Years of deadly pogroms followed by the dark clouds of fascism and anti-Semitism were ominous signs of the danger ahead.

When my wife's parents scooped up their two-year-old daughter and escaped communist Cuba, rumors of Castro's prisons and firing squads left little doubt about what would happen to them if they chose to stay behind.

What country they were going to mattered less than what country they were leaving. Or, as the ancient Italian saying explains, "The hungry aren't particular about which oven their bread comes from."

Those are not your problems.

The relative level of success you've achieved means that while you may not be picking between flying the Gulfstream or the Learjet to Europe for the season, it's not like you're deciding between buying medicine or food for your family. Things are pretty good, and most of the things that aren't pretty good are probably first-world problems.

But we don't always make changes because of ennui. Sometimes change is forced on us by circumstances we'd rather not have to deal with. Real estate professionals call those circumstances the Seven Ds—Divorce, Downsizing, Disease, Disability, Disasters,

Debt, and Death. Other than the blessings of a larger family or greater income, the Seven Ds are the main reasons people sell their homes and look for new places to live. They can also be the reasons why people finally decide to ditch their careers or their lifestyles and move on, especially if you add two more Ds— Dissatisfaction and Disappointment.

Maybe you are dealing with one of those events. Or maybe you're just sick and tired of being sick and tired. Either way, you have a choice to make…

Looking back over your life and kicking yourself for missed opportunities is never a good place to be. You know what will happen if you keep doing what you're doing, but imagine what could happen if you get fired up about doing something new?

9

Make Change Happen!

I T'S EASY to *talk* about change, but *doing* it is a different matter. What fears, concerns, habits, patterns, limiting beliefs, and undeveloped talents are keeping you from making the leap?

What's Bringing You Down?

Maybe you, like so many of my friends and my kids, find yourself dragged down by national and world events you find undecipherable. If so, let me try to help you get some of those thoughts out of the way so you can start your new adventure on the right foot.

From Nicolas Kristof's NYT op-ed, *This Has Been The Best Year Ever:*[10]

In the long arc of human history ... (this) has been the best year ever.

The bad things that you fret about are true. But it's also true that since modern humans emerged about 200,000 years ago, 2019 was probably the year in which children were least likely to die, adults were least likely to be illiterate and people were least likely to suffer excruciating and disfiguring diseases.

Or, as Israeli historian Yuval Noah Harari pointed out in *Sapiens*,[11] and *Homo Deus*,[12] for the first time in human history, more people died throughout the world from their indulgent diets than from the violence of war and crime combined. In other words, sugar is now more dangerous than gunpowder.

Max Roser, an Oxford University economist puts it this way:

If you were given the opportunity to choose the time you were born in, it'd be pretty risky to choose a time in any of the thousands of generations in the past. Almost everyone lived in poverty, hunger was widespread and famines common.

Back to Kristof:

> As recently as 1981, 42 percent of the planet's population endured 'extreme poverty,' defined by the United Nations as living on less than about $2 a day. That portion has plunged to less than 10 percent of the world's population now.
>
> Diseases like polio, leprosy, river blindness and elephantiasis are on the decline, and global efforts have turned the tide on AIDS. A half century ago, a majority of the world's people had always been illiterate; now we are approaching 90 percent adult literacy. There have been particularly large gains in girls' education—and few forces change the world so much as education and the empowerment of women.

"We are some of the first people in history who have found ways to make progress against these problems," says Roser, the economist. "We have changed the world. How awesome is it to be alive at a time like this?"

"Three things are true at the same time: the world is much better, the world is awful, the world can be much better."

Do You Have Too Many Choices?

Popular culture is full of conflicting advice on how to accomplish your dreams.

"Haste makes waste," and "Good things come to those who wait" face off against "The early bird catches the worm," and "He who hesitates is lost."

With all this chatter in our heads, it's no wonder that we're conflicted. Not only do we not know what to do with our lives, we don't even know if we should proceed with caution or throw caution to the wind and go for it—whatever "it" turns out to be.

Worse, while we don't know how much time we have left and we don't know what we should be doing between now and then, we do know what common fate awaits us all at the end—and it's the same end whether it comes in 20 minutes or 20 years.

"No matter what you do, it's all just going to run together by the time you're 50." said Blythe Danner's character, Carol Petersen, in the coming of (old) age dramcom, *I'll See You in My Dreams.*

"People can spend their whole lives ... waiting to find that feeling, trying to find that feeling over and over. And at the end, everybody gets it. We wait our whole lives for something and we get it. And you know what that is?"

"Happiness?" her hopeful young friend Lloyd asks.

"It's death,"[13] she deadpans.

There's nothing we can do about the inevitability of death. Sure, we can try to put it off as long as possible by watching what we eat, exercising regularly, trying to reduce our stress levels, and doing all the other things we're constantly reminded about on the covers of the magazines lining the grocery store checkout lane. But sooner or later our time's going to run out. And it's going to run out no matter how much kale we've choked down or how much we've actually accomplished in our lives.

That being said, it is a fact that our life expectancies are almost twice as long as they were only 100 years ago. And not only have our lifespans increased drastically, but so have our expectations of how we're going to live all those extra years we've been given. Today we are obsessed with both adding years to our lives and adding life to our years. One without the other feels like a raw deal because as much as we don't want to die young, who wants to live to be one hundred years old if we have to subsist on dented tins of BOGO cat food?

Over 160 artists have recorded the popular country song that twangs, "Everybody wants to go to heaven but nobody wants to die," everybody wants to live forever but nobody wants to grow old.

What does this mean for you?

Now is the time to move, the time to act, the time to change.

Now is the time to prove that you don't have to be defined by what you've done but instead by what you're yet to accomplish.

Now is the time to prove that not only must the show go on but that you're exactly the right person to make that happen.

After all, considering everything you've accomplished so far, what's the worst that could happen?

My grandfather's family left Poland and came to the United States a few years before the First World War. I have to believe that my grandfather's expectations of what his work would provide him with centered around money and security. Beside needing to find his way in a country where he didn't speak the language or understand the customs, my grandfather needed to earn enough money to feed himself and support his family. Education, purpose, enjoyment, and the like must have all taken a backseat to immediate opportunity and cold hard cash.

So imagine if you or I were to try to explain to my grandad exactly why we were dissatisfied with our careers and our lives. My grandfather had escaped the deadly pogroms of Poland and later returned to Eastern Europe to save three of his sisters from near certain death at the hands of the Third Reich. By the time he retired, he owned a home, a business, and a Cadillac. Plus, he had put his three children through college and was still able to buy a condo on Miami Beach and spend his remaining days playing pinochle.

Would any of those experiences have given my grandfather any understanding of your needs for fulfillment and self-expression?

Of course, that question is rhetorical. My grandpa Nat could no more live your life than you can live his. And while his problems and concerns might seem more existential through the refining lens of history and experience than our own, who's to say they were more real or troubling to him than yours are to you? We're each dealt the cards we get and we each have to play the best hand we can manage.

To start playing the game, and playing to win, you just have to ask yourself your own personal version of a simple question: *Is That All There Is?*

Doing It Differently

What things do you do a certain way only because you've always done them that way? What opinions, perspectives, or viewpoints do you hold just because you've held them for a long time without reconsidering? What habits, practices, or rules constrain your future simply because they helped you create your past?

Maybe it's time to reconsider what you're doing and the way you do it. Maybe it's time to start looking at new solutions and new viewpoints.

160 years ago Charles Dickens wrote opposing opinions and contrasting viewpoints in his masterpiece, *A Tale of Two Cities:*

> It was the best of times, it was the worst of times, it was the age of wisdom, it was the age of foolishness, it was the epoch of belief, it was the epoch of incredulity, it was the season of Light, it was the season of Darkness, it was the spring of hope, it was the winter of despair, we had everything before us, we had nothing before us, we were all going direct to heaven, we were all going direct the other way—in short, the period was so far like the present period, that some of its noisiest authorities insisted on its being received, for good or for evil, in the superlative degree of comparison only.

My running group meets bright and early at 5:45 AM to get our sweaty miles in.

When we invite new runners to join us, or when I tell people about our regular runs, they want to know why we meet so early. One of the reasons is so the young parents in our group can make it home in time to get their kids ready for school. A second reason is that if we start before 6:00 AM we can usually finish around 7:00 and get back in our cars before Miami traffic gets too congested. And the third is that if we wait until the sun rises, it gets too bloody hot to bang out five or seven miles without passing out.

Because meeting for these early morning runs is a four-time-a-week ritual, and because I've been doing it for at least 15 years, getting up early and running has become an ingrained habit. That's why I find it odd to be in another city and see people running at noon or later.

That's not when you're supposed to run, I think. *You're supposed to run early in the morning.*

You already know this makes no sense. If you don't have to get your kids to school, if you're not worried about traffic, or if it doesn't get Africa-hot once the sun comes up, there's absolutely no reason to drag yourself out of bed at o'dark-thirty in the morning just to pile on the miles. It only makes sense to *us* because we've been doing it that way for so damn long.

But does that make it right? Comedian Steven Wright said "I'm not afraid of heights; I'm afraid of widths." If I keep running in the morning simply because I've done it that way for 15 or so years, does that mean I'm afraid of lengths?

What other misconceptions have I developed? What do I do simply because I've been doing it that one way for so long that it's become ingrained as the *only* way to do something?

For example, I only drive cars with manual transmissions. I think automatic transmissions take the pleasure and control away from the fun of driving. *But do they really?*

I refuse to wear a tuxedo if the party invitation says, "black-tie optional." I do have a tux hanging in my closet, and it's actually a pretty easy wardrobe choice — I know exactly what shirt, shoes, socks, and tie go with the suit. The problem is I've always thought that if it's black-tie optional and everyone's not wearing a tux I'll look like a waiter. *But will I really?*

In the 12 years I've been writing my weekly blog, I've never allowed guest posts. I write everything myself (even though sometimes I don't have anything to say or I don't have the time to write). I figure if I let others write on my blog, I'll lose some level of the intimate relationship I've developed with my readers. *But will I really?*

And don't even get me started on which way I insist on hanging the toilet paper!

Realizing all of that, I'm going to go running at 4 PM one day soon.

Ask yourself:

What are you going to do differently in your life? Because living the rest of your life differently is what this book is all about.

Make Your Scar Your Star

Feeling dissatisfied is easy; no one has to work at that. But figuring out what to do next presents a real conundrum. By now you've probably identified and leveraged a number of strengths, but consider that your real power may lie in what you've always thought of as your weaknesses.

So, who are you?

Up until now you've probably been taught that you're the sum of all your parts. A big, coherent whole made up of your talents, your abilities, your diplomas, your certificates, your accomplishments, and your superpowers.

The best of the best.

But what if that assumption is wrong? What if it turned out that your liabilities are actually more descriptive than your assets? Who would you be if, instead of presenting from strength, you were actually presenting from weakness? And what if your weaknesses were actually your strengths?

What if your scar were actually your star?

When I present to corporate conferences, I often talk to my audiences about turning their liabilities into assets. But because I want them to have some skin in the game. I usually don't explain to my audiences how they can do it. I want them to go out on a limb, raise their hands, and ask how it should be done. Because when they do that they're more likely to listen and look for ways to apply the lesson in their own lives than when they just hear a new idea thrown at them.

By the time we get to Q&A, most of my audience has heard that they need to make their scars their stars more than once, but they still don't know *how* to do it. So, when the first person in the room asks the question, everyone pays attention.

That's when I know some real discovery can take place and when I tell this little story:

Energetic and Enthusiastic

"When this presentation is over and you get up to leave, you're going to be handed a yellow sheet of paper. It's the speaker evaluation form the organizer wants you to fill out. You'll get to evaluate how well I did up here on the stage and how much value you got from my presentation. The form will ask questions such as, 'On a scale of 1–10, how well did the speaker meet your expectations?' and, 'Was the subject matter appropriate to your business?' and maybe, "How well did the speaker explain the concepts they discussed?"'

Below those questions there is usually a box where you get the chance to write what you thought of the presentation in your own words.

Obviously, I've read a lot of these forms. And I generally find that most people say the same things: I get high marks — eights to tens usually — in the top section. And they usually use the same two words to describe my presentation in the comment box: "Energetic" and "Enthusiastic."

That makes sense, of course. I *am* energetic and enthusiastic. But being energetic and enthusiastic is not something I plan on; it's simply who I am. Before I got up on stage, I didn't stand in front of the mirror in the green room and repeat "Be energetic. Be enthusiastic." I just am. It's my gift. It's my superpower. Being energetic and enthusiastic is my asset.

But it's also my liability.

From an accounting point of view, the distinction between assets and liabilities is simple: Assets are the items you or your company own that can provide future economic benefit: Money in the bank, property owned, equipment, proprietary systems, account receivables, goodwill, inventory, brand value. All of these are assets.

Liabilities are what you owe other parties: Mortgages, debts, taxes due, accounts payable, and more are all liabilities.

Spoken like an accountant: Assets earn you money; liabilities cost you money.

But when it comes to your life, the distinction is less clear.

You see, being energetic and enthusiastic might be a great way for me to enchant an audience today, but it was a bit different when I was 12 years old: My audience back then also filled out a form that rated my performance. That audience was made up of my elementary school teachers. The evaluation was my report card.

I got pretty good grades for my presentation and content—As and Bs mostly—but down in the section where the teachers could fill in their description of my performance, they would write something like: "Bruce is a very good student. If only he could talk less, draw fewer pictures, sit still, and pay more attention he would do much better in class."

Today my behavior would probably be diagnosed as some sort of attention deficit disorder. Back then, being energetic and enthusiastic didn't work so well for me, but somehow I found a positive outlet for my liabilities. It wound up defining my performance and my value and it works really well for me today.

Why?

Because I made my scar my star.

Turn Your Liabilities into Assets

Every four years we get the opportunity to watch the world's most important branding contest— the United States presidential election. There's a lot to learn from studying the best of the best without letting your political opinion cloud your judgement.

In the 2012 election, statistician Nate Silver and then-governor Mitt Romney tutored us on the importance of precise research— both accurate and inaccurate. Four years before that, Barack Obama, Chuck Grassley, and Sarah Palin gave us a masters' class on messaging with "Yes we can," "Pulling the plug on Grandma," and "Death Panels." And as far back as 1960, Kennedy and Nixon's debate provided us all with a great lesson on how media can change public opinion and create or damage a brand.

The 2016 race was no different. That year the candidates on both sides of the aisle were also living laboratories for how to build a brand and relate to your audience.

Or how not to.

Hilary Clinton and Jeb Bush showed us what branding looked like for an established, mature product. Donald Trump and Bernie Sanders offered examples of how challenger brands generate passionate customers. Marco Rubio demonstrated how dangerous it is to allow your competition to create your persona and then reinforce that brand image with your own actions. And Ted Cruz was a shining example of what happens when you don't turn your liabilities into assets.

It's not like we hadn't seen it done properly before. Ronald Reagan created the masterclass back in 1984 when the then 72-year-old president was running for reelection against a 56-year-old Walter Mondale. Reagan ended speculation that he was too old to be president with one funny line: "I will not make age an issue of this campaign. I am not going to exploit, for political purposes, my opponent's youth and inexperience."

But it's not just politics where turning a scar into a star is so powerful. There are plenty of business examples, too.

3M did it when they turned a glue with weak adhesive properties into Post-It Notes.

Avis did it when they applauded their also-ran status with the line, "We're number two. We try harder."

Harley Davidson did it when they bragged about their customer waiting list and their inability to produce more motorcycles. They suggested it proved their commitment both to their uncompromising quality and the undying loyalty of their customers.

Paul Masson used the same strategy with their tagline, "We will sell no wines before their time."

Harland Sanders did it when he promoted extra greasy fried chicken with the line: "Kentucky Fried Chicken. It's finger-lickin' good!"

So how could Ted Cruz have turned his liabilities into assets? Quite simply by accepting his obvious liability—that he was not likeable—and turning it to his advantage. While Trump and Sanders were busy exploiting voter anger and criticizing their competitors for their establishment stands, Cruz could have risen above it all. He could have used the disdain his fellow senators have for him to his advantage. He could have confirmed his anti-establishment bona fides by celebrating his lack of popularity. He could have positioned his unlikability as the unfortunate result of doing the right thing instead of the popular thing. He could have demonstrated his undying commitment to his constituency by making his scar his star.

Unfortunately for Cruz, this alchemical exercise of turning emotional lead into gold is very hard to do. It not only requires the profound self-awareness of knowing what your actual weaknesses are, and having the willingness to face them, it requires the courage to expose your vulnerabilities. What's more, it demands the creative foresight to pursue a less-than-popular strategy.

Scratches, Scrapes, Scars, and Scuffs

The gouges and discolorations on my 1952 Gibson guitar were put there by all the players who played it before I did. They coaxed their own personal music out of an inanimate box of wood and wire long before I ever played it. Hell, they were putting marks on the guitar before I was even born. Needless to say, I can't hear the music they played, and I certainly don't know where the guitar has been or who held it. But I can see the effects their care and carelessness left all over it. The arc of gouges beneath the sound hole tell a story of frantic strumming. The circular abrasions on the back suggest frenzied encounters with a belt buckle or the arm of an old metal porch chair. And the miscellaneous scratches and dents might be the result of clumsy (or drunken) nights when my guitar wasn't yet a classic or vintage heirloom but just someone's old guitar.

My parents gave me a beautiful watch for my 20th birthday. 42 years later it's still on my wrist and still bears witness to all the moments in my life—both momentous and mundane. While I have taken it to the watchmaker for regular maintenance, I always tell them not to touch up its nicked and chipped finish. After all, the collection of scratches, scrapes, scars, and scuffs are not imperfections, they're reminders of miles traveled, and times measured.

Beautiful new things are just that—beautiful and new. And my kids will surely roll their eyes as they confirm that I can be as finicky as anyone when it comes to keeping new things pristine and perfect. But it's our marks and blemishes that make us interesting and unique. Just like the scratches on my guitar tell a story of use and adventure, your own wrinkles and idiosyncrasies are hard-earned symbols of a life well-lived with lessons well-learned. The accumulated marks of pain, experience, and lessons learned the hard way show us the way to a better future.

The Danger of Perfection and Success

Many of us become crushed under the weight of our own high standards. We're accustomed to raising the bar. We see excellence as its own reward.

We're all taught to do things to the best of our ability. "Practice makes perfect," we're admonished. "If at first you don't succeed, try, try again." "The good is the enemy of the great!"

But sometimes this adopted or inherited need for perfection keeps us from trying whatever it is we need to do to move forward. After all, if we believe everything has to be done perfectly, how will we ever find the guts to try something new, especially when we might fail, or not reach the lofty heights we're hoping for.

"To search for perfection is all very well, but to look for heaven is to live here in hell," sang Sting in "Consider Me Gone"[14] and he's right. Sometimes we have to accept that the pleasure, and possibly the reward, is simply in doing something, not necessarily in doing it right.

Canadian writer Ian Brown recorded an introspective journal the year he turned 60, cleverly subtitled, *The beginning of the end or the end of the beginning?* In it, Brown explained the debilitating price of striving for perfection: "If you feel you have to do something perfectly, you will never attempt it. If you know you will fail but figure what the hell, you might just try."[15]

Knowing we won't always succeed, Brown considered the inevitability of failure as a potential benefit: "If I were a gardener, a serious gardener, someone who lived for gardening, I would never again worry about having wasted my life. The gardener has a built-in engagement with failure because Nature always beats you down, but then you never expect to succeed, and are always slightly pleased when you occasionally do."[16]

But admirable though they may be, these values can prevent you from moving forward. You may have to allow yourself to be mediocre at something new for a while as you make your transition. With time and practice, you can become just as adept at whatever you do next as you were with whatever you're ready to leave behind.

When it comes to trying something new and changing your life, maybe Nike was right. "Just do it."

Make an inventory of your life's biggest fails, nearest misses, and greatest escapes. Think about what lessons you learned from each. Maybe you were a terrible spouse who learned to be more compassionate in your second marriage. Maybe you survived cancer, addiction, or bankruptcy? Maybe you experienced war or a natural disaster? Whether or not you gained any skills from these experiences, you gained meaningful insights and perspectives.

How can you use this wisdom to guide, encourage, or inspire others? Scratches, dings, and dents like yours have formed the foundation of many profitable enterprises and coaching practices.

Make your scar your star.

10

Don't Worry; You're Not Alone

WHATEVER IT IS that's holding you back, know that you don't have to set off on this journey all by yourself. I'm going to introduce you to some very successful people who reached the unknown just like you have. Each of them had to decide what to do about it. And each of them decided to move forward to discover a brave new world.

Some of them made it successfully across the chasm and settled comfortably into their new lives. Others had to try more than once before they reached the promised land. And still others made the trip across, continued along their new journeys, and then found they needed to make life changes over and over again. As you'll see, each individual's trip is their own. What they share in common is that they're all willing to be your guide and tell you about the trips they've taken.

Keep this idea of a *journey* in mind while you read their stories. Be an active traveler and experience the journey along with them. Don't just stare out of the car window at the scenery whizzing past. Roll the window down, feel the breeze on your face, and smell the air. Put on your guide's shoes and sense what their experiences would feel like if they were happening to you. Listen to new music. Taste new food. Try on a different version of yourself. Your mind and your imagination are about to go on a magnificent expedition.

These stories will show you how some very special people navigated the minefields of their own evolution and figured out how to create the lives they wanted to live. You'll probably notice that as they moved toward a better future, they were also moving away from a less-than-ideal past. Their lives became the canvases they used not only to create their new pictures, but to paint over old pictures they no longer wanted to look at anymore.

Each storyteller's reason for retelling their story and changing their own personal ending was different. Some wanted to overcome poverty; some insecurity. Some wanted to right a wrong.

Some wanted to prove a point. Some wanted more excitement. Some wanted to relax. Each wanted to change something they weren't happy about.

Singer/songwriter James Taylor (who calls himself "a professional autobiographer") explains:

> Memory is tricky. We remember how it felt, not necessarily how it was.
>
> Songs grow out of memories. I have a running joke that I keep on writing the same six or seven songs over and over again.
>
> I think many of us keep trying to work out exactly what happened in our early years. We want to go back and fix something that has already vanished and can never be corrected. But we can correct it in a song, in a book, a poem, a play.
>
> One of the nice things art does is to make things rhyme, tie up loose ends. Sometimes you can even slap on a happy ending.[17]

And that's the point of this book—to give you a different way to plan the rest of your life and help you slap on your own happy ending while you're still writing your own story.

There's no Right Way.
There's Only Their Way and Your Way.

The people you'll meet in these pages present different examples and offer different opinions. And often, those opinions conflict with each other. Robert Mazzucchelli went from being a professional tennis player to an advertising agency owner to a menswear retailer and manufacturer to an online entrepreneur. Alex Fraser moved from basketball to the mortgage business to credit card processing to urban development. Nathalie Cadet-James went from practicing law to event planning and was successful at both.

On the other hand, real estate investor Seth Werner says you should "stick with what you know." According to Werner, "The few times I ventured outside of what I really do and tried to do things that were outside my wheelhouse, I either lost money or didn't enjoy the experience." Werner believes that "people who consistently make money in one business after another are the people who are able to use the experiences they have rather than having to learn a new business from scratch."

The question is not which of the people you'll meet are correct, but which of their routes makes the most sense to you and your life.

The depth of change you decide to undertake is not just what you do with your physical situation and your relationships. It can also be measured by how you see your life as a part of the greater whole of the world and history. One of the great questions that has plagued mankind throughout history is, "Why are we here?" Your exploration of the rest of your life could be your own personal search for that answer. And the success of the changes you choose to make can also be measured by the way you view spirituality and a higher cause for your existence.

So what are the first steps you should take on your own path to real change?

The Question You Should Ask

No matter how you choose to digest *Is That All There Is?*, do it with one question in mind: How can I apply these tips and techniques to *my own* life? Not only have the people you're reading about been to the pivot party and lived to tell about it, they're sharing their real solutions with you. That means you might be able to find a shortcut to your desired outcome. Use what you learn in the following chapters to help guide your journey and avoid the pitfalls others have already discovered. And because nothing succeeds like success, why wouldn't you want to give yourself the best chance to progress toward the optimal outcome you've been searching for?

Per Harvard's Teresa Amabile and Steve Kramer, progress is the most motivating force you can use to move yourself forward: "This pattern is what we call the progress principle: Of all the positive events that influence inner work life, the single most powerful is progress in meaningful work; of all the negative events, the single most powerful is the opposite of progress—setbacks in the work. We consider this to be a fundamental management principle: facilitating progress is the most effective way for managers to influence inner work life."[18]

If at First You Don't Succeed...

We've all heard the stories:

Thomas Edison reportedly tried over a thousand different filaments before he found the perfect material to illuminate his light bulb.

Wimbledon and Davis Cup champion tennis player Stan Smith was turned down when he first applied to be a ball boy at a Davis Cup tournament.

Fred Smith explained the concept that ultimately became Federal Express as his senior thesis at Yale and received a C on the paper. The story is that his teacher wrote, "Your concept is interesting but in order to earn a better grade, your ideas have to be feasible."

J.K. Rowling's *Harry Potter* was rejected by twelve publishers before becoming a monster best-seller and catapulting the author to enormous fame and fortune.

Twenty-seven publishers rejected Dr. Seuss's first book.

Walt Disney was fired by a newspaper editor. Charles Schultz (Peanuts) had all his cartoons rejected by his high school year-book editor. Comedian Jerry Seinfeld was jeered off his first stage. Robin Williams was voted "least likely to succeed" in high school. Vincent Van Gogh only sold one painting during his entire lifetime.

Madonna, U2, and even the Beatles were turned down by the first record companies they contacted.

Uber-consultant Alan Weiss' bestseller, *Million Dollar Consulting* was rejected fifteen times before being accepted by McGraw-Hill with no changes. As Weiss says, "If you don't make a sale—your proposal isn't accepted—it may simply mean that at the particular time on that particular day a particular buyer decided not to say 'yes.'

"We can learn from our setbacks, be resilient and move forward as better, wiser people. Or we can choose to suffer longer-term, engage in bad habits, seek solace in all the wrong places.

"It's really a question of how well you choose to control your life."

We've all heard the old saw, "If at first you don't succeed, try, try, again." Andy Andrews, the author of *The Traveler's Gift,*[19] listed perseverance as the ultimate point of his *Seven Decisions:* I will persist without exception. I will find a way where there is no way."

What you'll learn from the people you're about to meet is that there are as many different responses to "How long will it take?" as there are people who try to answer the question. But what they all share is the willingness to try, try again.

Some people pivot on a dime, abandoning what they were doing the second they even get a sense of it not working. Some people continue to bang their heads against the wall until they start to see some progress. And some people decide to move forward or move on somewhere in the middle.

There is no one right answer. The only answer that matters is the answer that's right for you.

The Truth, the Whole Truth, and Nothing But The Truth

When I interviewed the people you're about to spend time with, I kept this thought in mind: I wanted them to tell us about their successes and share the tools, tips, and techniques they believed helped them accomplish their goals. But I also wanted

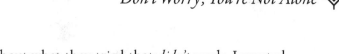

them to talk about what they tried that *didn't* work. I wanted to know where they hit a wall, where they made a mistake, where they wasted their time, their efforts, and their money. It seemed critically important that they provide an unvarnished report of how they got to where they are today, so you could weigh the costs and potential benefits of following their advice for yourself.

How to Get on TV

After appearing on national TV news programs over 400 times, I created a workshop entitled "How to get on TV."

I was given two-and-a-half hours to expose conference attendees to exactly what they needed to do to get on television. And two-and-a-half hours was just barely enough time to share all the tips and techniques needed to effectively cover the subject. After all, there's a lot that needs to be done in order to end up with the coveted spot in front of the camera.

The outline for the talk was systematic and thorough. It started with a quick overview of why I had the credibility to teach this course in the first place. Then it covered the reasons someone would actually want to be on TV.

From there we moved into actual the actual strategy of what to do — day in and day out — to get on TV.

We talked about how the TV news business works, about which professionals at a network make the decisions about who gets on the air, how they make their decisions, and what they do once they decide whom they want to work with.

We talked about how to write a "concept segment," how to reach out to the bookers, how to get into the bookers' "Golden Rolodex," and how to follow up on their initial requests.

The curriculum included information on how to prepare for a segment, how to research the subject, how to know what questions you're going to be asked, and how to demonstrate your value to the booker, producer, and anchor.

Next we role-played what to do once you're at the studio, what to do when the "On-Air" light comes on, what to do while you're on the air, and what do do when the producer tells you, "You're all clear."

Finally we discussed what to do immediately after the interview, what to do the next day, what to do the next week, and what to do to generate the next opportunity.

Though the workshop was exhaustive, it gave my audience a real overview of the TV experience and the tools they needed to actually generate opportunities.

After the seminar, I was walking down the hallway toward the reception, when a friend of mine stopped me. She wanted to tell me what she thought about the workshop.

"Wow," she started. "Your workshop on how to get on TV was wonderful. I've wanted to be on TV for years so I've attended lots of classes before, but yours was different. You see, they only talked about theory and told us why we should be on TV. Your class was the first one I've ever attended that showed us exactly what we need to do to get on the tube. Now I know that if I do what you taught us, I will achieve my dream and get on TV."

"Thank you," I answered. "I appreciate your kind words and I'm so glad you liked the presentation. Thank you for telling me. Please make sure you tell me when you actually get on TV."

"That's the thing" she said. "After you explained the whole process to me so carefully, I realized I'm not willing to do the amount of work it takes to get on TV. The price you've quoted is just much more than I'm willing to spend. While I was taking notes, I realized I just don't want to get on TV that badly."

I looked a bit disappointed but she went on: "But that's the good part. You see, I've always been mad at myself because I wasn't on TV. I figured I wasn't smart enough, I wan't pretty enough, I wasn't connected enough. But now that you've shown me what it takes, I realize that I haven't gotten on TV because I just haven't done the work. And since I now know that I'm not willing to do the work, there's no reason for me to be mad at myself anymore."

I've been running marathons for years. And I've always been embarrassed by my finishing times. Recently I read *Let Your*

Mind Run by Deena Kastor. Don't know Kastor? Wikipedia says, "Deena Michelle Kastor is an American long-distance runner. She holds American records in the marathon, half-marathon, and numerous road distances. She won the bronze medal in the women's marathon at the 2004 Olympics in Athens, Greece. She is also an eight-time national champion in cross-country."

In her book, Kastor clearly spells out the training she did to become one of the fastest runners in the world. She wrote about the 120-mile weeks, the six years of total focus on her workouts. She documented the effort and the pain.

Guess what? Even if I had a modicum of Kastor's talent, I'm simply not willing to put in any of the hard work Kastor did. Knowing that, why would I still be mad at myself for my slow times? I've simply accepted the fact that if I'm not willing to put in the effort, I shouldn't expect better results.

My friend Michelle is no longer going to be upset about not being on TV. I'm no longer going to be disappointed by my marathon times. What's going to get better for you?

While you read the tales of our life-changers, make sure you pay attention to the prices they paid for their successes and decide if what you want is worth the amount of work it might take to accomplish it.

Sometimes you can eliminate aggravation by overcoming whatever is holding you back. But look for aggravations that you can logically discard from your life because you're not willing to do what's required to make something happen. Learning what you're not willing to do will help you stop beating yourself up, give yourself a break, and treat yourself a little bit nicer.

All Roads Lead Home. Where Do You Want to Live?

As I conducted the interviews, I was also careful to make sure that they were telling their own stories, not simply offering philosophies they knew I would agree with. I want to be a true chronicler of their experiences and I didn't want to judge right and wrong based on my personal view of the world. My goal was to provide you with many proven paths to success with the hope that you'll find the route that is best for you.

For example, Susan Ford Collins and I have very different views of how the world works. Simply put, Susan is a "Universe will provide" person and I am not. Susan believes in magical thinking and I don't. Despite our differences, however, Susan is a very good friend, and was a critical coach and advisor to me when I was looking to free myself from my business.

I remember asking Susan how I would know when something I was trying out for the first time was on the right track.

"Watch for the little explosions," she'd say with a twinkle in her eye. "That's how you know the Universe is working on your behalf."

"But I don't believe in the Universe!"

"That's okay," Susan answered, undetered by my skepticism. "The Universe doesn't care whether you believe in it or not."

Some of the advice our tour guides share contradicts other's. One person is going to tell you to stick with what you know, saying that they believe in sticking with what made them successful in the first place. Another will tell you that they only did something once—just long enough to gain experience before moving on. And a third is going to suggest that you just stay open to whatever happens and "go with the flow."

How can you move forward if the map you're given has different routes and all of them are leading you to different places?

It's simple.

Just like the people in the interviews, you are heading out on your own unique journey toward your own unique destination. A one-size-fits-all solution won't work. The purpose of these interviews is to expose you to the tools our travelers used to reach their own goals. They'll not only tell you about the good and wondrous things that happened to them along the way, they'll share some of the mistakes they made and the failures they experienced. Their stories will suggest that maybe you should zig where they zagged, or perhaps you should keep your eyes open for the specific pitfalls and dead ends—actual and metaphorical—that made their trips that much more difficult.

It's up to you to decide what makes sense to you and what doesn't. It's your responsibility to use the ideas you like and discard the ones you don't. After all, their journey is not your journey. Since they drew their personal treasure maps, life's tradewinds might have shifted and the shoals might have moved. Plus, your boat might be faster—or slower—than the metaphorical ones they were sailing in. But despite your differences, these guides can still help you set your path and uncover your own buried treasure.

Or, to paraphrase a friend of mine's father, a gentleman with the wonderfully dramatic name of Broadway Haywood, "Been There can tell Going There how to get there."

Bon voyage!

The Interviews

Robert Mazzucchelli,
Founder, SportsEdTV

I met Robert after he had just completed another one of his pivots. When we first spoke I thought he was following a rather typical path—Robert had sold his business, gotten divorced, moved to Miami, and bought a sports car.

Once I got to know him and heard his story, I realized that the common stereotype I saddled him with was just that—both common and stereotypical. Instead, Robert told me a fascinating story of dreams, talents, failures, and successes.

Most of all, Robert told me a story of constant reinvention.

Robert Mazzucchelli

Growing up I knew I was going to be a tennis player. My entire life took place on the tennis court. I went to college with the intention that my career would be five to ten years of playing tennis. I studied a little bit so I'd have a backup, but the truth is I didn't really have a backup. I was going to play pro tennis.

That was it. *That* was my plan.

After school of course I went to play tennis. And my goal was to get ranked at least 200th in the world and I didn't make it. I got to 600 and—*BAM!*—I hit a wall. I hit a wall in my ability level, and I hit a wall financially because I needed to pay to improve my level. I was 22 years old and I realized that all 22 years of my life had been in only direction. Tennis. My whole life was geared towards, "I'm going to be a professional athlete" and all of a sudden, I woke up one day and said, "No I'm not."

The panic attacks and the stress were unbelievable.

I had no choice but to look for something else. I was leaving college with $10,000 in debt on my credit cards and I was losing on the court, and I knew this wasn't going to work. I mean I knew that even if I got a little better—I could spend three years moving up 300 more places—but I was still never going to make a living at tennis, so I'd better quit while I still had a chance.

I left tennis a few months after my 22nd birthday. I just picked up my stuff—I was living in Miami at that time, sleeping on the floor of my coach's apartment—and I got in my car with everything I owned, and I drove home to DC.

Now what was I going to do?

Within a month I had reconnected with my oldest and best friend and we decided that we were going to open up a marketing company. We had no clients, no experience, we just had an idea and brass balls. And we did it. We just said, "okay, what are we going to specialize in?"

We looked at the whole market. We were so naïve, if I ever thought to do that again with what I know now I'd call myself crazy, you know? But I didn't have the benefit of that or maybe the impediment, so it just worked.

We started the marketing company, we carved out this unique niche which was sponsorships and strategy for sports. No one was really doing that back then. And over a six-year period, my daily concern was that I needed to learn this business because I didn't go to school to study advertising, it was just a thing that was out there.

I went to Barnes & Noble—there was no Internet back then—and I'd pull all the marketing books off the shelf and sit in the coffee shop and read them. I went through at least 200 books on advertising and marketing. My plan was to read them all because when I got to talk to someone about their business, I'd better know some things about marketing that they didn't know. I'd need to get smarter than them. And I needed to get smarter fast.

I was speed-reading all these marketing books, and my partner was speed-dialing all these potential clients. We didn't know what we were going to pitch them, but we had a little script and every time we got a meeting I would go in and I would say "Okay, what are we selling, what are we doing for them? How are we going to help their business?"

Over that six-year period Steve and I built that idea of a business into a five-million-dollar company from zero, from nothing. And that was awesome, right? And we got to the point where we sold it. We were young, I think I was 30. I had just had my daughter, Ariana, at the time.

So now we're selling the business and Steve is moving to California, and I'm like, "Okay, what am I gonna do now?"

During the last three years Steven and I ran our company we would get calls from guys who'd ask if we wanted to sell our company or merge with them and I always used to joke with Steve that I wasn't interested unless I could work in The Chrysler Building. That became my standard response because we were young and naïve and brash. We thought we were going to build this monster company and I really loved The Chrysler Building— it was my favorite building in New York City. The irony is that when I was offered this big job and decided to go to work for Saatchi and Saatchi Holdings, their office was in The Chrysler Building, so I thought maybe it was a sign.

I had gone from playing tennis to running my agency. We got lucky and the business actually worked. And all of a sudden,

I'm 30 years old and I was offered a job as the president of a division of one of the biggest companies in the advertising world. With a big salary and lots of benefits and perks and things that when I had owned my own company I never really thought about or knew existed. So, there were a lot of things I transitioned to. They were good things, but it was still a huge change that I had to learn to deal with.

That was transition number two: I had gone from being a tennis player to starting a business. Now overnight I was going from being a small entrepreneur to working with one of the biggest ad agency groups in the world. That was a big adjustment for me because I had never worked for anybody else before.

The very first day I reported to my new job I walked into the lobby of The Chrysler Building. It's this incredible Art Deco lobby filled with marble and metal work. It's just gorgeous. The elevators are paneled with incredible wood inlaid with metal, and when I looked at the directory, one of the old-school directories where they push the white letters in, my name was right there on the panel: "Robert Mazzucchelli, President."

We didn't have cellphones with cameras back then, so I had no way to take a picture of the directory. My dream had come true and I had no way to memorialize it. Today I would have taken a picture and it would have been posted on Facebook the same day!

My transition went from "What the hell am I going to do?" to "How the hell am I going to function?" I was going from someone who had spent six years calling his own shots and running his own business to having to navigate this big world where I wasn't in control. I mean, even though I was president of the division, I reported to this guy who reported to the head of the company. And boy was that a massive change because office politics were never my thing.

I said to myself, "I don't own this company. I work for these other people. And no matter what I do they're going to make decisions I don't like. Right or wrong, I'm not going to work the way I did when I owned the company. I'm going to work hard and just do the best I can do." I made a conscious decision that I would never work on weekends unless I was traveling for business. And for six and a half years I worked my ass off all week long—I went in early and I stayed out late entertaining clients. But on Friday evening I went home, and I didn't pick up a piece of work until the next Monday.

My way of coping with it was, "I'll put up with this corporate bullshit"—and there was a lot of corporate bullshit—"but I'm just a hired gun; it's not my sandbox"—and I devoted myself to having a balanced life.

After about six months, the chairman of the holding company asked me to create a global company based on what I was doing in New York. He wanted me to partner with this guy in London and make a huge company. It was a rapid fire transition and I went from working for a subsidiary of a well-known ad agency to being president of a division of that company. Then all of a sudden, they were saying I would be the global guy. And this all happened in the span of a year. It was like a dream come true, a real Cinderella story.

I was rising, rising, rising and the global thing got me excited. Back then we had 114 offices around the world, and they picked a few where they thought I could grow the business. From that point forward, I spent three and a half years travelling around the globe. That was my job—I'd get up on Monday morning and jump on a plane. I'd travel somewhere, go from office to office, and come back at the end of the week and take the weekend off. I was travelling constantly and I loved it. *I loved it!*

I don't know how I managed it, but it just seemed to work. It took so much energy and adrenaline that my time at Saatchi and Saatchi went by really fast. It was a whirlwind and it was really fun. I was going full speed and I was in demand and meeting new people and visiting a new city every day. I was like the Messiah coming to a new country and telling them how to do marketing the American way. From Eastern Europe to South America to Asia they didn't know what integrated marketing was. And I was the guy to lead them to the promised land. I'd fly into their city, show them how we did things in New York, have a great dinner, and then fly off to my next destination and start all over again.

We built a massive company, offices in 50 countries with over two-hundred-million dollars in revenue. And then one day I saw even more growth opportunities and I went to the board to ask for more money to continue to grow the company.

They said "no."

I was stunned. I'd done everything they'd asked me to do and built a big operation that was making lots of money for them. But not only did they say no, they told me they were going to use the money to do something else, something I thought was absolutely ridiculous. I had just grown the business to more than $200,000,000 in revenue while the rest of the company had eroded about a billion dollars of market cap. So, when they said no it came as a complete shock to me.

I told the president that his decision was the stupidest thing I had ever heard. But even as I was saying it I was thinking I had just gotten myself fired. And sure enough, as soon as I walked out of the room my counterpart in London chased me into the hallway and screamed at me.

"What in the bloody hell are you doing?"

The next day they wrote me a check and wished me luck. And there I was, 38 years old and out on my ass.

I didn't know what I'd do next.

This was a really hard moment because I didn't realize that the advertising business was collapsing all around me. I'd had a lot of success really young but for my next job I'd be competing with guys with 20 years more experience than I'd had. And I was stuck. I was in a really tough spot.

The headhunters told me, "Robert, the chance of you getting another job like the one you just had with that salary level is really slim. There are 50 guys out there with much more experience than you have, and they'll work for less money than you want."

I didn't believe them at the time but when I went on several interviews that's exactly what happened. The HR people kept telling me the same thing: "We love you Robert, but we have this guy who's run companies for ten years more than you, and he wants $200,000 less. So we're going to go with him."

After about six months of this I gave up.

And it was quitting that prompted my next transition. I had no idea what I was going to do, by the way. I won't say that I was petrified that my career was over at 38, but I remember thinking, "Ok, this is going to be kind of a new adventure for me."

Fortunately, I had made a bit of money so I didn't have to worry about immediate financial pressure. One day I was sitting at home thinking about my future when a friend of mine called. He was in the fashion business at an English company called Ted Baker and he invited me to lunch.

I remember sitting with him in this garden restaurant and ordering a cheeseburger. My friend told me we were at the beginning of a renaissance in men's apparel. It had been really bad for the past few years, but he thought the business was about to take off. He believed there would be about five or six years of incredible growth and I should think about going into this business. He told me it was all marketing-based and my personality would be great for it and he liked my sense of style.

Of course, I had never even thought about the fashion business before.

But my mom had a degree in fashion and it was her passion, so I'd been around the industry a little bit. My mom had gotten a scholarship to the Rhode Island School of Design when she was 16 but her father wouldn't let her go. Instead, he told her, "You gotta have babies."

So she had this frustration that I thought maybe I could fulfill for her.

I went home and bought all the men's fashion magazines I could find. I went to all the men's clothing stores in New York. After some research I decided to get into this business. But instead of looking for a marketing position at a fashion brand, which would have been the smart way to get into the business, I did it like a crazy person and opened my own store.

I'd never been in the retail business before, except for a short stint behind the counter at a little tennis pro shop when I played ball in college. I did have a number of retail clients when I had the agency, so I figured I understood it a little.

Looking back, I realize I knew nothing about tailoring, I knew nothing about the fashion business, I knew nothing about nothing. But I did know men needed better service and that no one was taking care of them. So I just dove in.

I created a store called Robert's — very original name — rented a space, threw my money into it and went to a tailor I knew. He was this little 5' 2" Italian guy who used to make suits for me and I told him I needed to apprentice with him. I needed to learn. No, I wasn't going to sew anything, I was just going to watch and have him show me how suits were made, how to fix suits, what suits are all about. Everything.

And I did that for a few months before my store actually opened. When it did open I hired him to do my alterations. His name was Pino, I don't remember his last name. He had bright red hair and his hands were like a butcher's because he must have stabbed himself with the needles at least 1,000 times. But he just loved everything about men's suits — from the fabric to the tailoring to all the little touches. He was the real deal, a tailor's tailor.

Pino and I went to a couple of menswear shows. I didn't know anything about buying either — remember, I didn't know anything about anything. Instead, I learned all the mistakes you can make by making each one. I probably did have a little too much cash from my agency buyout, so I was able to weather my mistakes, but looking back it was a recipe for disaster.

I finally opened the store and the deal I made with my friend at Ted Baker was that the first third of my store would be a Ted Baker shop. He agreed to give me the fixtures and all the merchandise on consignment. In the back of the store was everything I had bought from Italy. The store was kind of like my closet. Since I didn't know how to buy merchandise, the only thing I knew was how to buy for myself. The only things in the store were things I liked.

I'd spend hours merchandising everything in the store just right so when I came in the next day everything would be perfect. It was just me. I didn't hire anyone; it was my store. I like to throw myself into whatever I'm doing, and I love clothes. I loved going to Italy on buying trips, and I went to all the showrooms. I would go to the factories. I fell in love with the business.

I literally spent three years of my life in that tiny store and I was there every single day. I was helping clients. I learned how to do fittings. I learned how to mark-up suits for alterations. I learned how to buy. I learned everything you can learn about retail by doing it.

Business was good. I had a growing clientele and it grew 25-30% every year. I also had some marketing savvy, so I opened right down the street from Mitchell's, the most successful men's clothing store in the country. It was a gigantic store of like 40,000 square feet and I assumed that any business that big has pissed off some of their clients. I'm going to offer them an alternative and let them shop with me. I learned my survival was serving people who didn't find what they wanted at that big store. And that's how I grew my business.

I'd find new things in Italy that weren't a brand name people knew and I'd sell to people who hadn't seen those things yet. And I'd have two or three good seasons with a manufacturer before Mitchell's would catch on. Then they'd go to Italy and order five times more merchandise than I could and the manufacturer would tell me, "I'm sorry, we can't do business with you anymore." But that was okay because by then I had moved on to something else.

After my third year, I found a niche and decided I'd go into the wholesaling and manufacturing of very high-end clothing. So, I went from being a tennis player to an ad guy to a retailer who sold clothing to a fashion company owner who did everything from design to wholesale and retail. That was another big change.

I don't know what it is about me and transitions. But the excitement makes the fear of going through them very minimal to me. I only transition if I like what I'm involved in so that the enjoyment of doing what I'm doing takes away any reluctance I have of doing it in the first place. And I think that's part of making these transitions successful.

Don't transition into something you're wishy-washy about. Transition into something you really can get passionate about. Then you won't think about how crazy it is that you're doing something completely different at that point in your life.

So I went into that wholesale manufacturing and in a year we launched a brand called Roberto da Carrera. Carrera was my family's hometown in Italy, so the name was Roberto of Carrera. I bought a company to bring in the designer of a really special shirt brand and he was a real hip young guy.

Within a year of launching the company we were nominated for menswear designer of the year by an organization called Fashion Group International. And every year they have a competition to pick the best menswear designer, women's wear designer, accessory designer, and so on. Because we were nominated, we had to give them a whole portfolio of our clothing. They had a committee who voted on it, and we came in second.

That was kind of cool because I had never even contemplated being in that business. It was a nice nod that our stuff was credible, and our business kept growing. Before long we were selling to 50 of the best stores around the country. The retail business was growing, and I thought I was going to spend the rest of my life in the fashion business. By now I had two stores and I was really enjoying the rhythm of the fashion season—going to Italy for the buying shows and making a lot of friends in the fashion industry.

Life was great.

And then the financial crash happened in 2008 and my world stopped dead.

The finance industry was based on all of the mortgage-backed securities that crashed the economy. And that killed the hedge fund business. I was living in lower Manhattan at the time, and it was Ground Zero for the hedge fund industry. And all those guys were my clients.

One day, about a month before Lehman Brothers crashed and the whole thing dominoed down, the chairman of Morgan Stanley, who was a customer of mine, walked into my store and asked, "How're things, you okay?" I had a really good relationship with him and asked him why he was concerned, and he said, "I can't get into details but something big is about to happen and the economy is going to have a really tough patch. It might affect your business."

That's all he said. It should have been enough. But I didn't think too deeply about it at that time because business had been really good. My clients had been very loyal, and my customer base was growing.

A month later the hedge fund industry blew up, Lehman Brothers shut down, the economy imploded, and my business went from growing 30% a year to not even being able to get one customer to walk in the door.

All the hedge fund managers, all these 35-year-old guys who were making four million bucks a year and used to shop in my store every weekend with their wives –I had woman's clothes by then too. They cut off their wives' credit cards, stopped shopping, and literally headed for the hills.

Overnight my business ended, two stores and everything. And my only thought was, *How do I exit with the shirt on my back, no pun intended?"*

It got so bad that for a month I was in shock. No one would even come in the store. I would call my customers and say, "are you okay?" and they'd say, "yeah, we're fine" but I didn't see anyone.

So, I sat down with my wife and told her we had to get out of this business because we were about to lose all the money we had invested. Luckily, one of my leases was up –I'd been renting month-to-month– so I told my landlord I wasn't going to renew. But I also had a lease that wasn't up, and I had to break it. I had over a million dollars-worth of merchandise in the store that I was not going to be able to sell, but still had to pay for. I had to go and negotiate, vendor by vendor, for ten cents on the dollar. And I ended up losing over a million dollars.

This was an important transition for me. It took me about four or five months to wind down the whole business. I remember one day just sitting in my house. I had lost more money than I ever thought I'd even have. I looked at myself in the mirror and said, "OK, this is not such a big deal. I did it once, I can do it again." And it was the most empowering feeling. Here I was on the brink of disaster and people around me were committing suicide and doing all kinds of crazy things. And I'm just looking in the mirror saying, "all right, I guess we have to do this again."

Of course, I had no idea what THIS was.

While I was liquidating the business, I started calling my old friends in the ad business and letting them know I was available for some consulting work. I told them, "whatever you have, I'll do consulting projects, whatever you need." And fortunately, within a few months I started picking up things and getting my feet back into the business.

As soon as I had officially closed both the stores and all the merchandise was liquidated and out of my possession, I decided to move.

I was 45 or 46 and I had been doing this for a long time. I thought I don't have to live in the Northeast anymore. I don't have to live in this rat race. Everyone around me is chasing nothing but money, and I need a break. Plus, I don't like the cold. So just like that I decided to move somewhere warm.

One of my old customers lived in Sarasota, Florida. I had been there two or three times and I always thought it was a nice place, so I decided to move there. I picked up everything and moved and started running my consulting business from there, doing a little bit of project work, and doing yoga because I needed to calm everything down. I worked part time and tried to unwind.

We stayed there for three years. That transition was a different one. The first one was in New York and there was frenetic energy and abundant opportunities. This time I needed to be alone. I walked on the beach every day and try to figure out what I should do.

My daughter was older, and that responsibility was off my shoulders a bit and I thought I'd enjoy the easier pace. But after three years I missed the energy and I missed doing something exciting, and living somewhere exciting, so I moved to Miami.

I'd been to Miami a lot for business and pleasure, but the reason I moved to Miami was that while I couldn't go back to the cold, I needed to be in a city, I wanted to be near the beach. I wanted to live somewhere international, so where could I go? So I just picked up and moved to Miami.

And I came by myself because by this time my wife was tired of moving, tired of my transitions. She wanted stability which, ironically enough, caused another transition.

I had my existing consulting business, but I wanted to start another business.

I had a client who had an interesting germ of an idea and I decided to throw my energy into that endeavor. I wanted to keep the consulting, but I also wanted to do one more big thing.

That's how I wound up doing what I'm doing now, SportsEd.TV.

That decision was a nice combination of a lot of passions—sports, marketing—things I enjoy. That transition was tough though, because I had to decide to give up a lot of my consulting to spend time raising money and getting the new company off the ground, instead of earning some money that wasn't so difficult to make.

I think it all starts with really knowing yourself. If you make transitions without knowing yourself—what you're good at, how much risk you're willing to take, what you don't want to do—it's really difficult. Fortunately for me, my experience as an athlete and working with coaches and sports psychologists and all those times where I had to perform under a lot of pressure gave me a good understanding of who I was and what I was capable of doing.

Tennis is a lonely game. You're out there by yourself and there's no hiding when you're on the court. It's just you out there and you have no one helping you. These transitions feel just like that.

Making the decision to change is the easy part of managing the transition, right? You decide you're going to go in a direction. It seems like it's the logical decision. Not a lot of emotion in it yet because you're not in it dealing with all the problems that are going to come your way.

Knowing how you're going to react to the stress is the hard part. I think I said earlier—there are just two responses: You either panic and then you have to go backwards, or you say, "damn the torpedoes" and you move forward. You need to know yourself ahead of time and you need to ask yourself, "Am I cut out for this?"

When you dive in it starts to get real, and the emotions start to sink their teeth into you. And you start thinking to yourself, "Can I do this?" Will I do it? Have I thrown away my whole life to do something I'm not able to do? And that's the part people wrestle with.

When that happens you either have one of two reactions: You get scared shitless and you try to run back to your old life because you can't do it, or you get a sense of calm, mixed with adrenaline, and you just go. And that's the transition. And it lasts anywhere between three months and three years.

The part people get wrong—and it's so funny that you're writing about this subject now because I was thinking this would be an interesting story to tell—is how you manage yourself during that time.

My stress management is exercise. If I don't exercise twice a day, if I don't stop what I'm doing and jump in my pool and swim laps, go hit tennis balls, go for a walk, anything—I just get worn out. I'm working 12 hours a day, but I need to stop and get all the adrenaline out of me because my body is coursing with it. If you don't do something to bring the level down and relax then you'll burn out.

A good friend of mine was a great client at a major wine and spirits company. After lots of success he went to another spirits company and did very well there too. Then one day he called and said, "Robert, I'm thinking of starting my own business." I don't remember how old he was, but I don't think he wasn't quite 40 then, and he said, "what do you think?"

I hesitated to answer him for a minute but finally told him that I thought he had the brains of an entrepreneur, but he didn't have the heart. I told him that he could easily start the business but based on what I know about what it takes to do it emotionally, and knowing the way he operated, he was going to panic.

He was taken aback and couldn't believe I said that to him. I think he was pissed at me for a while. But he listened, and he waited ten more years before he started his company. Since then he's become enormously successful.

I had lunch with him recently and he said, "you know, I never thanked you for your advice. You were right, I didn't have the heart back then."

You need to know that about yourself. You need to know that you're going from this point to that point and the trip may not be very smooth.

Back when I was playing college tennis, I was chatting with my sports psychologist and he asked me, "What do you think is the objective of a tennis match?"

I was a brash young kid then, so I blurted out, "To get the most points and win the game."

He looked at me for a minute and said, "Not really. The object of a tennis match is to create more problems for your opponent than they create for you. Your job on the court is to become a really good problem solver because all you're going to get is one problem after another and the way you manage that—emotionally, physically, intellectually—is going to determine whether you succeed or not.

"You have to love the problems."

If you don't love dealing with the problems you're going to encounter, you'll transition poorly.

I'll never forget this. I was 21 years old and I was struggling to find my way in tennis, and he gave me this exercise to do: He told me to go home and look in the mirror and repeat, "I love problems. Bring me the problems. I am the problem solver."

From that day forward, I saw myself as the problem solver. I embrace problems. I love problems.

If you have that type of mentality, you're cut out for transitions. If you don't, you're not going to be able to handle the things that are going to happen.

That's it. If you can become a great problem solver, transitions aren't had.

There's a great saying, "You can't cross a wide chasm with two small jumps." All you get is one. You have to know that if you don't make it you can't get back to the other side.

Susan Ford Collins, Founder, The Technology of Success

You already met Susan back in the beginning of the book when we talked about how she helped me pivot away from a business that provided me with my livelihood as well as a lot of my own sense of self-worth. What you don't know (yet) is that Susan also lived a life of transitions and pivots. Some, such as moving to China to consult, were her own decisions. Some, like suddenly being a newly unemployed, newly single mother of two small daughters, were not.

Susan Ford Collins

When I was young, I always wanted to be the best student in the class. I sat in the front row. I put my hand up to answer every question. I did all my homework. I prepared for every test. And, as a result, I was a good student. But when I went out into the world to find a job, I learned something really useful—useful, but really painful.

My first job interview was with the telephone company in Washington DC. I thought that having all the right answers was what they were looking for from me, but they weren't. As a test they had me role play a customer service issue with a man who couldn't pay his bill and wanted to pay it over time. In my "do everything perfectly" world that simply wasn't acceptable.

So when I told my mocked-up customer, "I'm sorry, but you have to get your payment in today," they ended my interview saying, "Susan, we wanted to hear you negotiate and come to some kind of agreement because we'd rather collect some money than nothing at all."

That's when I realized, "The right answers aren't going to get me where I want to go."

I was disappointed. But a few days later I was offered a research position at the National Institutes of Health and I was excited. I thought I would learn how to be successful and healthy there. Instead, I learned that NIH was focused on illness and dysfunction.

After a year and a month of sleepless nights spent rehearsing what I wanted to say, I finally raised my hand in one of our prestigious weekly conferences. I was excited and nervous when I stood up in front of two hundred of my peers. I told them that I thought we were on the wrong track. I told them we should be studying highly successful heathy people, people who are making contributions to their families, society and world. We needed to understand what they were doing that the rest of us weren't.

The whole room laughed.

Red-faced, I had to make a life-changing decision on the spot. Were my colleagues right that my idea was laughable and I should abandon it immediately? Or was my idea important and they just didn't understand it? Silently I committed to my idea and vowed to devote my career to studying highly successful people. Looking back, this was the most important decision of my life.

If highly successful people were using skills the rest of us are missing or misusing, then I needed to know what their skills were and how I could teach them to others.

Twenty years later, when I finished telling that story at the National Grant Management Association Convention in Washington DC, a group of a dozen-or-so participants headed my way. They told me that they were currently deciding about grants at NIH, and if they'd been in their positions all those years ago, they would have funded my research with pleasure! Their news was a little late, but heartwarming none the less.

Committed to my plan, I spent the next six months designing my research and doing preliminary interviews. Then, out of the blue, my husband got a job offer he couldn't refuse. And so we moved to Jenkintown, Pennsylvania, where we bought a huge Victorian house and started the work of restoring it. Since that was before working remotely was possible, I had to resign my position at NIH.

My husband and I were so busy parenting our two young daughters, building our careers, and restoring the old house that we didn't see the expanding fractures that were developing between us. Then—*BAM!*—our marriage fell apart.

Suddenly there I was—a single, divorced mom in my mid-thirties who needed to find another way to make a living and continue my research. I wanted a schedule that was compatible with my daughters' lives, so I took a job in their middle school, giving me the same hours, the same vacations as them. Plus, summers off to continue my research.

I taught graphic arts, photography, and the gifted program and I soon realized that the highly successful teens in my classes were using the same skills I was observing in highly successful adults.

I was anything but a "Universe will provide" thinker growing up. My mom and dad looked at the dark side of every situation and I had learned to do the same thing. It was only when I started shadowing highly successful people that my point of view began to change.

And even though I am a "Universe will provide" thinker today, my approach is far more scientific than that... just one of the many side benefits of my years as a researcher at NIH.

Our brains contain a part called the Reticular Activating System (RAS) which works like the "search and find" function in a computer. When we want an experience and we pre-experience or program our brains in detail—what it will look like, sound like, feel like and even smell like—our RAS begins monitoring sensory data and alerts us to potential matches. We sense that "match alert" as a jolt, a gut feeling, an aha moment or an insight. Whatever you call it, you know it when you feel it.

Our RAS was probably designed to keep us safe from lions and tigers, but if we use it correctly, it can also keep us on track to fulfill our plans and dreams. Or, if we use our RAS incorrectly, it can alert us to every potential threat or disaster or pitfall or failure and keep us in a state of chronic fear and anxiety.

With my mission to study highly successful people still clear in mind and a growing list of people I wanted to study, I went about teaching my 7th and 8th graders. Then one morning my principal asked me to attend the World Games Conference at the University of Massachusetts. When I arrived at World Games I bumped– quite literally—into Buckminster Fuller in the hallway of the opening session!

Bucky was short, so when we collided I found myself looking down at this bald-headed elfin man smiling up at me. Fortunately, I had the presence of mind to blurt out, "Ah Bucky, I want to study you." And Bucky had the presence of mind to immediately ask, "Why?"

Looking back, I guess being laughed at NIH had prepared me for this very moment!

I told Bucky about my experience at NIH and emphasized that I didn't want to just interview him for an hour or so, I wanted to shadow him for at least three months… in cars, meetings, whenever and wherever he went. I told him I understood that outstanding people didn't know and couldn't tell me what made them successful. Instead, I had decided to spend time with them and figure it out for myself. I told him, "Bucky, you're on my list!"

Bucky responded with a nod. "Okay then Susan, you live in Jenkintown and I work in Philadelphia at the University of Pennsylvania. That's just a train ride away. I'm sure we can figure something out."

Over the years highly successful people repeatedly told me that as you head for a goal, you must be willing to suddenly spin around, stop, and head out again in whatever new direction seems appropriate. And it's not only the new direction that matters. The stop phase is important too, but most people don't bother to stop and re-think and re-strategize. They just keep trying to go in the direction they were going, like one of those wind-up toys that bangs into a wall and stays there trying to move forward until its batteries run out and the fun ends.

When I completed my three months with Bucky, I detailed the success skills I had observed him using. He listened and quickly said, "Susan, you're right; I do do those things." Then he added, "But doesn't everyone?"

"No, everyone doesn't!" I said. That's the point. My mission is to identify the skills you and other highly successful people are using and teach those skills to the rest of the world.

Finally, with a chuckle Bucky added, "I like you, young woman. You've got spunk!" And Bucky recommended the next person for me to shadow. And the next person recommended the next one, and so on and so on. It was astounding!

Looking back, I did have spunk. I can't believe what I did, but I did it. And I spent the next 20 years following the greats of the planet and I discovered *The Technology of Success* skillset that I've taught in over 4,000 conferences and business sessions around the world. I even went to China and India to teach. It's been one heck of a ride!

Early in my research, I realized that most people never stop to think about what success is, or how it shifts and changes. They know what the dictionary says. They know what their parents want. They know what their teachers want. They know what their bosses and spouses want. But when you've made enough money to make you feel safe and independent, when you've saved some and you don't have to take every single piece of business that comes your way, you need to begin asking new questions, such as "What do I want?" "What makes me feel good?" "What makes me happy and healthy?" "What makes me wake up early in the morning all revved up and excited?" "Which ideas of mine do I still believe in, and which ones do I want to fulfill?"

Then, instead of waiting for someone else to tell you what to do, you need to sit down in your own executive chair and tell yourself what you want. And you need to start exploring because there's no map for that, no spelled-out itinerary. It's trial by success, not by error.

The first skill I observed highly successful people using consistently is the one I call *Success Filing*. Each and every day, these successful people set aside time to acknowledge themselves for the small successes they are having, according to their standards. Success Filing frees them from needing others' praise and acknowledgment and reminds them that they're on course and making progress. Or if they're not then they need to re-think and re-strategize.

Today's kids are asking these life-defining questions much sooner that we did. My grandson Sam is climbing mountains around the world and broadcasting his treks online, while also studying mechanical engineering at Georgia Tech. Many teens are creating startups that are revolutionizing industries and disrupting old products and supply chains.

But most people resist the risk of newness. And so they inevitably wind up at a point in their careers where they're stuck in a rut and bored to tears because they think they're doing what they have to do. This happens because they have confused what they've done with who they are.

When I look back at my life, I see that some of the people who've been most important to me have been ones I've bumped into in elevators or collided with in halls. Think that's crazy? Where did you meet your spouse, business partner or best friend?

I was invited to be on a major TV show because I got to know a man from the neck up. He and I were taking a water aerobics class together and, after weeks of conversation about the book I was writing, he told me he was headed back to New York. Then he added, "Susan, when your book is published, give me a call. I'm a producer of *The Today Show* and I'll get you on."

I did, and he did too.

We need to be open to an unexpected kick in the ass from our Universe… and our Reticular Activating System. When these events occur, most people grumble, "Why did that happen?" But I suggest telling yourself, "That happened for a reason." Lean into it to see how it might reveal your next step.

One morning I woke up early knowing it was time for me to start doing weekend Technology of Success seminars. I had been facilitating small exploratory two-hour sessions for several years, but it was time to go big.

Each time I presented *The Ten Success Skills,* they unfolded like pages in a book. After a few months, HR directors started calling me. "Susan, we don't know what you taught our employees who took your weekend seminar, but whatever it was, we want you to teach it to the rest of our team." And I did.

My audiences begged me to write a book about the Ten Success Skills so they could share what they'd learned with their spouses and their kids' teachers. So I wrote *Our Children Are Watching: 10 Skills for Leading the Next Generation to Success.* And I traveled across the country working with parents, teachers, police, and local governments.

When businesspeople learned how to use the skills they literally shouted, "Why hasn't anyone ever taught us this before?" What was so important to them and their organizations?

By observing highly successful people, I discovered that success has gears… three distinct ways of thinking and behaving, all of which are needed to reach goals and create new directions.

1st gear is for learning the basics of new skills. 2nd gear is for producing and competing. 3rd gear is for breaking through familiar ways to discover new products and approaches and new ways of living.

The three gears are easy to recognize when you learn their keywords. 1st gear keywords are right/wrong, good/bad, have to/must, possible/impossible. 2nd gear keywords are more, better, faster, cheaper. And 3rd gear keywords include aha, insight, create, and innovate.

Here's a critical question? Do you regularly gear up to 3rd gear to detail the future you want and program your RAS to alert you to opportunities? Or are you so busy in 2nd gear… making money, paying mortgages and credit cards, working longer and harder… that you keep putting it off and opportunities slip by unnoticed?

Ten years and 4,000 seminars later, I woke up in a hotel room one morning unable to remember where I was, what kind of rental car I was driving or where I had parked it. I suddenly realized, *I've traveled four days a week for long enough. I need to find new ways to teach The Technology of Success.* By the time I got home, Hurricane Andrew had devastated many of my clients' businesses and I suddenly found myself with an unexpected chunk of time.

That's when I started writing *The Joy of Success.*

The writing experience was fun because it made me remember all the people I had shadowed, everything I had learned from the people I'd worked with, the stories they had told me. And these experiences soon became the book.

When *The Joy of Success* was published and the PR campaign began, I got lucky again. After a radio interview my host said he wanted me to meet with Stuart Gelles at CNN. When I called Stuart, he invited me to have dinner with Lou Dobbs and his team the next time I was in NY. Lou invited me to be on his show.

After interviewing me, Lou asked me to teach The Technology of Success skillset to his entire financial news team. Thanks to the work I did there, CNN called me "America's premier success and leadership coach." And even though I no longer needed the world to acknowledge me, it was damn nice!

One morning, I received an email asking me to teach The Technology of Success to business leaders in China. I learned that businesspeople in China were good at doing what they were told to do and giving back the answers they were taught. They were also efficient at doing more, better, faster, cheaper, and they were even able to copy American products overnight. Those were my first two gears. But when it came to my third gear of success, creative thinking and breakthroughs, Chinese businesspeople were still far behind.

As kids, their family structures and school systems taught them that it's wrong to ask questions or suggest changes. It was fascinating to understand what success meant to them, and for the most part it meant first and second gear. So, I enjoyed the challenge of showing them what else was possible.

Next I taught *The Technology of Success* in India. Then I taught it in South America and even signed 1250 copies of *The Joy of Success* in Port au Prince, Haiti.

Now I am focused on consulting on leadership issues. What do the people you work with need? What do the ones you live with, your spouse and your kids, need? Not what are you comfortable giving them, but what do they need?

Do they need more input from you? Do they need less input? Do they need praise? Are you too controlling? Are you not allowing their own creative ideas and breakthroughs to thrive?

Today I am in the most fulfilling phase of my career, working one-on-one with CEOs and leaders around the world. And I'm still chuckling over all the ways the Universe, and my clients' Reticular Activating Systems, have assisted them—the bizarre circumstances where they met their partners, the ridiculous coincidences that led them to create new products, services, mergers and spinoffs. I help them live their dreams and help others live their dreams, too.

Lemme tell you, if you lean into your life and trust the process, it's thrilling. When people say, "I'm bored," I say, "Life's exciting." You never know when you'll bump into an astounding opportunity. And be ready to grab it on the spot.

Today I'm called "The People Whisperer" because over the years I've developed a sixth sense about who people are and what they need to think and do to find their own fulfillment.

Chris Crowley,

Author, *Younger Next Year*

I read Chris's book, *Younger Next Year,* long before I met him. After I followed his instructions and changed my life, I reached out to Chris and licensed his book for a client of mine. Through the process of monetizing his concepts and looking for speaking opportunities for Chris in order to promote my client's business, Chris and I became friends. One of my favorite things to do with Chris was to ask him a question and sit back and listen to him weave a great yarn. I think you'll see what I mean.

You should know that Chris practices what he preaches and lives the life he talks about in his books. When I called Chris to discuss this project with him, I caught the 84-year-old "on the top of Ajax Mountain in Aspen and having a grand old time skiing."

Chris Crowley

Back in college I was bit of a bust, which was a surprise. I'd done well in prep schools but I'd gotten married as a freshman and it didn't go terribly well. I was a lackluster student at best. I mean, I was smart and whatnot but I didn't do anything with it. And when I got out of Harvard, I got exactly one job offer. Just one.

So when I graduated I had a series of dreadful jobs for five years. I was a banker for three years and I was awful at it. I was at a second-rate bank and I hated it and they weren't crazy about me. And then I did some other stuff which was even worse.

I'd always wanted to be a lawyer. During the war and in the years right after, my three older sisters were always surrounded by guys from Harvard and MIT and whatnot. The ones that I always gravitated towards where the ones in the law schools. They were the ones who were the most attractive, they were the smartest, blah blah blah. And I just somehow knew that that was what I ought to do.

And so somehow I got some self-confidence a ways out of college and I said, "I'm going to law school." And, woohoo, my poor parents, they couldn't afford it, but anyways I felt like I was coming up from underwater.

I hadn't done a whole helluva lot in the five years I'd been out of college. I had been married as a freshman and we had three kids and we did a good job of it in a way, but my schoolwork suffered. So I applied back at Harvard and they turned me down in a heartbeat—the rejection came by return mail! And so I thought, *Hmm, this might be a little harder than I expected.* Out of sheer desperation I wrote a letter to the dean of admissions at the University of Virginia law school—one of the things I can do is write a good letter—and they took me in.

I later learned that UVA had already turned me down also. But the guy who read the letter said, "You know, if he feels that strongly about coming here, what the hell, let's give him a shot."

And he turned out to be right. I finished in the top handful of kids in my class.

Because I'd was already a parent in undergrad, I hadn't been part of the pack. I wasn't part of any tribe; I was just out there somewhere. I was not part of the clubby world of Harvard undergraduates. And that experience, being sort of an outsider, helped me later on in life, when I went to law school. Because then along comes the Sixties, and everything changed socially. And a lot of people my age were just knocked sideways by it. They couldn't believe it, they just hated it. But I thought, *Oh good. Fundamental change? You bet.* I didn't have that deep a stake in what was otherwise going on. I just loved it. I wasn't a hippy or anything, I mean I was a guy going to law school, but it was very easy for me because I'd already been an outlier once and it was easy-peasy.

I just loved the idea of everything that was going on around me. Turns out I had a wonderful time in law school. I was good at it. I was the articles editor of the law review. And remember, when I got out of Harvard, I had been almost unemployable. But when I got out of law school everybody offered me jobs and they even offered me jobs with bonuses and God knows what else. And I had to choose. So I picked what I thought was the best law firm in the country, Davis Pope. It was a very civilized place in addition to just being a hugely powerful law firm.

I started out as a corporate lawyer, which turned out to be a misunderstanding of my gifts. So I shifted over to litigation. And that I had a real flair for. I made partner in almost record time and I had a wonderful, wonderful time.

Being a litigator is very demanding work, it's very stressful, but I just thrived on it. I was a bit of a star for a while there and it was marvelous.

Let's talk a little bit about practicing law.

A lot of people don't like it, but I just loved it.

Is it hard? Oh mercy! A big law firm like Davis Pope hires a bunch of smart kids, and they've all done well in law school, and they're just like you. And then only one out of ten becomes a partner.

But for the next eight years before that you work your ass off trying to be that one person and you're competing with folks who are a lot like you. And it's a helluva competition and good grief, I worked like crazy.

But I had great luck. I worked with this guy, S. Hazard Gillespie. And he was a lawyer and a rock star. He was a wonderfully successful practitioner. He was the US Attorney, not a US Attorney, but the US Attorney for the Southern District of New York, and he was one of the best lawyers in the country and also a mightily engaging man.

Gillespie was six foot two, imperially slim in his marvelous London-tailored double-breasted suits. He had the kind of accent that in general would make people furious but he had some extraordinary charm. Everybody liked him and he got along with everybody. He was not haughty, he was elegant. He didn't have any dough, the family money had disappeared during the Depression, but he'd still gone to Yale before he joined Davis Pope. And everybody just loved him. In fact, no matter how hard I worked it often seemed like it didn't matter. Because judges just wanted to be on Gillespie's side. He was the king of the WASPS.

I found myself working for him on a case. It was just a doomed case; we were fighting off a corporate takeover thing. And I had an idea for a strategy and I stuck it in the papers, over the objections of the firm partner I was working for. And he marched me right down to Gillespie's office to get me fired or some damn thing.

The partner tossed my brief across the desk and Gillespie picked it up and read it and said, "Hmm, hmm; not so bad."

We finally won this case, to the astonishment of everyone. We won by the skin of our teeth in the Court of Appeals by a two to one vote. The only argument they agreed on was the one I'd stuck in the brief against everybody's wishes. And so all of a sudden, I was looking pretty damned good. From then on, the big change was that I went from sort of just doing it to being just plain on fire.

I worked nutty, insane hours, I cared like the devil. I was working so hard that sometimes you have to go to the bathroom but you want to make another call, you gotta take a leak like crazy but you think, *I just gotta take one more call before I do it.* And you really start to worry that you're going to piddle in your pants but you can't bear to stop for even a minute—it's that level of intensity.

Thanks to winning that case—and working like a madman for the three months it took—Gillespie took me under his wing. We never really became friends, Gillespie and me. But the great blessing of my career was that he became my mentor. He took me on and just marched me along. I worked only for him for four straight years—it was terrible hard work, and he wasn't cozy, but there I went.

After some twenty odd years I got a little stale. It was a wonderful life and there were just lashings of dough in it but I thought, *You know, you oughta live more than one life,* and that's what I always tell people: "You oughta live more than one life." And it's a luxury, but it was one I could afford. I figured that even in retirement I would have enough dough to live pretty comfortably. Yeah, it would have been a tiny fraction of my old income but…enough.

So I up and quit—which was terrifying.

At about the same time I met Hilary, to whom I've now been married for 27 years, and she just got roped in with me.

When I had decided to quit it was just me, and having limited dough seemed easy. But now it was the two of us and it was a little harder. But the decision to quit after those 25-or-so years was, in retrospect, the smartest thing I've ever done, I'm truly grateful. But at the time, I gotta tell you, it was scary. You don't realize how much your persona, your whole self, is caught up in what you do until you stop doing it.

You don't think of it consciously but hey, there you are, you're a partner of Davis Pope and you're a helluva guy and you do serious work and chairmen of the board want to hear what you have to say and blah blah blah. And now all of a sudden, it's the middle of the day and you're walking the streets and you oughta be in the office and you're afraid that someone'll see you and you feel like a guy in a suit coming out of a dirty movie and getting caught by your mother-in-law. It is *hard*.

I didn't have a firm plan; I didn't have one idea. I thought, *You know, I have a house in Aspen.* I had a bunch of houses because

I did make some dough for a while and I had a house in Aspen, so I thought I'd just pick up and go out there and be a ski bum while I reset myself and do some writing.

I'd always wanted to be a ski bum but I couldn't afford it when I was younger. So I did that and that was wonderful, if I may say so. I mean it's like guys who want to go play golf for the rest of their lives and I wanted to ski and it was a great luxury and I truly loved it. And Hilary loved it too. She learned how to ski and so on and so forth.

And I just loved skiing. I couldn't afford to do it in those early days but later, when I was a partner and had some dough, I'd go off to Europe for a solid two weeks, and then spend two weeks in Aspen and in that month I took lessons every stinking day. I treated skiing just like practicing law, just work at it crazy hard. And at the end of the month, I was a good enough amateur skier. And then when I lived out there for five years and skied as much as 100 days a year I became a good recreational skier. I mean, I'm leagues away from the professional guys but I can get down a mountain. It was one of the great pleasures in my life; I loved the feel of it. For a guy like me to be cantilevered out there over the ski run and get a little blip of what it's like to be graceful, oh my! I get going 100 miles an hour, or 40 miles, or whatever it actually turns out to be, and lean downhill into the gravity it's just a joy and a privilege. It's as if all of a sudden, I could dance, which is something else I couldn't do but having that sensation in my life was just terrific.

But after a while, even that clearly wasn't going to be enough. That's when I started casting around. I'd always wanted to be a writer. I've always been good at it and since grade school people have always talked about it and I wanted to write something.

You use that gift a lot in the law, but I'd never really written anything else and I felt guilty about it and so I took a shot. I worked on a novel which never worked and then eventually got the idea for the book that's been responsible for the rest of my life, *Younger Next Year.*

The basic notion was "Change your behavior and you can have a massive impact on the quality of your life." Health, wellness, energy, effectiveness, all kinds of stuff. You can put off 75% of aging until you're 80 and beyond. Eliminate 15% of the worst sicknesses and conditions, it's just miraculous stuff. And it sounded like nonsense, except it wasn't. It was really true. Truly.

I came to New York to find a partner to do it with. I had the great good fortune to have someone I knew introduce me to Dr. Harry Lodge, one of the smartest guys I've ever met. And that was a great watershed moment in my life, finding Harry. It took a year to talk him into doing the book, but once we started, that next year was about the most fun that either one of us had ever had. Most writers will tell you that collaborating with a co-author is just an agony and in ten days you're at each other's throats, but not me and Harry.

The old gag is that when you go to book-signing events you have to take two cars because you can't even sit in the same back seat together, but Harry's and my experience was the exact opposite of that. We took a great shine to one another and became very close friends in no time at all. That year that we spent working on the book was just a joy.

We thought almost the same way. I mean, he was a doctor and I was a lawyer, but we grew up in the same intellectual traditions, I guess. We came from the same part of the country, the Northshore, above Boston, and we'd gone to similar schools and maybe that was a negative for the book, but it was a positive for us because it sure made it easy for us to work together.

Anyhow, we had great fun writing it and then it was easy to sell. And when you look back at that you say, "It's a miracle." We had wonderfully enthusiastic editors and supporters and stuff and a short time after the book came out it was a *New York Times* bestseller.

Harry and I were down in Washington doing a tour and we got news of that and we said, "Oh my gosh; we're gonna have quite a story here." Because we both believed like crazy in the book but you never know, who can tell?

It was a great bestseller; it sold over two million copies in some 23 languages and it's a cult book for baby boomers and others and 15 years later they rolled out a new version with stuff about the neuro side—there was never anything about the brain in the first version—and we got some nifty guy from the University of Arizona, a professor of neuroscience. He wrote a chapter and I wrote a chapter about the brain science, so the journey continues.

What Harry knew and I knew was that steady exercise, six days a week, can have a profound impact on your quality of life. Health, fitness, vigor … just everything. But you go tell someone, "Hey, you need to get up off your butt and exercise six days a week," we knew that wasn't going to fly. It was going to take a little persuading.

So we worked hard at trying to make it more persuasive. And we did it. We made it oddly persuasive, it's been a sticky book. A lot of people have changed their lives, and I get a tremendous amount of mail saying, "Hey man, thanks a lot for writing that book. You saved my life."

We tried to put stuff in the book to motivate people. Harry told a story about a guy named John who was in his office. And he was fat as butter. He was miserable and he was about to retire. He hated his job. He hated his wife. He hated the idea of retiring to Florida and he was just in despair.

He was fat as butter and he was bone idle and Harry said to him, "Listen John, if you don't get some exercise you are going to die." So our guy's on the beach in some Godforsaken place in Florida. And he walks a mile the first day and he felt okay. But the next day he felt as if he'd been hit by a truck; he was almost bed-ridden. But he managed to walk a couple hundred yards the next day. He changed his clothes and got up and went for a walk on the beach, in the sand, every day, and a year later he'd lost 50 pounds; he was in remarkable shape. And he no longer hated his life; he no longer hated his wife; he didn't hate Florida; he was just a happy man. It was a wonderful transformation.

The point of the story is that even if you start off in awful shape and hate the idea of exercise, it can be transformative. It's worth giving it a serious shot. There's such profound changes out there. A 50% reduction of risk in heart attacks and strokes? There's nothing in medicine that comes close to that. Nothing.

Does it make sense to do that? You bet! Is it hard to believe? Sure it is. But it's just nuts not to do it. And we felt that with such strong conviction. Everything goes to hell unless you do stuff. And that starts with regular exercise. Sarcopenia is the loss of muscle mass. You lose 10% of your total muscle mass every decade after you're what, 35? Well shit, by the time you're my age, half your muscle mass is gone unless you do something about it. Ditto on bones. Ditto on balance, coordination, and your proprioception. The only way anyone knows to avoid Alzheimer's is serious aerobic exercise. Regular aerobic exercise reduces the risk by half. That alone is enough to get me in the boat.

But with all that, we managed not to lecture people. We made it fun. We weren't complete assholes. You didn't hate the guy who was telling you what to do. As Harry used to say, "People want to be with us, they want to be like us." It looked like we were having fun, our lives were fun. And people could relate to that.

It was just like being with my old mentor, S. Hazard Gillespie all those years before. Remember that everyone loved Gillespie and judges just wanted to be on his side. People wanted to be with Harry and me too. I was singing a song I believed in and people started singing right along with me.

Years later we found that it turns out the same behavioral changes that make your stronger and fitter also do great stuff to your brain and your emotions. They make you a better person, more decisive and more energetic—which I think is the great secret to life. And, if you can believe it, you'll be 10% smarter too.

Anyhow, that book, the new one with the brain stuff, is selling well. It's just flying off the shelves.

I have a wonderful friend named Goldie whom Hilary and I just spent time with down in Key West. Goldie charmed us 40 years ago by saying, "Look, all of life is a series of breaks and beatings, breaks and beatings. Today you get a magical break—and you're like, 'Oh boy this feels good.' Tomorrow you get a terrible beating—'Oh God, I can't get through it.' Breaks and beatings. Breaks and beatings. They're incessant, like the waves on the beach." Goldie always said, "If you don't like today's beating, just wait for tomorrow's break." And I think there's some truth to that.

I won't say I've had more fun writing these books than the other things I've done, but it's been radically different. I've repotted myself again and again and it's been a true joy. I couldn't be more grateful. I set out to lead more than one life and I did. That really, really happened.

I'm a bit reluctant to tell this story because everyone vaguely wants to write a book. It's not the answer for everybody these days, there are very, very few who succeed, but it was an answer for me. I do think that my experience has some general application—that is to say, that I quit doing what I was doing and started doing something I really wanted to do, which was also using my gifts at the highest level and the best kind of use that I could make of them.

And that, by the way, is my notion of the secret of life—using your best gifts at the high end of life. I think that's the great secret to happiness. And so I had a ton of it, and there you go.

Seth Werner, Entrepreneur

I worked for Seth long before we became friends. Seth was already a very successful serial entrepreneur when he founded what turned out to be the biggest company in his history of brand building; Mortgage.com. Seth built the company to over 800 employees and then sold it during the first dot-com bubble in 2002.

Throughout the very exciting ride Seth and I became and remain very good friends and we have started a number of projects and businesses together. One, The Strategic Forum, is still going strong more than 15 years after we founded it. Others less so. But throughout it all, good times and bad, I've always considered Seth a mentor, a friend, and a great source of business knowledge and advice. I think you will, too.

Seth Werner

My earliest recollection is also what really molded my life and personality in a very dynamic way. It happened after my father died. We lived in New York City in a 21-room apartment on Central Park West. My father was a successful attorney; we had chauffeurs, full-time live-in butlers and maids and so forth.

And then one day when I was six years old, I came down with the chicken pox. I was in bed and I remember my mother coming in the room and telling me my father had died. I had no idea what that meant.

I was in the end of second grade and the middle son of three brothers. My mother was 39 years old and decided she needed to start her own business to support us. So she got together with another lady and opened a high-end woman's dress shop in New York City. My mother determined that she could not give us the attention we required and so, at the ages of three, seven, and nine, we were sent away. My youngest brother was sent to live with my mom's sister on Long Island and my older brother and I were placed into a boarding school in Connecticut.

I was enrolled at that boarding school at the age when most people begin to form their personalities. I entered at the beginning of third grade and stayed through seventh grade. There were about 250 boys and girls who lived on the premises. We were totally cocooned inside the institution with the people who were responsible for us from the time we woke up in the morning until the time we went to bed at night. They were in charge of both educating us and running our lives.

Every other Sunday was Parents' Day, but because my mother was running her business and couldn't visit very often my brother and I were even more isolated than many of the other kids. We were there together but because he was three years older, my brother lived in a different dormitory and I didn't see him very often.

It was a very, very traumatic experience for me. The trauma was that not only did I lose my father when I was too young to understand what that meant, but also that I was removed from my mother. In a very short period of time my life changed drastically. I was thrown in with a bunch of kids I didn't know, in an unfamiliar environment I didn't know, and not with the friendliest teachers or house parents either. They were all very strict.

The result of all of that was that over a period of a year or two I was extremely unhappy. And then one day—literally—the light bulb went on. I said to myself, "If I'm ever going to be happy, I've got to change what's going on." Somehow I knew I needed to take a leadership role to mold the environment to the way I wanted it to be. And that was a life changing experience for me. It turned out to be the way I conduct myself to this very day.

Even at such a young age I was extremely athletic and there were lots of opportunities for sports at the school so I became the organizer. I organized the baseball team and I made myself the captain and the pitcher. I organized the basketball team and

I made myself the captain and the point guard. I organized the football team and of course I was the captain and the quarterback. I would call other schools to set up games and convince the teachers and the coaches to get the transportation necessary so we could play games at other schools in the area. And that was because I hated the environment I was in and decided to mold it to please myself.

In the five years I spent at the school, I was always at odds with the teachers and house parents. The owner of the school called my mom more than once and threatened to kick me out because she couldn't control my activities. Somehow my mother was always able to convince them to let me stay, promising that I would behave. I think what really upset them was that the other kids would follow me instead of the school employees they were supposed to listen to. I would come up with an idea of something fun to do and all of a sudden, 50 kids were following me.

That molded my leadership skills. But at the time the school authorities didn't see that as a good quality. I was disruptive and always pushed against the tide and my leadership talents were not appreciated. To this day I can remember the name of every coach, every teacher, and every school administrator I had to deal with because that's what it took to get things done the way I wanted.

I remember my 20 best friends at the school—both girls and boys—so well that I used to tell my own children bedtime stories about these kids I went to school with. Even today my kids remember me telling them stories about Stevie and Mike and Teddy and Sammy and all of the crazy things we did. We bonded because every one of these kids had something off about them—just like I did. We were all thrown into this environment because our parents couldn't handle this kid or we don't want to deal with that kid or they couldn't afford to take the time to care for their kid. I wouldn't say we were misfits, but we were one-offs, that's for sure. And I became the leader.

For example, some other student would come up to me and say, "Seth, I'm gonna run away tonight."

And I'd say, "Good idea. Run away."

And they'd go.

They'd get as far as the train station and they'd get picked up and brought back to school. There were no gates. You could just walk out, but there was nowhere to go.

We were too young to be interested in sex, and even though the girls were on the floor below us nothing really happened. But the high school kids, that was a different story. They were in the next building and there were all kinds of crazy things going on. That's how we learned about sex, hearing stories about what happened with those kids.

In a strange way I was blessed to be in that school. Because I had decided to be a leader, it required me to get along with everybody.

If you wanted them to follow you, you had to get them to like you and you had to get them to want to be around you. And that was a very important part of building my personality.

When I reached the eighth grade, my mom sold the business she had in New York and got a job as the manager of the high-end lady's dress shop in a new hotel in Florida. And that's what brought us down to Miami Beach.

Miami Beach was a very affluent neighborhood. My school was 90% Jewish, 9% Italian, and about 1% Hispanic—that was before the Cuban exodus to Miami. There were so many rich kids on Miami Beach living in mansions while we lived in a little 700-square-foot, two-bedroom, one-bath apartment. My brothers and I shared a bedroom, my mother had a bedroom, and we all shared a bathroom. It was very uncomfortable.

My senior year of high school was in 1963. I was in a fraternity and most of my frat brothers were from very successful families and most of them had new cars they drove to school. Just imagine going to high school and your friends drove new cars. I shared a 1956 Ford with my older brother and my mother. I found that living in such an affluent environment convinced me I never wanted to live three-to-a-bedroom again. There was nothing I could do about it at the time and I knew my mom was doing the best she could.

While I was a senior in high school, I made money delivering bagels to those big, beautiful houses up and down Miami Beach. Every Sunday morning at 6 AM, my partner and I would pick up one hundred dozen fresh hot bagels from the bakery and we'd deliver them to our customers who lived in homes on Pine Tree Drive or on North Bay Road, a very affluent neighborhood.

One Saturday I told my mom I was going down to the new grocery store because they were interviewing for bag boy jobs. I think it paid two dollars an hour. I was on the way out the door when my mom said, "Go put a tie on."

And I said, "Why would I put a tie on? It's just for a bag boy job."

She said it again. "Go put a tie on. Because you want to look good and you want to stand out, and you're better off wearing a tie than not. It's no big deal, just put a tie on."

I whined, "Awright," and went to my closet and put a tie on.

I go down to the grocery store and there's a long line of kids, maybe twenty kids, all standing there waiting. And the manager's looking up and down the line of kids and he looks at me and says, "You" and motions for me to come with him. That's all he said. My whole job interview was, "You."

I was the only one who wore a tie and he picked me out for that reason. There was no other explanation for why he picked me out of the line-up. A lesson learned.

When I started working, I had many, many jobs from the time I was 12 or 13 years old. But I always had a problem working for other people. Because of what I'd been through in boarding school, I just didn't like people telling me what to do.

I had put myself through high school and college and when I graduated, I went to California and worked at a company I hated. I thought the boss took advantage of everyone and even though I learned the real estate investment business I couldn't stand being there.

I had moved to California to follow a girl I met in college and after working at that company, I figured, "They gotta be making a profit off of me. I know what they do; I can do this myself."

Things in California didn't work out. I hated my job, and things with that woman didn't work out either, and I wanted to go back to Miami. I came back and I called one of my college fraternity brothers who was finishing up his studies at Stanford and I convinced him to go into business with me. He didn't know anything about real estate but I convinced him that I knew enough about it that I could teach him and he'd quickly learn the business.

I started this company when I was 26. The business was simple: We'd identify a property we wanted to own, we'd raise the required equity from investors, we'd buy the property, we'd manage the property, and we'd ultimately sell it. We'd make money both purchasing and selling, and we'd make money managing and operating the property while we owned it.

About four years into our business, the country experienced a major real estate recession. All of a sudden, properties were selling for 50 cents on the dollar. It dawned on me that the best time to buy real estate was when everyone else didn't want it. So I went to a Florida-based securities firm and convinced them to help me raise the capital to create a fund. We set out to raise five million dollars and only raised four, but it was enough. For the first time we could buy eight or nine properties at a time instead of just buying one here and one there. That gave our investors diversification because we'd buy shopping centers, apartment buildings, and warehouses all over Florida.

For the second fund we raised ten million and the third we raised 15. Generally speaking, it took about a year to deploy all the capital in a fund and we couldn't start a new one until we'd completed the previous fund. So for the next five years we raised the amount we needed every year and then built real estate portfolios. Along the way, more and more securities funds around the country joined our selling group and so by about 1980 we were raising a couple hundred million dollars a year. That meant we could buy twice that amount in real estate because the equity matched the debt we put on the property. For example, a $10 million property would cost us five million in cash and we'd put a five-million-dollar mortgage on it.

By then we were buying real estate all over the country and had offices in four or five major cities. But as time went on my partner and I found we had very different interests. He was more intellectual and wanted to write articles on how well we were doing to get our name in lights and I wanted to put selling groups together, raise capital, and buy more real estate. I had depended on him to run the business and oversee the operations while I was out doing deals and now he was busy getting us PR coverage. So in 1980 I bought him out and brought in a new partner whom I had bought some real estate from.

In 1981 we took the business public. A few years later, we were approached by a fellow in Chicago I had met through one of our board members. Turned out he was interested in buying our entire business.

When we sold our company to him, I had my first exit. I hadn't planned on it being an exit, though. Part of my deal was that not only would the buyer pay me, my partner, and all our shareholders a very nice profit, but I'd have a five-year contract to continue running the business. All the people who worked for me stayed on and I entered into an agreement to be the vice-chairman of the parent company.

That worked for about six months, until I started getting directives coming down from Chicago that I didn't agree with. "You gotta do this." "You gotta do that." "You can't do this." "You can't do that." And as we've already discussed, I didn't like taking orders and I didn't like working for someone else.

So one day at a board meeting in New York we let the board know what was going on. We each told our story and what we were unhappy about. After we each said our piece, someone on the board asked me to step out of the room so they could discuss the situation. About an hour later I came back in and they told me that they had instructed the new owner to take all his people back to Chicago and let me run the company the way I wanted. The board member said that "one of the reasons we agreed to buy your business in the first place was because we wanted you to run the firm."

And I'll never forget this, I looked over at the buyer and he was just boiling mad.

I got in a cab to drive to LaGuardia to head home and one of the board members caught a ride with me. He said, "You know you'll be hearing from the buyer tomorrow?"

And I said, "Sure, I talk to him almost every day."

And he said, "No, no; you'll be hearing from him and I'm sure he's just going to pay you off and end your contract. He doesn't like people telling him what to do. There's no way he's going to put up with the board's decision."

Sure enough the next day he calls me up and says, "You know what? Why don't I just pay you off and end your contract?"

So I like to say he bought my company twice—once when he bought the firm and the second time when he bought my contract. I was 39 years old and for the first time ever I didn't know what to do with myself. But I was very happy and financially set.

That was phase one of my business career.

When they hear me tell my story, people always ask me, "How was it that you decided to own your own business at such an early age?" It's funny, when I sold my business, I asked myself the same question, "Why would a 25-year-old start their own company?" I realized that I really don't like anyone telling me what to do. And that came from being in an institution where from the time you woke up until the time you went to sleep, they told you what to do and where to go and what to eat and how to eat and so forth. Rather than becoming regimented, I revolted.

When I think about all the things I've done and wonder what made me tick and what drove me to do those things, it was those early years in school and the realization that I really didn't like to work for someone else. Someone once told me that "Only the lead dog in the dogsled team gets a change of scenery," and that really resonated with me.

I wanted to have freedom to do what I wanted to do, when I wanted to do it, and how I wanted to do it. I also found that many of the people I did business with weren't very ethical and I didn't want to have to deal with people who conducted themselves that way.

I wanted to figure out what had motivated me. So I went to the dean of the business school at the University of Miami and convinced him that I could teach a course called, *The Psychology of Entrepreneurship — What Goes On Between the Ears of an Entrepreneur and Why*. I figured this would be a way I could learn what made me want to start my own business at such a young age, especially an investment business where I was competing with people who were much older and more established than me. For instance, I can remember going to buy a piece of property and the people I was buying it from would ask me, "When is your father coming to make the deal?"

And I'd ask, "What are you talking about?" even though I knew damn well exactly what they were talking about.

I went to the library and picked out every book I could find on entrepreneurship. I had my students read them and that forced me to read them too. And I learned many interesting things — two of which stuck with me.

What drives an entrepreneur?

1. Fear of failure and 2. Guilt.

Fear of failure is pretty obvious. Entrepreneurs, especially the successful ones, will do anything not to fail. They'll sacrifice anything, they'll put up with anything, they'll do whatever they have to do to be successful. And often there's a very big toll to pay—whether it's their family, their marriage, their health, and so forth.

And guilt is the second driver because many people who became successful did so because their families gave up so much for them to go to school and to have opportunities. And these entrepreneurs want to reward their families with their success. I remember story after story that supported that notion. And it was like that for me, too. I clearly remember how hard my mother worked to support her three boys and it was very important to me not to let her down.

As time went on, I met many people who exposed me to other opportunities. When we built Mortgage.com, for example, we were the first to actually originate a residential mortgage online. But we didn't start out to do that, we just morphed into the business as people and opportunities presented themselves.

That was an incredible experience. We had 800 employees in offices all over the country and we were so on-target with what was going on at the end of the nineties that our venture capital partners realized they could make huge profits by taking the company public or selling us outright. In 1999 we got to the point where the marketplace was so hot that we had to take the company public.

Within five days of doing that the valuation of the company was about 900 million dollars. We were on top of the world. But within six months the dot com industry just imploded. And our stock went from a high of $25 a share down to about two bucks. That resulted in a domino effect where our partners, customers, and vendors didn't want to do business with Internet companies. Mortgage.com was ultimately sold to a Dutch bank, but for nowhere near the amount of money we had originally been valued at.

After that I returned to my roots and started working back in real estate investing because it was the business I knew so well. Around 2007 or 2008 when the great recession hit, I was able to replay my strategy of buying real estate when no one would or could and once the market turned around that turned out to be big.

One of the sayings I remember was a quote by the great financier Bernard Baruch. When Baruch was asked how he made so much money he said, "I buy my straw hats in the fall." In other words, when people aren't buying is when you should buy.

The few times I ventured outside of what I really know and tried to do things that were outside my wheelhouse, I either lost money or didn't enjoy the experience. I read an article about that some years ago. It said the people who are the most successful over time are the people who stick with where they made their money in the first place. That's not always the case, and of course there are stories about people who are successful in whatever they do. But the people who consistently make money in one business after another are the people who are able to use the experiences they've had rather than having to learn a new business each time.

I credit my success to two things that I learned from how I grew up:

1. Because of what happened in that boarding school, I can walk into almost any social gathering and connect with everybody I come in contact with in a positive way. And I can do it relatively quickly.

2. And because when I went to Miami Beach Senior High I saw what people had that I didn't have, and that motivated me to do whatever it took to be successful. I think people who grow up in poor environments have almost no shot. Lack of education, connections, role models, even what they don't get to learn around the dining room table, all contribute to lower expectations and abilities. So those who make it out of a poor environment are 100-to-one. Ironically, they can credit that poor environment with their ultimate success.

Gayle Carson,
Founder, SOB (Spunky Old Broad)
Radio Network

Gayle Carson is the person we all hope to be when we reach her age. She's vital, active, involved, and constantly meeting new people and doing new things. What's more, Gayle is always pursuing new projects and getting the people around her excited by them.

I've never seen Gayle uninterested, fatigued or out of her element. She is always the life of every gathering, the one who charms everyone in the room, and the one who leaves with the most business cards, the most new contacts, and the most new opportunities to follow up on.

Gayle calls herself a SOB, a Spunky Old Broad. After you spend some time with Gayle, you might too.

Gayle Carson

My first stage appearance was at the age of three and I have been on stage ever since. They were doing a dance recital of the 12 months of the year and I played January, so I was the first one on stage. I went out and I did a somersault and my crown fell off and I put it back on, but I put it on backwards and everybody was laughing at me. My mother told me this (of course I don't remember) but she said I stopped the music and I put my hands on my hips and I waited until everybody got quiet, put my cap back on the right way and finished my dance. She said to me, "Gayle, I knew right then I would never have to worry about you."

That was how it all started. From then until I was 13, I was always dancing. I was dancing in the backyard. I was making up routines. I was dancing in the house when it was cold—and it was almost always cold because I was born in Albany, New York. So when it was cold, I had the record player on and played MGM musicals and I would dance to the musicals. That was my life.

When I was 13 years old, I had already broken 22 pair of eyeglasses. My father was sick of constantly replacing my broken glasses. So he told me that if I broke one more pair, I was going to buy them myself. I went to the optometrist, picked up my 23rd pair and my dad was waiting for me by the curb. I opened the car door and put my new glasses on the seat of the car. When I got in, I sat on them and broke them and we had not even pulled away from the curb yet.

My dad said, "Young lady…"

And I said, "I know."

So I had to figure out some way to make money. The only thing available to a 13-year-old girl was babysitting, which I was horrible at, so I decided I would get a real job. Back then, in the '50s, people still read the newspapers and they still had help wanted ads in the back. I went through the newspaper and saw openings for Avon ladies. I started selling Avon cosmetics door to door from the age of 13 on and became the top salesperson in the area. Why? Because I was little and people would let me into their homes. When I knocked on the door, they'd let me in and I'd sit right down on their couch. Once I sat down, I didn't get up until they bought something.

Then, at 14, there was a camp I wanted to go to. I decided I that I could teach dancing and drama and music and my parents wouldn't be able to say, "No." And because I had been studying piano since I was four or five, I figured I'd be good at it. I went to the guy who owned the camp and told him my plan.

He said, "Well, we don't have anybody who does that."

"I know." I said, "That's exactly why you need me."

He brought me in and I worked at the camp all summer and I produced a show at the end of the year. I choreographed it.

I wrote the music. I did a lot of stuff like that. After that first year he wanted me to stay on but I'd already done that and figured I should only do something once to get experience.

When I was 15, I got it in my head that I wanted to be a model. My mother told me that if I wanted to model, I had to earn my own money. So being interested in fashion, I went to work in a department store. That was the time of PBX and so forth and I worked on the switchboard, like on *The Marvelous Mrs. Maisel*. I was terrible; I disconnected everybody. But I earned the money I needed for my modeling course, took it, and started modeling.

I was short and I couldn't do fashion so I started doing photography modeling.

Of course, by the time I was 16, I wanted to do something new. This time I decided I wanted to work in a radio station. They had no interest in me but I was determined. So I went there every day for two weeks and just sat in the lobby. It wasn't easy because It took me two buses to get to the station and two buses to get home. But I wanted to work there.

I was in the lobby one day and the general manager came out and said, "You're here every day. Who are you?"

I said, "I'm here to get a job."

And he said, "Well, we don't hire anybody like you."

I said, "I know you don't, but I will sit here every single day until you do."

He finally hired me and I did everything they needed. I was the record librarian. I did the station traffic and things like that. I answered the phone. I did everything but sweep the floors.

One day the producer needed a young voice to record an ad and he asked me. After that he started using me to do some commercials. As I said, I did everything there— commercials and managing the record library and whatever else they needed.

At 17 I went off to college. I went to Syracuse University and I hated it.

To stay busy, I joined the dance program. I found a good dance partner but we eventually got blackballed because the school administrators said we were doing what they called "risqué" dances. The director of the program brought us in and was going to suspend us. I said, "I won't apologize because there's nothing wrong with what we did."

He said, "They were very dangerous things."

And I guess they were because I would jump up on my partner, wrap my legs around his waist, turn upside down and he would swing me around—and they found that outrageous. Well, it was tame compared to what you see on *Dancing With the Stars* today but it was a different time then. Still, they let us continue.

In fact, they had my partner and I audition for a musical thing. After we finished, they asked us if we would split up. I said "yes", and he said "no" because we both thought they wanted me,

but they didn't. They wanted him because they had no male danc-
ers. I was crushed. I called my mother in tears and started blub-
bering, "I don't want to stay here anymore. I don't want to do this
and I want to leave this school and they're all terrible."

I thought she'd drop everything and come get me and hug me
and bring me home. Instead, she said, "Grow up. This is not the
big time. This is college. What are you going to do when you get
out into the real world? You are just not going to make it. You've
got to stay there for a year. Then you can go wherever you want,
but you are not leaving now."

So I stayed for a year and then transferred to Emerson College
in Boston. While I was there I worked as a model for wholesale houses, taught modeling, was the accompanist pianist for
the choir, and did three radio shows. One was for the community station and then two more were for the FM station
there: WERS.

Funny thing is that I really never graduated high school because
I had finished early. When they scheduled the graduation cere-
mony, I was already at Grossinger's Resort in the Catskills. I was
competing in a dance contest. Then at college, I was done before
my class graduated. So I had already moved to Miami.

My parents were going out of their minds because nice girls
didn't do that. They didn't move that far away from home, but
they knew it was too late for them to complain. And besides,

I only gave myself two weeks to make it. If I didn't make it in two weeks, I was going to move to LA. Why only Miami and LA? Because they were the only two warm places I knew and I was done with the cold.

On the 14th day I was in Miami I got the job I wanted. I was teaching in a modeling school and I think they paid me $13 a week. I was trying to figure out *How am I going to live on this?* Then, the woman who ran the school called me up and said, "Forget teaching; you should be an agent. I'm going to fire my other girl. I'm going to hire you. I can tell you're going to make money for somebody and it might as well be me."

She started me at $35 a week.

After that, I didn't see her for two weeks. I was in her office not knowing what I was doing. I had a big yellow pad that I kept with me all the time. Anytime anyone called and had a question, I would write it down. I'd say, "I'll get back to you." Then, when my boss called in, I would ask her for the answers. Once I knew what to say I would call the people back. Well, in 30 days, I had a year's education because I was writing everything down. Within 30 days later I was making $100 a week. That went on for eight months.

When the holidays came around, I went home to see my parents. My boss called me while I was home and said, "Do you want to buy the business?"

I said no because I had no money. But then, I thought about it for 24 hours and thought, "Well, why don't I? This is exactly what I wanted to do. I want to own a modeling school."

I called her back and I said, "Yes, I want to buy it, but I have no money."

She said, "Well, come back and we'll work it out."

We worked out a deal so that I could pay her off over three years and it was a good deal for her, too because she taught the classes at night, so it gave her a double income.

Then after three years when I had paid it all off, I took the money I'd used to pay my debt to expand the business. I opened my second school, then my third and my fourth and my fifth and I developed them into an actual career school. We taught real estate, court reporting, legal and medical secretarial, fashion, merchandising, travel. We had the largest talent agency in Florida and we did all the movies and TV commercials that came to South Florida. Before long we branched off into convention services because we had been supplying models to the Doral Hotel and we had been doing fashion shows at the Fontainebleau.

One day my client at the Doral said to me, "Can you do other things? We need spouse programs. We need spokespeople for industrial shows. We need entertainers for theme parties. If you can do as well as you've done supplying us with these models for our golf tournaments and so forth, we'll give you an exclusive contract."

Before long I was also doing programs for the Fontainebleau, the Eden Roc, the Deauville, the Carillon, the Diplomat, the Boca Raton Resort & Club, the Breakers, and most of the other big hotels in South Florida. I did that for 21 years.

During that time, I became president of the Modeling Association of America. My company put on conventions at the Waldorf in New York, in the Fashion Mart in Dallas, in Long Beach on the Queen Mary, in San Francisco at the Fairmont, and so many more. I also started the first Model of the Year pageant. That was interesting because I just walked into a Madison Avenue advertising agency and tried to sell them on this idea of the pageant.

It was just an idea, just a concept—and they bought it! The show was on ABC Wide World of Entertainment with George Hamilton. You know, he's the one who is tan all the time. Barbara McNair was my co-host.

After a year I sold that pageant to Eileen Ford. In the meantime, we also created the Mother-Daughter Beauty Pageant. We had Dick Van Patten as our host and his wife, Patty was our hostess. I was also the director of the Miss Florida World Pageant for 13 years. Larry King was my emcee for I think seven or eight of them, and so on and so forth.

While we were producing these pageants, we were also working on our convention service business. One of the things we would do was book speakers for conferences. One day I booked Bill Gove, who was the first president of the National Speakers Association (NSA) and Sam Edwards. My clients always loved them so we did a lot of work together. Bill and Sam would always tell me that I had to go to NSA meetings because according to them I did a better job at speaking than they did.

But I was always so busy running the business I never went. Finally Sam said to me, "You are going to this next convention and that's that." So I went to my first convention in 1980 and I watched what was going on and I thought, *Oh, my gosh, I can make a living at this!*

I came home on Friday, put my business up for sale, and sold it in no time. My husband asked me, "What are you going to do now?"

I told him I was going to be a speaker. And he said, "What's that?"

I said, "Well, that's when you get up in front of people and you talk."

And he said, "Gayle, I hear you talk all the time. Who on earth would pay you to do that?"

I got on the phone and I called a hundred meeting planners a day. I called 500 a week and I didn't care who said no, I only cared who said yes. Within nine months, I was doing 135 programs a year. I did that for 20 years. I spoke in 50 countries, 49 states, and I was getting my doctorate at the same time. That's how it went for 21 years. I had a wonderful time, went through all kinds of outlandish travel.

I even drove a taxi once. There was a terrible snowstorm in the Northeast and I had to get from New York to Philadelphia for a speech and all the planes were canceled. But there was no way I was missing my speaking engagement. So I hopped in a cab and told the driver I'd pay his fare and pay his return fare if he got me there on time. Somewhere along the way the taxi driver started falling asleep at the wheel so I told him to lay down in the back and I drove. It was a crazy time.

I don't want it to sound like everything was fun and games. I am now going through my fourth round of breast cancer. It started in 1987. I've been having reoccurrences for 33 years, and every time I think they're over, they're not. I had an occurrence in 1987, I had another bad report in 1988, a third in 2004, and then I was diagnosed again two years ago. I've had 16 surgeries. I've gone through radiation three times, more chemo than I can count. I've had to go through surgeries to get fat put back on my chest because my blood vessels were coming through. I had an implant burst, so they had to scrape all this silicone off of my chest and I'm on chemo right now. Throughout it all I've lost a son and I lost my husband. But I keep going no matter what because I just don't ever give up.

I really believe in positive thinking; I believe that my positive mindset has a lot to do with how you get through life. I believe in exercise. I work out for two hours every day. I worked out this morning—I did the treadmill from 9:30 to 10:00, then I did two classes from 10:00 to 12:00. I believe in moving. I think it's very important to move. I was a Silver Sneakers Fitness Award winner. I don't tell anybody about my surgeries. I just go about my day, do my stuff and work out because if I didn't work out it would be worse.

I will tell you that life is not as grandiose now as it's been. It's tougher to make a living now for me because people don't want to hire you when you're my age and I'm going to be 82 this month. But I have had some inquiries from a senior living facility that has about eight or ten units here and then they've got one in New Jersey and they're talking about maybe having me as a spokesperson or something and maybe sponsoring my radio shows.

But I'm not waiting around for them, I'm always busy doing different things. Did you know I have three different radio shows on the air right now? I have *Women in Business,* I have *Living Regret-Free* and then I have *SOB Radio.* SOB stands for Spunky Old Broad.™ I own the Spunky Old Broad Radio Network and

I have women over 50 doing shows for other women over 50 on my programs.

Why SOB? I was in the back of the room at a conference with two friends and we were kibitzing in the back, which we shouldn't have been. I said, "We really need to be quiet." They said, "Yes, yes, we do." Then I said, "We're just a bunch of SOBs—spunky old broads," and it stuck and I trademarked it and I've built a business around it.

I think the thing that always earned me success is that I am extremely persistent and I'm extremely dedicated. If I want something, I won't stop until I get it. You can tell me "no" a hundred times, but I'll keep figuring out how can I get it. I think it's the dedication and the persistence. It was the way I was brought up. It was like when I wanted to leave college because I didn't get the role in the musical and my mother said, "Grow up. You're not going anywhere. This is not Broadway; this is life."

What would I do differently? I would not listen to as many people as I did. I should have followed my own head and my own heart more. I do believe in mentors. I do believe in coaches, but I should have listened to myself. I should have not followed the path that a lot of people said to follow.

That first 21 years, modeling and so forth, I really listened to my heart and I went after everything I could possibly get. When I went into speaking, I got on that phone and I called 500 people a week and I had a really great follow-up system. I had all kinds of irons in the fire. Then when I left speaking and I created the Spunky Old Broad Network, I listened to too many corporate bigwigs and I stopped doing the leadership and team building and customer service and all the things that I did so I could concentrate on the women over 50 market. But their advice was not appropriate for me and nothing came of it and I just should never have done it.

Women over 50 love me. They don't know where I get my energy from. They don't know why I think so positively. They don't know how I've gone through everything I've gone through. But what they do know is that I'm going to keep going for as long as I can—maybe even a little longer.

Alex Fraser, President, Smart Merchant Processing

The first thing you notice when you meet Alex Fraser is how big and imposing he is. At 6'8" tall with the physique of an athlete, Alex stands out almost everywhere he goes.

The next thing you notice is Alex's smile — it's almost as big and broad as his shoulders. It may be an overused description, but Alex Fraser truly is a gentle giant. After you read about how Alex grew up and made his way in the world, you'll see why.

Alex Fraser

I was born in Kingston, Jamaica and was brought to the US when I was about two and a half years old. As I recall, my mom and dad had a great relationship, but I guess the 17-year difference in their ages didn't work out too well for them, so they went their separate ways. My dad moved to New York and my mom decided to move to Miami.

She moved to a new city with her two and a half-year-old son and only $42 in her pocket. Of course she had to find a way to make a living for herself and her little boy, so she took any odd job she could find until she finally got a good gig at an insurance company.

When she got the job, she decided to send me to a school called the Pan American Institute, which was in the heart of Little Havana. Little Havana was the Miami neighborhood where Cuban immigrants had settled when they escaped Castro's revolution. I guess when she went to the parent-teacher night everybody spoke English, but the minute she walked out the door, English went out the door with her. That meant I quickly had to learn how to live my life as a Spanish-speaker from when school started at eight o'clock in the morning until she picked me up at 2:30 and my life returned to English. It was a very tough transition, but it helped me learn Spanish, and knowing another language was very helpful to me as I got older.

When I was around eight or nine years old, my mom decided I needed to have a man in my life and she felt that the perfect person was my dad. He was still living in New York and doing very well as a professor of economics at Brooklyn College. I started going to New York during my summers and then lived there with my dad and my stepmom in their apartment in Brooklyn.

New York was a very different lifestyle than I was used to. When I had grown up in Miami I would go outside and play and my mom didn't worry about where I was as long as I was home in time for dinner.

But it was very different in New York. It was a very intense city and my dad was a strict disciplinarian and I had no freedom. Later in life I realized how many good times I enjoyed in New York, but when I first moved there it was like I was in jail. I was stuck in their apartment and if I walked outside, the doorman told my parents what time I left and what time I came back. I felt trapped.

There was also this odd dynamic there that I had trouble understanding. My mom was in Miami by herself, working her behind off while my father was living in New York and, at least from what I could tell as a kid, in a much better financial state.

When I wasn't in school, I used to enjoy taking the train to Citibank where my stepmom worked. If she worked late, we got a car service to take us home and I loved that because I felt like I was living large in the big city.

One day when I was around 12 years old, I was walking home from school and I got stabbed. I was always the tall kid in class and some bully wanted to prove how tough he was so he picked me to fight with. He pulled a knife out of his pocket and waved it around at me, finally slicing my arm open. I needed 20 stitches and today I have a scar that serves as a constant reminder of how fortunate I am to be alive.

When my mom heard what happened she was horrified. She had sent her baby to New York to have a relationship with his dad, and now he had almost lost his arm and could have lost his life. So for eighth grade I was back in Miami full time. I was one of the youngest in my class but I was big and tall so all the coaches wanted me to join their teams. I thought I wanted to run track but since they didn't have a team, the PE coach told me, "Alex, you're going to play basketball."

I tried out for the team and I wasn't very good, but they picked me simply because I was big—I mean I was already six-foot-four. I really sucked, but the coach kept working with me. From the time I got to middle school until the time I moved on to high school, he kept working with me and teaching me the game. At some point he realized I was pretty athletic, and he must have seen some real potential in me.

When I was almost done with middle school, high schools started talking to me. By this time I was committed to playing ball and I even went to basketball camp to get better. I was still big for my age, but I still sucked and I knew that if I didn't get better I wasn't going to make the good teams. Also, my mom wanted me to be in a more controlled situation, some type of private school or Catholic school because after my life-threatening experience in New York she was very worried about me.

Coincidentally, some guy in my neighborhood played football at a well-known Catholic school in town called Pace, and he knew the basketball coach. He told him about his neighbor. "He's tall" he said, "and I think he plays hoops and went to basketball camp."

So the coach called me and never even asked to see me play. He just told me that if I passed my admissions test, I'd be on the team. Not only did that help me avoid a tryout, it worked for my mom too because she liked Pace. Before I knew it, I was enrolled and I started playing varsity basketball right away—as a freshman.

There were two other freshmen on the team and I was definitely the worst. I had a miserable go at it my freshman year but I kept at it and something happened between the end of my freshman basketball season and the start of my sophomore year. I was playing basketball constantly and starting to get more comfortable on the court. And I started developing a little more self-confidence because I had found something to excel at besides just academics. It was good to be a smart kid, but I wanted more—I wanted to be good *and* cool. And I found that in sports I was able to express myself differently.

So I had a good sophomore season and even before my junior year I was being recruited by colleges throughout the country. At that point I had dreams of going to college for the next four years, and then I assumed I'd go on to play in the NBA.

I got recruited by a lot of very good schools and finally chose the University of Miami. I looked at a bunch of other colleges, but I liked the way UM recruited me the most. Coach Leonard Hamilton had a certain approach to how he did things, and when he finally recruited me, there was just no other choice for me to go anywhere else because I appreciated who Coach Ham was and what he stood for. I also felt good about what he could do for me and my athletic career.

Coach put me in the game my freshman year which seemed great. But I definitely wasn't ready for the much higher level of college play. And I probably posted the worst record in the biggies by getting on the court my freshman year.

Even as bad as I was as a high school freshman, I don't think I'd ever lost 18 games in my entire career, let alone in one year. I was devastated with our performance and struggled to decide whether I should stay at UM or transfer to another team. After a lot of sleepless nights, my roommate and I decided to stay with Coach Ham at UM and work even harder. Our decision paid off. The next year the University of Miami was Team of the Year and Coach Ham was named National Coach of the Year.

All of a sudden, things started to change. We played in more and more postseason games and we started getting bigger and better recruits. Even with my dismal freshman year, I had a great experience playing college basketball for University of Miami. I started all four years and I was captain of the team from my sophomore year until graduation. I got to travel all over the country playing basketball and I was recognized everywhere on campus and even all around Miami. Things were great.

But as good as everything was, the next step just never seemed to materialize. At some point in my senior year, I remember me and one of my college teammates noticing that we weren't getting the recruiting calls our teammates were getting. We realized that they were going to be drafted into the NBA and we weren't, so we figured that we'd probably have to go overseas and work our way back to the NBA if we wanted to live that dream.

For whatever reason, that was the first time the reality of life without basketball ever hit me. And even though I still had eight months of college and some basketball season left, I couldn't stop thinking about what that next chapter of my life was going to look like. The realization that I now had to figure out what life would look like without basketball hit me. And it hit me hard.

I did go overseas and I played basketball in Germany for a couple years which was a great experience. And even though I was invited to a few NBA tryouts, nothing real ever materialized. For whatever reason—maybe it was my injuries or maybe I just wasn't talented enough to make a roster—I didn't know. What I did know was that I had to make a decision because my basketball career was drawing to a close whether I liked it or not.

The decision was prompted not just because things weren't working out in basketball, but because I had seen a couple of guys who went and played basketball overseas, and I had watched what happened to them. Like me, they had enjoyed playing internationally, but then, at the age of 32 or 35 or whatever they were done.

Yeah, they had made great money overseas and they did get to travel and see the world, but when their careers ended they needed to decide what they were going to do professionally. And because they'd done nothing but play basketball 24/7/365, their professional options were limited. Worse, they didn't seem happy with what their opportunities were.

Whether the choices were to be a coach, a substitute teacher, a bodyguard, or a bouncer, I knew that wasn't the path I wanted to take. So after I tried out with the Lakers and that try-out didn't go well for me, either, I really started worrying about what I going to do next.

During that time I met a guy who owned a pretty prominent financial services company and I asked him if he'd give me a job. He told me he couldn't understand why he should hire me or why I even wanted to work for him because I didn't meet a lot of the criteria of the people that worked at his shop. I still had some basketball swagger left in me, so I said, "I can see why you think I'm not the right choice but you might as well give me a shot because if you don't, somebody else will and they'll get all the benefit." And he liked my moxie and he hired me.

I've been very fortunate to have good men in my life like my dad and Coach Ham. And this guy also became a great mentor and he helped me look at things differently. I worked for him selling municipal bonds for a couple of years, until I realized I didn't really like convincing people to buy things over the telephone. I'm a people person and I enjoyed face-to-face interactions. So I moved to a new company that had come to town from Atlanta, and I enjoyed the new job because it allowed me to use my personality.

One day a good customer of mine telephoned and said that someone he knew who owned a local bank wanted to talk to me. Turned out he wanted me to be his regional president. I was glad I took the meeting and flattered that they wanted me. But I was surprised to learn that if I wanted to take the job, I'd actually have to take a pay cut. Still, I figured the opportunity to become the regional president of a community bank that had branches in three different markets was too good to pass up. Especially because I had already decided that when I turned 30, I was going to open my own business and I thought this would be a great steppingstone. In the meantime, I enjoyed some great experiences, I wound up making good money and, best of all, I met the woman I would end up marrying.

I went out and got married and started my own business exactly on schedule. And we did well right out of the box. It seemed like everything was going my way again. But then, right after we got back from our honeymoon, something crazy happened. We went through one of the biggest financial recessions in history. Some financial experts even compared the Great Recession in 2008 to what happened during the Great Depression in 1929. I don't think it was quite that bad, but a lot of things changed. I had become a guy who was very comfortable and had seen a lot of successes and felt that things happened very easily for me.

And then, all of a sudden, I wake up and I'm 32 years old, I'm married, and I own a mortgage company that's hemorrhaging money every single day.

It dawned on me that not one of the people I looked up to because of their successes had been consistently successful for their entire career. Instead, most of the people I respected said that things happened in their life that caused them to change course again and again. I discovered that it wasn't enough to win or lose; you had to know how to bounce back—and that was the same in basketball or in business or in life. After a bad play or a bad call or even a bad game, you had to figure out how to get up off the bench and come back stronger.

At that point I started leaning on things I had learned over the years. When I was a kid I thought there was only one thing that

I was going to do for the rest of my life — play basketball. And I had to accept that even though my life hadn't turned out that way didn't mean I wasn't a success.

I learned that from sports. You see, people look at all the great things that athletes do, but most people fail to notice how much failing goes into that success. If you're a baseball player and you strike out 70% of the time, but you hit the ball 30 or 33% of the time, you're famous. You might not have gotten on base 70% of your times at bat but you're still good enough to be a hall-of-famer.

If you shoot a basketball and you miss 50% of the time, that means you will sink a basket only half of the times you shoot the ball. It also means that somebody will pay you millions and millions of dollars, and you can be in the Hall of Fame.

If you play football and you're a defensive end, you're going to try to sack the quarterback every single time the ball is hiked. If you knock him down only once per game for your ten-or-so years in the NFL, you've probably failed about 70 snaps per game. But if you find a way to tackle the quarterback one time in each game, you're considered one of the greatest defensive ends of all time.

Thinking about this made me realize that I had been in training to understand that failure is a big part of all the good that happens. So now that I had to turn things around, I realized that a lot of it had to start between my ears. I needed to change how I looked at things and how I approached things. Most importantly,

I needed to believe in myself more than I believed in the power of the situation I was going through

After hemorrhaging a ton of money, I came across the business that I'm in now. I learned about the credit card business and the merchant processing world and started the company that I've been running for 12 years now. I've seen some successes, been able to hire some friends, made some new friends within my business, and now I'm trying to grow something special. But even as I'm going through this, I'm feeling another shift happening and I'm thinking that I want to add some things to my plate—and that can be challenging with a wife and two young children. But this last year I lost my father and I've seen people lose family members and friends. And the one thing that I keep finding myself saying is that I don't want to look back and say, "Well, what if I didn't try this or why didn't I do that?" Because no matter how much success you may have, or how many times you fail, it's good to always be able to get back up and chase the dream. Funny thing is that I don't even know what dream I'm chasing right now. But I do know that I want my dream to be bigger tomorrow than it was yesterday.

Ed Wasserman, Dean of Journalism, University of California, Berkeley

I always say that if you were to look up the word "eloquent" in the dictionary, you'd find Ed Wasserman's picture. I never knew if Ed's eloquence was a result of his exemplary education, his journalistic experience, or his natural gifts. What I knew was that Ed had a way with words and a way of explaining things that was a whole level above anyone I had dealt with before. As such, I found it especially fascinating to interview Ed and learn both about how he developed and marshalled his prodigious gifts and how he never quite felt that he used them to their full advantage.

Ed Wasserman

When I got out of high school I was very inspired by John Kennedy in the White House. Thanks to him, I was taken with the concept of public service as a noble thing. So the thought of being involved in the public sphere took on a real attraction. I was also influenced by my older brother who was at the Georgetown University School of Foreign Service. Mindful of what important work had to be done in the public eye, I don't think I ever envisioned myself going into business.

While I was studying at Yale in New Haven, Connecticut, I experienced protesting the Vietnam War. By the time I got out in 1970, my desire was to put my shoulder to the wheel and seek solutions to big, big problems—war and peace, poverty and equality; all of that.

As I said, I was pretty heavily involved in the antiwar movement and campus mobilization. There was a student strike in May—that was after America had invaded Cambodia and after the Kent State and the Jackson State shootings. My brother was in East Africa on a Fulbright scholarship finishing up his doctoral thesis. And he invited me to join him traveling around Africa. But first I needed to raise some money to fund my trip.

So right after graduation, I got together with a group of people and we had this idea of starting a magazine that would tell stories about America and its past. The magazine would highlight struggles for social justice and individuals who distinguished themselves in ways that we thought were progressive and socially beneficial.

We really didn't know what we were doing, and none of us had ever done any real publishing before, but we were relatively successful. I had moved back into my parents' house and in time I saved enough money to go abroad. So I headed to Africa and met my brother and traveled around.

Somehow I ended up in Kinshasa where I ran into a college classmate of mine who was doing alternative service for a Mennonite group. So I wandered around looking for a job and found work on the construction site of the Intercontinental Hotel. Bechtel was the contractor and they needed somebody who spoke French and I told them I did even though it was really only college-level. Truth was, my French wasn't actually helpful because I couldn't talk about business or construction issues, but I stayed for six or eight months and earned a bunch of money.

While I was in Kinshasa I read *A Moveable Feast* by Hemingway and became enamored of Paris. I was also inspired by Angela Davis, who had gotten her degree at the Sorbonne. And at the time it was cheap to go to school there so I spent a year in Paris and worked on my French and earned a graduate degree in philosophy.

I came back to the states in late '72. It was just after the presidential election when McGovern was defeated by Nixon. I went back home to DC and started looking for work. I didn't really know what I wanted to do, but I did have a degree in politics and economics from Yale. So I thought maybe I should try to find something social science-related, and I sent out some resumes and got a few nibbles, but nothing great.

I was having dinner one night with some friends and one of them was a teacher at Montgomery College, and she taught English and journalism and had just collaborated on a project at a newspaper called *The Montgomery County Sentinel* with a reporter named Bob Woodward—yes, that Bob Woodward—and she said that maybe I should go to the *Sentinel,* they're great people and they do good work. Before that I hadn't really thought about journalism at all.

It's old history now, but at the time, the whole Watergate thing hadn't happened yet. Well, the break-in had happened, but this was 1972 and the story hadn't come out and it hadn't become the kind of historical moment it would become. So I went to the office of *The Montgomery County Sentinel* in Rockville Count, Maryland and knocked on their door.

I'd done a little writing before; I'd been the editor of the humor magazine in college and written one piece on an anti-war demonstration for the Yale Daily News. But aside from that I'd never really been published and never really thought about journalism. But I went in there and met the news editor and he hired me. Later on, I found out he told one of my colleagues that the last untutored Yalie he had hired off the street had been Bob Woodward. And that was a real coup because that hire was starting to distinguish himself with the coverage of the Watergate break-in. So I guess indirectly I got my job because of Bob Woodward.

I wound up working at the *Sentinel* for a couple years. I had started as news editor but that was not what I wanted to do. So I moved into reporting and was doing general interest reporting and really loved it. And I thought, well, you know, the usual pattern was to go from there to a paper such as *The Washington Post*. In order to do that I thought it might be useful to go back to college and get a PhD. I also thought it would be a good idea because I had a thought for a project that I could write my thesis on. And so I figured I had a leg up on getting that thesis done. I presumed it would be kind of my union card. If I ever wanted to work at a university, having a PhD would be a handy thing to have. So, long story short, I started looking around for the right school and I ended up in Europe again.

I didn't have any money and I discovered that getting my degree at The London School of Economics would be very, very inexpensive. Plus, I was so naïve that I actually thought I could do my PhD in two years. It turned out to be five. You see, I had met a woman in Paris and in the meantime we had gotten married. So instead of me quickly finishing my PhD and writing a book from the thesis, we had a baby and various things happened. It also turned out to be very hard to get a PhD at The London School of Economics; they made you really work for it.

It also turned out that I didn't get my book published. The University Press did show some interest, but after five years I was so sick of the project that my heart wasn't in it. And I felt bad about being 30 years old and not making money. So we came back to the states and I got a job, which turned out to be the only job I could find.

This was back in the day when we didn't have Craigslist or anything like that. To find a job you had to write letters to people asking for references, and they had to send you letters with names of people to send résumés to, and they'd have to write you back with an invitation or a rejection and it just took forever. The best I could find wound up being a job as a business reporter at *The Casper Star Tribune* in Casper, Wyoming.

Back then Wyoming was booming thanks to the energy business. Oil, gas, coal, and uranium were all going bonkers and newspapers were trying to cover business effectively and they had a new editor from *The Wall Street Journal* and he brought me on. Unfortunately, he left before I even got there so I never worked with him. And just like London, I went to Wyoming planning to stay for only two years and I wound up staying for five.

In the meantime, my wife was going crazy living in that high plains windy town and we had had another baby by then. So we had two little kids and I was only making about $30,000 a year, which even in 1981 was not enough money to raise a family.

So we're broke, and my wife is unhappy, and we're living in the middle of nowhere, and I'm not setting my career on fire.

And then I got an offer from *The Miami Herald*.

An editor who had worked with me in Casper had relocated to Miami and he recommended me. I came to visit my mom who was living near Ft. Lauderdale, and I took advantage of that trip to interview with the editor at the paper and we hit it off. I went back to Wyoming and my wife and I packed up our family and moved to Miami.

Once we got there, I became the deputy city editor, which got me involved in interesting projects and put me on longer, more thoughtful work. It was good training and after some successes I ended up as the executive business editor of *The Miami Herald*.

Thanks to the work I did there I got the call about a job from a guy I didn't know. There was an editor named Marty Baron and he'd been the business editor of *The Miami Herald* and then he'd gone on to be the business editor of *The LA Times* and he'd heard of me and wanted to know if I wanted to come out to LA.

There was this strange harmonic convergence because at around the same time I also got a call from another guy I didn't know named Steven Brill. Turns out Brill had recently bought a chain of newspapers based in Miami and was looking for an editor to run them.

So I went out to LA and I loved *The LA Times* and I really liked Marty Baron, but I was intimidated by LA and I was fearful that living in LA would be expensive, and we were broke. And, as you might have guessed, by that time we had had a third child. It was not great family planning on our part. We're sort of fans of the *"YOU'RE WHAT?!"* school of birth control, so I had a third child and I was making, you know, not that much — maybe fifty grand — and I didn't think I'd make enough to live in LA and support my growing family.

Brill impressed me as somebody who was serious about what he was doing and he offered me a lot of money. So now I'm looking at doubling my salary, and Brill was a very persuasive guy and I didn't know what to do. So I went out to see Al Checchi, an old friend of mine from high school days. We were student government presidents together at different schools in the same area. Al had been working for the Bass Brothers in Fort Worth and together they were basically responsible for turning around the Walt Disney Company. Al had gotten extremely rich and he ended up buying Northwest Airlines with some of his proceeds and getting even richer.

So I got in touch with him and said, "I don't know what I should be doing. I want you to look at this deal Brill's offered me and talk to me about how I should handle this negotiation." I flew out to see Al and spent the weekend at his place in Fort Worth and he gave me some great advice. I went back to Brill and I said, "I want this and I want that," and Brill said, "Okay, okay, okay" and those concessions made Brill's offer really irresistible.

Brill told me, "I'm going to give you a year's pay and if for any reason you don't stay, I'll still pay you for the year," which was a pretty sweet deal. He said that he wanted me to turn his chain of papers into local *Wall Street Journals.* He promised I could hire whoever I had to hire and I could pay them whatever I had to pay to make these really, really good papers."

This was kind of a dream opportunity for a journalist. So I took him up on it.

All of a sudden, I had a company car and a cell phone, and I doubled my pay. Even better, I was able to hire the best reporters from *The Miami Herald, The Wall Street Journal,* wherever. I hired from *Forbes Magazine*—which at the time was a great business magazine. I hired from wherever I wanted. And I conscripted the top, top editors from both Miami papers—*The Herald* and *The News.* I got them all to come aboard.

What I was doing was trying to send the signal out that there's a new guy in town. I was just editor for a few years and then I was made CEO of the company as well. So I was running a chain of three daily papers and we're doing work that I found immensely satisfying. We won a bunch of national awards for business reporting. A number of our people went on to do great things. We did some very fancy investigative projects. We kind of took down the person who was head of the biggest savings and loan in the Southeast. This was the time when the savings and loan and lending industries were in turmoil and we were able to do very, very powerful and important work on all the major lenders in South Florida.

I got the papers involved in commercial and industrial real estate which had gone unreported. We covered some law issues and we put out special sections on the Florida Supreme Court's best and worst cases. We brought a new level of sophistication to covering business, real estate, and law that I was very proud of.

I credit Brill with quite a lot. He had a certain amount of disregard and contempt for people who were thought to be experts. He believed that if you're smart, you can learn what the experts can do, and he was a tough boss. But he never wavered in his confidence in my ability to do whatever it was I needed to do. That included running the company, which I had never done before.

We also had a commercial printing company. I can't say I knew a lot about printing when I started, but we expanded it and brought in new web presses and I learned something about it. I was also in charge of ad sales and promotions and we were successful there, too. We made a lot of money.

We didn't accomplish everything we set out to do, though, and I had my share of disappointments. We did not succeed in

diversifying our revenue base into the kind of help-wanted advertising and display advertising that would have enabled us to really
benefit from our increased circulation. Almost 45% of our revenue
came from public notice advertising which is the same way those
papers have functioned since they were founded in the 1920s and
that didn't really change too much.

But 15 years went by, and by the late '90s Brill had sold out. He
created *Court TV,* and then Time-Warner bought him out there,
too and he left. Time-Warner didn't want to retain control of the
Review Newspapers so they put them on the block. They were
bought by a venture capitalist named Bruce Wasserstein, and his
team installed new leadership.

They decided that they were going to heavy-up on covering law.
And they had some new ideas that were not really compatible with
the directions we had gone in terms of the aggressive editorial
offerings, and the kind of quality we wanted, because they realized that the editorial quality did not make them any additional
money. They believed that we would be able to make more money
by getting more subscribers and raising our ad rates to get more
advertising. As they saw it, a lot of what we were doing came at
the cost of profits and the new owners wanted to see those profits. They also wanted to install leadership that was going to cost
them less money. So in spring of 2000 they told me to leave. That
was not a great moment.

By the fall of 2000 the competition from the Internet had not yet kicked in, and we didn't fully appreciate just how the fuse was burning down on the newspaper industry. But it was still not a great time to be in your 50s and on the street looking for a job in the news media.

So I found some temporary things to do. I was working at Money Laundering Alert, which was a company that specialized in publishing for the anti-money laundering community. And some other opportunities came my way. At that time Dow-Jones was looking for a new editor for their *Far East Economic Review* and I had some interviews and I was very excited about going to Hong Kong, but it didn't work out. Thinking back, it probably didn't help that I had a family of six that would need to be relocated. But within a few years they sold that out anyway, or I think they may have just shut it down.

I actually spent a year commuting to New York every week, because Brill had called me and said he needed an editorial director for this company called Media Central that he had created in partnership with another media company called Prime Media.

I worked for a year as his editorial director there, which was interesting work because Brill had conscripted some amazingly talented writers to cover different areas of the media industry—Hollywood, publishing—it was a very broad-brush effort. But the whole thing was running out of steam because by then the economy had gone into a serious recession. Of course, after 9/11 things were just apocalyptic in the media world.

I was in New York for 9/11, and I remember Brill's secretary had a place in Battery City near Ground Zero, and we walked the length of Manhattan to try to get in there and see what happened to her apartment. It seemed like the whole world was just crumbling around us.

So this media central gambit in New York fell apart by the end of 2001. They just weren't hitting their numbers and advertising was disenchanted with us. I think they just sold off what they could and shut down the rest.

Brill left and I was gone. I had some money left over and I had some severance pay, but I was not in a very rich place. I tried my hand at creating a prospectus to start a city magazine, and I poked around with a friend who had a very successful city magazine in Memphis. I thought that Miami was just a vain-enough place that a city magazine couldn't fail, but I didn't really have the money-raising chops to interest investors. Even though I believed the concept was a viable one, I didn't have the skills to do it very well and it never really went anywhere.

Back in my old *Miami Review* days I had become friendly with Hodding Carter, who was now the president of the John S. and James L. Knight Foundation. He told me that Knight had funded various professorships at different colleges. The Knight

Foundation didn't have anything to do with filling those jobs, but I should look into them because I had substantial news experience and I had a PhD and Carter thought it might be something good for me.

The job turned out to be at Washington and Lee University in Virginia. I put out some feelers and indeed they were looking for somebody to be appointed to the Knight chair in journalism ethics. All of a sudden, my little degree in philosophy that I did on a lark, you know, 25 years before, meant I could claim to have some knowledge of moral philosophy. And I got this PhD and it turned out that the person heading the search committee was someone I had vaguely known back in *The Miami Herald* days. So I sent an application and a cover letter and they invited me to the next step.

When I flew up there I brought one of my kids along. I wanted somebody else to do a reality test because this was a small town in Virginia. And it was different from anything I'd experienced before.

The interviewer and I hit it off and I ended up getting the job. My family moved, somewhat under protest and we got there in 2003, which was the same year the Mel Gibson movie about Jesus hit the theaters. That was interesting because here we were, Miami Jews, going up to a small town in Virginia where the nearest synagogue was 40 miles away and services were actually held in a facility borrowed from the Methodist Church. At the time, interest in the Mel Gibson movie—which was generally regarded as anti-Semitic—was intense. Because the theatre in Lexington, Virginia was closed for renovations, they were chartering buses to go down to Roanoke, Virginia to see that movie. The change we'd been through already seemed so abrupt that watching people line up for this move made me feel so unwelcome. It made me wonder if we'd made the right decision.

Making the transition into academics was hard. They don't do a lot of tutoring, you know? They don't tell you what a syllabus is. No one shows you how to organize a course. There's a lot of learning by doing and it was an extremely stressful, difficult time.

I spent the first six months in Lexington Virginia in a rental house by myself except for my cat and dog. My family had gone back to Miami; my wife was trying to fix up and sell our house. My youngest daughter, who was the only one left at home, had come with me but she lasted only a couple of weeks before she went back home to Miami, too.

So it was tough and I certainly felt like I had failed. You know, when you can't afford to stay in your home, the home where your children grew up and where all your friends were, it's a tough transition, going to a place where you didn't know anybody and didn't really care to be.

But I was there for the next ten years and it turned out to be a very rewarding time. I liked being a professor. I liked writing. I liked the fact that the professorship gave me program funds so I could host twice-yearly symposiums on journalism ethics and bring interesting people down to talk about ethical challenges.

I was writing a monthly column and I developed a readership. For the next 10 years I was a relatively influential media columnist and I lived as a professor. I liked the teachers. I liked the people I worked with and that sort of helped as well. Plus I enjoyed the work.

But I still kept my eyes open for opportunities and I was contacted for several jobs. I tried out for a few while I was there because I didn't think staying in Virginia was a sustainable thing for us. And what became clear to me was that it would be hard for me to make the transition as a professor in the journalism and ethics world because I was competing with people who had done very solid scholarly work in ethics.

My columns didn't really qualify even though I was covering the work I was doing in peer-reviewed research in ethics. I was doing academically respectable work, but I didn't have volume. I didn't have books. I didn't have publications in that sphere. My PhD was in political politics and economics. It was about media technology. It wasn't about ethics, and my field was really about ethics. That meant that for me to move to a larger opportunity it would have been in administration because I had a run a chain of newspapers and I could lay claim to having stronger executive and management experience than to being a respectable academician.

In the meantime, the media industry was dying. My time at Washington and Lee, from 2003 to 2013, was an era of an almost uninterrupted tailspin by the news media. Not only were the employment opportunities drying up, but the nature of news was undergoing fundamental transformation. And I no longer had a modern set of skills for that, for the World Wide Web. The time I spent being a professor was the decade when the news media was both shrinking and undergoing significant changes.

Of course I was aware of the changes that were going on. I was working very hard to keep abreast of what was happening. I was talking to people all the time. I even spent a month with *The Miami Herald* because I wanted to get reacquainted.

I went to a lot of conferences. I was keeping as up-to-date as I could. But watching it closely is not the same thing as doing it. I stayed in academia because that's where it looked like the opportunities were.

One thing I learned is that you have to work very hard at keeping your network of contacts broad and up-to-date and with you. That's one of your most valuable assets and you need to be a responsible steward of the people you know.

As a case in point, there a person I met through another friend was an investigative reporter and filmmaker at CBS' *60 Minutes*. He was running an important program I'd been attending thanks to my acquaintance with him. Around that time the University of California, Berkeley happened to be looking for a dean and my friend invited me to speak at a symposium that had a lot to do with endearing me to the people at Berkeley.

When they contacted me they told me there was a search going on. I had been somewhat acquainted with people there and I was impressed with them. Obviously, Berkeley sounds like a pretty good idea when you're in rural Virginia, and I thought this was something my wife would like. I didn't want to end my academic career as a professor at Washington and Lee. So being in a world-class university like Berkeley sounded like a pretty good idea and to some degree, maybe I felt it was kind of the place where I belonged. I felt that my combination of management experience, academic experience, and journalism experience would make me a natural fit for the deanship.

While I didn't have extensive fundraising experience, I had some experience in sales and I had some acquaintance with the art of getting rich people to part with their money. So it just seemed like a good fit. And the position would come with tenure, because I wasn't going to go out there unless I had a tenured professorship as a fallback position. And that worked out, too.

It's astonishing how you make choices and the things you have in mind—the things you're pursuing when you make those choices—turn out not to be the goals you end up achieving. None of us can see around corners, so we do something with a certain outcome in mind and make lists of pros and cons. But if you hold on to that list and look back at that decision point in your life, maybe five years later, you're probably going to find out that the things that were inducing you to do what you did aren't really particularly operative at all. Those things don't turn out to be important.

When I think about what I was hoping to accomplish by doing something, oftentimes those plans didn't turn out to be what happened. I made a decision to go to graduate school when I was 25 and then did nothing with it. But hey, my journalism career was going really well. You know, I had won some awards and I really was on course to get a job with *The Washington Post*. And I could have done that, but I don't know that I would have ended up as editor of *The New York Times* and probably not since there are very few of those opportunities. But when I was at *The Miami Herald*, I didn't get the kinds of promotions I thought I should have gotten. And who knows what that kept me from them?

When I was working in Casper, Wyoming I already had degrees from three of the best universities in the world, including a PhD from The London School of Economics, I had a wife and two kids, and I was working for $14,000 a year. This looks like the result of a pretty stupid set of decisions.

And then, in the fullness of time, that PhD saved my life when I was 57 years old and looking for something in academia. And that PhD probably gave me a big leg up over other people that might have grabbed that job at Washington and Lee. And that job at Washington and Lee turned out to be a real gift. When I look at the quality of people who don't have a prayer getting a job where I work now, and I look at just how strong their résumés are as journalists, and how difficult it is to get jobs in academia, well, I got really lucky. And so what I thought was a kind of a career-mutilating choice that I'd made in my mid 20s where I could have put those five years into my career instead of studying for my PhD, turned out to be a real lifesaver.

To pursue my career I just needed to be far nimbler and far more willing to abandon my family than I was. So something I thought I was training myself for, which was to be an international roving correspondent, I never actually did. Instead, I found I needed the money and I had supervisory chops, so I gravitated toward editing and supervising as the best position for me in the news organizations I was in.

It's about the agony of choices and how hard it is to make these transitions, even when you think you've got the prerequisites in terms of your skill set. You need to believe that you can do this.

And that kind of confidence is under siege every time you make one of these choices. I certainly can tell you that being dean out here at Berkeley has been very, very hard. It's a tough environment. It's a difficult culture to read and to learn. The kind of authority you have as dean is dramatically different from the authority you have running a news organization or running a company in the private sector. It's easy to get things wrong, and it's a very difficult, demanding, and stressful job. You're at a point in your life you think you should have a lot of confidence in your ability to weather these things, and next thing you know you're up at three in the morning chewing your cheek.

I don't regret any of this. I do have some disappointment that I didn't do more or matter more, but often I took jobs—or didn't take jobs—because of my responsibilities. I didn't go abroad as a foreign correspondent. We moved from rural Virginia to a more cosmopolitan city so my teenage daughter could attend a school that looked like something she recognized. I do feel like I've been blessed with a lot of capacity that I haven't used to my satisfaction, but when it comes to my wife and children, I realize how blessed I've been. I'm happy to have given up what I gave up raising my family.

I look rearward now from the vantage point of being a few years older. I've seen so many people who have been looted and pillaged by their career aspirations. And then they're given early retirement after having devoted themselves, their evenings, and their weekends, to building a career and a professional calling or for an institution. They sacrificed all that for an organization that is totally without gratitude, and they're just wondering what the hell happened. I imagine there are also people who raised families and gave up their careers for their families who feel the same way but I sure as hell don't. I am enormously grateful.

I am really glad that I never decided that family was going to get in the way of my great career. I'm glad we never said, "Let's make sure we're really careful and have zero or two kids," that kind of thing. I'm glad I never did that.

But there are still things I want to accomplish, so I'm about to change my life again. One of the reasons I'm leaving the dean's office is that I want to get back to writing. Being dean is a great title and the job is a great forum for publishing, but it doesn't give you the intellectual time or space to develop your thoughts and put them on paper. I want to get back to that. I have several years' worth of work that I want to be doing.

After all this time I'm still trying to find my voice and make a difference.

Ian Wolfe,

Communications Sergeant,

U.S. Special Forces, Middle East

A friend of mine asked if I would speak at a conference for a group he was involved with called Your Grateful Nation. According to their website, the "organization assists special operations forces veterans with the successful transition from the military into their next career."

Before I spoke I went around the room and asked each participant to tell the group who they were, what they had done in their military careers, and what they hoped to get from the evening we were going to spend together.

Each story I heard was more interesting, more dramatic, and more heroic, than the one that came before. When I heard how Sergeant Ian Wolfe had changed his life—and continued to do so—I knew he had to share his story with you.

Ian Wolfe

I was born in Los Angeles, but Colorado's where I mostly grew up. My dad is a Colorado native, so I guess when we lived in LA he and my mom got tired of cops knocking on their door at two in the morning and asking if they could search the backyard for somebody. So we moved to Boulder.

I was a pretty outdoorsy kid, went skiing most weekends when it was cold, went hiking when it was warm. I was also good at school and didn't have to work very hard at it. I did a lot of my homework ten minutes before class. Back then I thought of myself as somebody who worked pretty hard in high school, both in academics and sports, but it probably wasn't true. I mean I wasn't a straight A student or anything, but now I remember thinking that school was easy, and maybe that's just because of what I went through later on in my life.

I played soccer from the time I was little, probably six years old. When I first joined the program, they put me on the white team which was the second-ranked team and I hated that. I was on the white team for probably three or four years, but I decided I would work harder than everybody else on the team until I could climb my way out and make the first team and wear the red jersey. I think I probably got my work ethic from sports.

When I was in high school, I joined the whitewater canoe kayak team. That turned into one of the more formative experiences of my youth. The team was a very small and tightly-knit group of people. We traveled all over the state, all over the country. Some of the kids I paddled with raced internationally. So there was this drive and passion, because people were trying to make national teams and stuff, and that was the first time I was ever exposed to that level of focus and competition.

When it was time to apply for college, I didn't know what I wanted out of school, other than leaving Colorado. I was excited to just get out of the state and experience something different, which I think is probably going to be a theme throughout my story—wanting to experience something different.

Until I left for college, all I'd known was the small town of Boulder, Colorado, and I knew there was all kinds of different stuff out there in the country waiting for me. I wouldn't say I was escaping in terms of the stories you hear of people joining the army, because that's the only way they're going to get out of town. But come to think of it, I did want change and I did join the army, so who knows?

I applied to schools all across the country. I applied to Boulder and I applied to some school in Minnesota. The process felt very considered and measured and rational but looking back, it feels kind of arbitrary. Clearly, I didn't have a good system for choosing which schools I wanted to go to.

Maybe that became my pattern of thinking. I *thought* I was being rational in my choices but actually I was strongly influenced by circumstances and emotions. My ultimate choices did seem to have a certain logic to them. The final three schools I had my narrowed search down to were Swarthmore, which is a little liberal arts school outside of Philadelphia, Cornell University, and MIT; they're all pretty much top of their field. Swarthmore is one of the most prestigious liberal arts schools in the country, Cornell is in the Ivy League, and MIT is one of the best tech schools in the world, never mind what those Caltech people say.

What the decision came down to wasn't looking at one school's set of programs against the other set of programs or comparing clubs or student activities or anything like that. It was based on my experiences. I went to a student day at Swarthmore and I had an amazing time there. I stayed overnight at one of the houses that was just off campus. I made friends with the people there. I just fit in immediately. I had gone to a private college prep high school and Swarthmore felt very much the same. It's a beautiful little campus with little cottages, a small student body, and you knew everybody in your class. But I realized I wanted something different.

Cornell was at the opposite end of the spectrum. I did a summer program for high school students there and I had a great time. But it was so big. Cornell probably had 10,000 undergrad students at the time, plus that many more graduate students. Also, it's in Ithaca, which is a nice town but it felt sort of remote. It's at the end of the world and cold as can be.

Then there was MIT. My experience there was interesting because the campus is this eclectic mix of buildings. The main buildings are Greco-Roman with columns and domes. They're huge imposing buildings, and the names of famous scientists are written along the top edges. But then you go to a different part of campus and there's this giant concrete monstrosity built in the '70s or '80s, and then there's Frank Gehry's State Center, and it doesn't look like a building is supposed to look at all. There's also a dorm called Simmons, which we called the SpongeBob Dorm, because it looked like a big brick with a ton of little holes in it.

MIT's campus style was just all over the place, and that's what my experience there was, too. I went and stayed with a friend of mine from high school. He was two or three years ahead of me and was also a paddler from the canoe kayak team.

The walls in his dorm were painted all these crazy colors by the students who lived there. You got the vibe that this isn't the normal campus experience. The administration was allowing the students to express their creativity in ways you didn't see other places. I thought that was both attractive and uncomfortable for me. I wasn't really used to what felt like rule-breaking, but in a sort of sanctioned, creative way.

I think I picked MIT because I knew I was going to be more uncomfortable there than any of the other places I was looking at, and that meant it was going to push me harder and further than I would go otherwise.

And it was hard. Later on in life I became a climbing guide and summited Denali with four clients. And I was a Green Beret so I've done a lot of hard things. But MIT was by far the hardest thing I've ever done. It was brutal, just psychologically brutal.

I went from being the smartest person in my high school to not having any idea what was going on at MIT. The information and the workload was coming at me so fast I didn't know how to handle it. I had a friend there who used to say, "I walk around campus and I know—*I just know*—I'm the stupidest fucking person on campus." MIT was soul-crushing. It completely destroyed my ego.

Since I was a child, I was always interested in aeronautical and astronautical engineering. When I was nine or ten years old I wanted to be an Air Force fighter pilot real bad. My oldest brother was in the Air Force. He wasn't a pilot; he was a radar operator.

We went down to see him and he took us to an air show and I was fascinated with all those airplanes flying around.

My brother said, "Hey man, come here." He took me inside the radar truck he worked in. It was like this box on wheels that's got a big radar dish spinning around on the top of it. So we go inside and it's really dark. There are all these cool, circular screens, like out of movies, with the little green sweeping radar beams going around, and I didn't have any idea what any of that stuff meant, but it looked cool, and he pointed to one of the dots on the screen, and said, "Hey, you see that right there?" I said, "Yeah." He said, "Go outside right now."

I stepped outside the truck and at that exact moment a freaking F-15 screamed by at 500 miles an hour and man, that was the coolest thing ever. From that moment on all I wanted to do was fly jets. In fact, when my brother was stationed in Saudi Arabia, I always sent him drawings of fighter jets.

Unfortunately, when we moved from California to Colorado, I had been tested for school and we found out that I was nearsighted. That meant being a fighter pilot was not in the cards for me. My little ten-year-old heart was totally broken.

I decided that if I wasn't going to fly jets, maybe I'd build jets. And that's what I started out trying to do at MIT. But my second semester as a freshman, I took this class—Statistics and

Probability—and I just didn't understand it. I don't think I learned anything, and I realized that I wasn't going to pass the final exam, because my score on the midterm was an 11, the lowest score I'd ever achieved on a test.

My physics class was Electricity and Magnetism. It was really hard, too. When finals came around, my Statistics and Probability and Magnetism finals were all scheduled on the same day. One of my friends still remembers looking over during the Probability final and seeing me with my head down on the desk sleeping. I knew I was going to fail Probability anyway, and since I had been up all night studying for my physics final, I decided to grab two or three hours of sleep before that exam.

I started in Aero-Astro the next semester. I couldn't organize myself or organize the workload I had. Instead, I got caught in this cycle where I would stay up all night working on a problem and then turn it in in the morning. I'd wake up to go to class but I'd fall asleep in class because I'd been up studying all night. That meant that I didn't understand the lecture, so that afternoon and night, I was trying to learn the things we had already talked about in class, which meant that by the time I got to the assignment, it was already late and I didn't understand the things anyway, and then it took me longer to do the problems, and then I was up all night again, and then I went to class, and then I slept through class again. That was a rough semester.

It finally got so bad that I had to take a leave of absence. MIT's got a pretty generous leave policy. I guess they know that they're soul-crushing. In fact, when I finally got my class ring years later, I noticed the letters I-H-T-F-P engraved on it. I think they stand for "I Hate This Fucking Place." The rigor is so much a part of the school that it's literally a motto. I think the administration recognizes this and that's why when I wanted to take time away from school, they let me go for up to two years with no questions asked. I didn't have to reapply. I didn't have to do any kind of process to come back. Once I was done with my leave of absence I could just go back and start my classes again as if nothing had happened.

I had done some climbing courses out in Washington state with a company called Alpine Ascents International. They taught me about climbing and alpinism—how to do stuff in the mountains. Remember that I had always been an outdoorsy person. I did lots of hiking. I had climbed mountains myself, but not technically. I had done the walking route up or worked my way through the boulder field to get to the top, but this was about rock climbing and traversing steep snow and glaciers and I loved all of that stuff.

Just outside of Vegas is a place called Red Rock Canyon National Conservation Area. It's gorgeous. There are 3,000-foot sandstone walls barely ten minutes away from Las Vegas and hardly anybody who goes to Vegas to gamble and drink even realizes that

Red Rock Canyon is just over the hill. So when I left MIT, I went to Vegas. I had a cousin who was teaching at UNLV at the time, and he let me crash at his place. I think he had gone through a divorce not too much before this so he needed some company and I needed a place to stay. And I just climbed for four months. I would stand at the parking lot and wait for people to come up and ask if they needed a partner and up I'd go with them.

My friend, Jason Martin was a working guide and he was studying for his American Mountain Guide Association (AMGA) rock instructor exam. That's the big ten-day technical exam that they put you through. It's kind of a big deal in the guiding community, and he needed a partner to do some long technical routes with him.

Jason was way out of my league, but I could follow at about the level where he was leading, and he would let me take the easier pitches and while we were doing that, he was teaching me his little guide tricks and how he does stuff. I learned a lot from Jason about being a climber. Eventually I signed up for the rock instructor course myself through the AMGA. There are three levels: the instructor course, the guide course, and the guide exam. If you pass the guide exam and all the disciplines, you become internationally certified; you can go do stuff in Europe. So I took the course and spent the three or four months before that just climbing as much as I could.

When I completed the guide course, I spent the next summer in the Cascades and in the Waddington Range up in British Columbia, which is a ten-hour drive north of Vancouver and then a 30-minute helicopter ride west into the range. That was my first experience in a big range with huge glaciers covering everything. It was a good experience for me. After that, I signed up for wilderness EMT certification, which I did through the National Outdoor Leadership School. They have the Wilderness Medicine Institute out of Lander, Wyoming. But a day before I went there for the next program, I got a call from the Winter Park ski patrol where I had applied to work.

They normally put all their candidates through a ski test in the spring, but they called me and I told them I had been a ski racer in high school and we went off of that. After I completed my EMT I moved near Winter Park, Colorado and patrolled for that year. It was my best ski season ever; I managed 150 days of skiing in one season and I got really, really good at skiing bumps.

After patrolling I worked for Alpine Ascents International. When I left MIT, I left to be a climbing bum and a ski bum. But my real goal was to become a climbing guide so I sent an email to Jason telling him about my plans. Jason emailed back telling me all the reasons I shouldn't be a climbing guide: You don't get paid very well. You're going to climb way below your ability. You're going to move around all the time. You'll live in campgrounds, that sort of thing. It was his attempt to convince me not to be a climbing guide.

While I was with Alpine Ascents, I would tell people that I'd left MIT and was doing all this stuff, and they're like, "What? Are you crazy?" Or some people would say, "Yeah. You're never going back to school, man. Once you've left, you can't go back."

Being a guide made me think about the value of the MIT education, what I was getting for being there. And so one day I packed up my stuff and I went back. I didn't go into Aero-Astro, because I had gotten double Ds in my last Aero-Astro class. Instead, I switched to physics where I thought I'd excel. I knew I was motivated to work hard and I figured things should work out. But it was still soul-crushing, I don't even know how to describe the amount of work and pressure I was under all the time.

When I got my first A in the spring of my junior year things started to improve. The next year I got four As and a B. I discovered that it had just taken me that long to figure out what I was doing and part of that was taking classes where I actually enjoyed the work. By the end of my time there I had even started to figure out how to manage MIT. Ultimately, I got through it and today I'm really proud of the work I did there.

I learned that having a vision of where I'm going or a high-level understanding of what my purpose in life is really important to me. Some people say life is guided by fate or some spiritual force, but for me it's not a higher purpose. I don't have that religious role to guide me but having a sense of vision or moral purpose matters. It turns out you can be an atheist and still believe in morals and have a sense of right and wrong,

I think that's really important so when I finally finished MIT, I didn't know what I was going to do with myself. I knew I wasn't ready to spend six more years in a basement lab to get my PhD, which is what I would need to do if I wanted to do anything in physics.

I became an EMT in Boston. I had decided to join the Army but I wasn't ready to tell anybody yet. So being an EMT would serve as my testing ground where I could go out and put myself in high-pressure situations and do something to help others. I wanted to see if I was capable of doing that.

When I finally made the decision to join the Army, I had more than 100 different reasons. I wrote a 20-page paper to my dad to explain what all of the reasons were, because how do you explain to your parent who just sent you to MIT where you got a degree in physics, that you're planning on enlisting in the Army? I didn't know how that would go over. I knew I had to have all my ducks in a row. I had to have all of my arguments well laid out, because otherwise that's crazy.

On the one hand I was trying to take the mountain-guide-ski-patrol-kid part of me and combine it with the physics-computers-nerd-MIT-graduate-part and just smash those things together into a career.

I was also looking for a sense of brotherhood. That was something I had had on the canoe and kayak team back in high school when I felt really close to all the people I paddled with. I had been in a fraternity at MIT and I think I was looking for the same thing there but I didn't really find it. I wanted the "Band of Brothers" thing where everyone has everyone else's back.

Also, Boulder, Colorado was the liberalist place in the whole country outside of Berkeley, especially during the Bush presidency. Living there I had gotten tired of complaining about government. I felt like somebody needed to go do something about what my friends and I perceived to be the wrongs of government. That meant that I had to go join the government and make the change I thought was called for.

When I was training to be in the Green Berets we were sent to this school—Survival, Resistance, Escape—where they put you in a prison camp situation. They do all sorts of unpleasant things to teach you how to resist, but not get yourself killed resisting.

The actual prison camp portion was not that long, maybe four days, but they were the longest four days I've ever experienced in my life.

They fly this flag in the middle of the prison camp and it's for the People's Revolutionary Republic—The PRR; it's a fake communist country they made up. So they turn us around and they say, "Praise the flag." And we all say, "Good morning oh glorious flag of the People's Revolutionary Republic." And they'd say, "Not good enough." And we'd yell, "Good morning oh glorious flag of the People's Revolutionary Republic." And they'd say, "Insincere!"

And they kept doing this. They'd just screw with you and they'd knock you down and punish you and you'd praise the flag some more and then they'd punish you some more and you'd get back up and praise the flag again.

Finally, they appeared satisfied and they'd send you off to do your regular prison camp duties which were just menial and meaningless and degrading.

One morning was worse than every other morning. They just keep going and keep going and keep going until one time you turn around and look up and it's not the flag of the People's Revolutionary Republic anymore but it's the American flag flying up above the prison camp. And arrayed behind the flag are soldiers in immaculate US uniforms. They play the National Anthem and everyone snaps to attention and you've got your salute up. It's a really, really powerful moment.

Before all of this happened, the students had heard rumors of what we were in for. I'm not usually an emotional person so I was like, "Hey, I'm not going to cry when it happens."

But man, I cried like a baby. Because seeing our flag up there represented the restoration of every single freedom that I had enjoyed and had also taken for granted and had been taken away from me.

That's why believing in America as this place of liberty and freedom and inclusion is so significant. I'm not sure I recognized that when I decided to join the army, but it's something that has since become very significant to me. America is a place where people can come when they don't have anywhere else to go. For me that's a founding principal of our country and it's become really important to me.

My first overseas trip was to Lebanon. Being an ignorant American, I expected camels and sand dunes, but when I stepped off the airplane in Beirut, I saw beautiful snowcapped mountains that reminded me of California and Colorado, the places where I grew up.

I was also struck with how multicultural the country was. Lebanon had been a colony of France so they spoke French in school. Plus, they're naturally Arabic speakers, and then they learn English from pop culture. So it'd be really common to go up to talk to somebody and they'd greet you in three different languages in one sentence.

You could go down to Gemmayzeh Street, in downtown Beirut and go bar-hopping and there'd be all kinds of young Lebanese people from all different religions. It's a really cool melting pot kind of place, which also reminded me of the United States in terms of the diversity of people, the different religions, the different cultures. The one thing I encountered there that wasn't as apparent in other places that I'd visit in the Middle East was their deep sense of national identity.

They're all Lebanese first. It's a mistake to call the average Lebanese person an Arab because they'll immediately counter with, "Oh, no no, I'm from Lebanon; I'm Phoenician." Never mind that the Phoenician empire dissolved about 4,000 years ago, that's where they get their heritage. Not only do they have a national identity, but they have this cultural ethnic identity that's different from other places in the region. And I think that's part of why the country can survive as a melting pot, because people think of themselves with a strong national identity. Again, just like the U.S.

We worked with the Lebanese army, which is probably the most trusted institution in the country. And just like the country, there were people in the Lebanese army from different backgrounds and religions and cultures, even including some that were likely members of Hezbollah. That made things a little different than what we're used to in the United States, where everything is clearly defined in black and white: good guys versus bad guys, axis of evil versus NATO, that sort of thing.

The Lebanese' trust in the institution has really served them well. Since I left Lebanon there have been protests there. But when the government told the Lebanese army to clear the people off the streets, the army refused to do it. Instead, they protected the rights of the protesters. I think the work that we've done over there to help the Lebanese army become a professional, non-partisan, non-sectarian fighting force has done a lot of good for them as an institution. And when they were tested, I think they passed the test. I'm proud of my involvement.

After Lebanon I was posted to Syria. I was working with a partner force of ours and there were frictions between the partners and our team. Sometimes there can be the perception that our partner forces are lazy or aren't good soldiers, and some of that was exacerbated because there was an officer who truly exemplified those stereotypes.

One day we were doing our post-mission duties: cleaning our machine guns, making sure the trucks were all filled with gas, things like that. Our team sergeant angrily confronted the officer from our partner force and things got a little bit tense. That never creates a good working relationship for us.

It is important that we get along with our partners because as special forces guys, there are only a few of us at any particular place at any particular time. And that means we depend on these guys for our security, our safety. We need them to drive trucks, to man weapons, to do all of the sorts of things needed over the course of a mission.

I was one of the better Arabic speakers on the team so I decided to try and improve our relationship with our partner force. I started sitting around their campfires at night, drinking tea with them, playing dice games, asking about their lives.

I remember it was during Ramadan, so most of them were tired and grumpy during the day. They'd been fasting so they were calorie-starved. And they couldn't drink water even though it was 95 goddamned degrees outside. But once I started talking to them and showing respect, our relationships improved.

One of the things I always did was address them by their rank. Whether that's *Raqib,* which means Sergeant, or *Naqeeb,* which means captain or *Mulazim,* which means Lieutenant, I always addressed them by the rank they had earned.

In the Levantine dialect, the word *lazim* translates as "necessary." For something you had to do, you'd say, *"lazim"* which means, "I have to" and then you'd add the task. *"Mu"* is a negative and it turns the word that follows it into a negative. So I would joke with the enlisted guys, telling them that the lieutenant's rank *"Mulazim"* meant "not necessary," and that would always get a big laugh from them.

When I needed help from our partners I'd say something like "Mulazim, can you help me with this? Can you help me put this box on the trailer?" Since I was speaking Arabic and I was using their titles respectfully, they'd just jump up and run to help. I found that they really wanted to help us, they just didn't necessarily know what we wanted from them or what they needed to do to please us. We didn't have a translator so I think caused some language friction. Most of us aren't translator-grade speakers. Special Forces guys are supposed to know how to speak a foreign language but we'd only spent six months learning how to speak Arabic. But once we broke through the language and respect barrier things changed.

My last name is "Wolfe." Once I changed it into an Arabic word that they recognized, they'd understand and they'd remember me right away. They'd come up to me and say: "Wolfe is a strong name, strong name." That was one of my better marketing moments and it really improved my relationships. They'd show up in the morning and ask, "Hey Sergeant Wolfe, which is your truck?" And they'd dump their bags in my truck because they wanted to ride along with me.

It was just about recognizing that people are people and everybody needs respect, whether you understand their culture or not. I was one of those guys who worked pretty hard on my language skills and it paid dividends for me overseas. And now that I'm back home in the States, it pays dividends for me here.

I'll get into a taxi or an Über and if the driver is an Arabic speaker I'll address them in their own language. As soon as I start talking, they'll say, "You speak Arabic?" And they're flabbergasted that a young white dude can speak Arabic. It's the last thing they expect.

When I was on leave I was flying home to Denver to see my parents for Christmas. I got off of the plane, and there was a family in the waiting area and there was this odd tension around them. The mother had a hijab on and her hair was covered, so I knew they were Muslim. And I heard them speaking Arabic and they seemed really disoriented. They didn't seem to know where they were or where they were going.

I stopped and turned to them and said, "Do you need help?" in Arabic. And they froze. They didn't speak any English and my Arabic was a little rusty. But I started a conversation with them and learned that they had recently fled Syria and were in the United States on a refugee visa.

The husband was wearing this cord around his neck and hanging from it was a clear plastic sleeve with a note that listed their destination and who they were supposed to meet. But they had to catch a connecting flight and they didn't know where they were going because they couldn't read any of the English on the card. They didn't know how to ask anybody what they were supposed to do. They were completely lost. I talked to them and together we worked through the process.

They didn't know where they were going and they didn't have a ticket for the next flight. So I took them to the ticket counter and translated for them. Eventually the airline brought over one of their real translators and they were able to get the family on their way.

It felt really good to me to be able to help somebody, not only because I could use the skills I learned in the army, but because I could help somebody begin their American immigrant story and head toward their American dream. Plus, it felt great to be able to do some good in the world without having to carry a gun.

Exactly what all that meant for that particular family I probably can't even imagine. I mean, I've been through a lot of stuff, but I've never been the oppressed victim of a fascist government that used me as a pawn. I've never had to take my family and flee with only the clothes on my back, travel across the sea, across multiple countries, and not have any idea if I'd have a place to land or not.

Their experience reinforced that moment in survival school when I looked up at the US flag and realized how much it meant to me in terms of freedom and liberty. It felt good to be able to reach out to somebody and say, "Hello. I'm American. I speak Arabic. I welcome you here."

When I had left MIT and enlisted in the army, I signed up for a five-year term. Near the end of that term I had to decide whether I was going to stay in or not. I had reached a point where I was earning more seniority and starting to have more of an influence on how things happened on my team. And like when I had returned to MIT, I felt I had finally reached a point where I really knew how to do my job. I reenlisted because I didn't want to have worked so hard to get to this point and then lose the very things I had worked so hard to achieve.

This time they sent me to Syria and things were awful there. But even amidst such destruction, one of my big takeaways was that everybody was just a human being trying to survive. For example, there were people we worked with who were former ISIS members. Our challenge was to figure out whether they were the real deal—ideological hardcore criminals—or just trying to put food on their table so their kids could eat and just doing what they had to do to survive.

I found that most people were just trying to survive. They didn't care who was in charge; they were just trying to live. I empathized with the situation they were in and I wanted to help them. I'm really proud of the work that we did there.

My problem was that even though I was now a staff sergeant, I didn't have the influence to accomplish the things I wanted to do nor make the changes I wanted to make. I had felt like I would be able to do a lot more good if I wasn't structurally limited by my rank, my position, and the overall structure of the army. I felt like my opportunities for growth and my opportunities to be able to help people were going to be limited if I stayed in for a 20-year career.

That's why I decided to get out. And those same reasons neatly sum up what I'm looking for now— a place where I can have a strategic impact on an organization. Looking back over all the experiences I've had, I think that's what I've always been searching for. Whether it was soccer or ski racing or paddling in high school, or climbing Denali, or getting through MIT, or working as an EMT, or making it to the Green Berets.

As I said, MIT crushed my ego completely flat, but it also taught me how to solve problems. And ironically, the Green Berets also taught me how to solve problems but specifically using soft skills—not what you'd naturally assume you'd learn in the military. I learned how to empathize, how to understand others, how to network with people, how to reach across institutional and cultural boundaries, how to collaborate, how to be a member of a team. I basically learned how to lead through influence when I couldn't lead through authority.

I had made the decision to join the Green Berets for the same reason I had decided to go to MIT—I knew it would make me uncomfortable. And it was; the army was a completely different world than anything I had known. When I signed on that dotted line and got on that bus in Denver, I left all of my possessions behind. The next thing I knew, I was flying up to Fort Benning, Georgia to start my new life.

As an MIT grad I could have commissioned and been an officer, I could have done a whole bunch of other stuff. Only 10 or 15% of the guys who start out to be a Green Beret actually make it. But being part of that 10% was my only choice. I kind of describe it as my Cortez moment—because when I signed on to the Army, I burned my ship behind me. The only way forward from there was forward. I know it sounds redundant, but the only path at that point was to keep moving forward.

It was that motivation that got me through the program. Being a Green Beret was not about being more physically fit than anyone else. There are a lot of guys who are built like freaking linebackers who don't make it because it's about mental discipline. It's about putting one foot in front of the other and never allowing yourself to stop no matter what. And if you know that you have no other alternative but forward, when you realize that success is your only option, there's no decision to make—you just keep going. No matter what.

You don't think, *Ah, I could go home, I could go back, I could do lots of things that are easier.* All you think is, *How am I going to make it through the next challenge, the next problem, the next mile, the next signpost, the next hundred meters?* It took the determination and discipline I learned as an athlete and that's what got me through and made me a Green Beret.

"Never quit." Lots of people ask me how to become a Green Beret. And that's the only piece of advice I offer. They want to know how they should train, what they should learn about, how they should study. And sure, you have to do all those things, but none of it matters. The only thing that matters is "Don't quit."

Never quit.

My first reinvention was leaving Colorado and going to MIT. And then I reinvented myself as a climbing guide. And then I had to reinvent myself back into being a college student, which turned out to be a lot more challenging than I thought it would be. I couldn't go back to doing the things that I did the first time; I had to radically change everything about myself, because the first time I tried getting through MIT, it didn't work out very well. It was about redesigning my approach to being a student.

My next goal was to be a Green Beret and that drove me through three years until I finally made it. And then my goal was to be the best Green Beret I could be. What drove me in the Special Forces was finding my way in order to have an influence bigger than what I was supposed to have. And when I found that even as a staff sergeant I didn't have that kind of influence, I transitioned again and enrolled in the master's program at Harvard.

I was stationed in Jordan when I started working on my MBA. I'd be awake at all sorts of weird hours trying to watch online lectures and do research and write my papers. It was more hard work. But I'll be done soon, and the great thing about Harvard's extension school is that it's an authentic part of the university and when they graduate you, you walk with your class.

Walking down that aisle to get my diploma will be the start of my next transition.

Nathalie Cadet-James, Founder, Luxe Fête Event Planning

I was emailing back and forth with a friend and prominent attorney, and mentioned to him what I was writing my new book about. He wrote back that I had to meet with Nathalie Cadet-James but he didn't tell me why.

When I met her for a cup of coffee and heard a bit of her story, I actually asked her to stop telling it to me because I wanted to interview her for this book and I didn't want to already know how her tale was going to end. You'll see why.

Nathalie Cadet-James

When I was in college, I thought I would go into advertising. I've always loved telling stories and I've always loved visuals. When I came home and told my parents that that's what I was going to do, my dad was like, "Absolutely not. I literally will have a heart attack if you do not go to law school."

That was his actual quote, and he exhibited physical signs of a real illness for about a week after that conversation.

I said, "Fine; not a problem. I don't want anything bad to happen to you. I understand; you've worked so hard to get us where we are."

We're from Haiti. My grandmother, his mother, did not know how to read or write, but somehow she knew enough that she figured out how to send my father to Argentina to become a doctor. When he went to Argentina, he didn't even know how to speak Spanish, but he was there however long it took him to figure it out, and finally graduated from medical school and then practiced medicine in Argentina.

Eventually my dad moved to Canada where he met my mother. She was a nurse in the hospital he worked at. Then they moved to New York together.

Leaving Haiti and moving to South America was a really big sacrifice for my father, so education has always been a key part of my family. You always pursued education and you pursued it with excellence. Advertising? He didn't know what that was.

By the way, he did say, "The day you graduate from law school, if you don't want to do it anymore, that's fine. Then go to your advertising copy school, whatever you want to call it, but you're going to go to law school first."

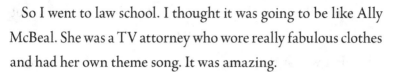

So I went to law school. I thought it was going to be like Ally McBeal. She was a TV attorney who wore really fabulous clothes and had her own theme song. It was amazing.

I thought that's what being a lawyer was going to be like. I actually thought I could be a lawyer like I had seen on TV, but I learned early on that it wasn't like that. I probably planted the seed in my mind that the law was not going to be something that I would actually do as a career, but I sure was going to try.

After law school I had an amazing mentor, John Koyzak. Thanks to his help and guidance I landed a federal clerkship in the bankruptcy court. From there I worked at an amazing law firm, Kenny Nachwalter, and then I went to work at the County Attorney's office.

Those are all three highly coveted jobs for attorneys. And guess what? Even though I excelled at all of them, I wasn't actually passionate about what I was doing. None of what I was doing at work kept me up at night at three in the morning.

But let me tell you what did:

When my friends would ask me to plan their weddings or help create dinner parties for them, doing that filled me with such, I don't want to say excitement, but it filled me with energy. I loved to be able to create ambiances that inspired people. When I did things like that, the people who attended always talked about how great they felt in the spaces I'd planned.

While I was at the County Attorney's office I became pregnant with my first daughter. Getting ready to be a mother made me shift my thinking. I started to wonder, "Okay, what happens now?" I knew that as an attorney I wouldn't be able to pick her up from school or read stories to her or wake her up because as an attorney my schedule was not really my own; it belonged to the court, to my cases.

Believe it or not, that realization was the only push I needed to wake up one day and say it would be my last day practicing law. I decided I was going to be an event planner because I had experience doing it and I did it really well. And just like Ally McBeal had pointed me to the law, the shows that I saw on HGTV suggested that my favorite hobby could actually be my profession.

As confident as I was, I did have nagging doubts and I didn't really see event planning as a profession. One of the things that was difficult for me was actually accepting myself as a creative artist. Up until then I'd been more right-brained with the law and so forth, and all of a sudden, I was projecting myself as an expert planner and designer—just because I said I was.

The skill sets I had learned from being a lawyer really did translate nicely into planning, and I felt that I could say I was a planner because I was a lawyer, but the designer part was where I felt like an impostor.

I have no background in art or design. I just know that I have a vision and I can see things. But it took me a long time to feel okay to speak with someone who is an expert designer and to share my views.

I had a lot of that imposter syndrome, but I had to get over that quickly because it's really hard to book clients when you don't believe in yourself. So I said, "Nat, you have a gift. You're talented and you're passionate, which is the most important thing. I think people book you because of your passion and who you are and what they believe you can do for them versus what you may have done in the past."

I started to build that business. My first big realization was figuring out that just being good at something didn't mean that you were necessarily good at business, too. They're two completely separate things. I thought if I had a pretty website—*BOOM!*—lots of money would come through the door. Of course that didn't happen. It was very tough for two years. I watched myself just wait for business and I realized, "Nathalie, you actually have to create a model. You have to think about how you're going to get business. Just because you can create great events doesn't mean you can run a sustainable company." Those things require very different skills.

I broke my business down into sections, like the four wheels on my car. Why a car? Because I thought, *How do I move this thing forward?*

I broke my business down into marketing, business development, and servicing my existing clients, and then I added the fourth section—my big picture—my why. *Why am I doing this? What is my big picture? Where is it going to lead me to?*

As long as I could keep those four things moving, it seemed to me that I might be able to build something special. Because my big picture, what I see myself doing and what I think my purpose is, is to somehow impact change in Haiti. I don't know if I'll do that through philanthropy or through the work I do now, but it's what I'm working to achieve.

It's crazy when I look at the work I'm doing now. My marketing is so much more than just a website. It is constant branding and making sure that I'm always true to my brand.

I've said "no" to clients who didn't fit within my brand, and I'm glad I did because I don't think I would have the clients that I have now if I'd taken some of the other opportunities that came my way.

Business development was the hardest part for me because I realized that I had to seek out business; it wouldn't just show up. Seeking business meant figuring out, "Who do I know? Who's doing an event? What's my dream event? Who's my dream client? Who do I know there?"

I also learned how important it was to do the best job servicing existing clients. You can't have a client and half-ass it; it just won't work. Things fall through the cracks. You have to make sure everyone's happy because the people who attend your event can be a source of business or they can turn people away from you.

So I always try to check on the air in those four tires, so to speak, to see if I'm doing what I need to do. Sometimes I spend a lot of time on one area, sometimes on another, but I do try to keep a pulse on everything. That's the formula that helps keep me focused and moves me forward.

It sounds so simple but it took me a long time to learn that. Once I figured it out was when I started getting the clients that many people wish they had. It's nice to see that happen, but of course it wasn't enough.

Hitting eight-to-ten big events a year was my goal Why that number? Because every time I plan an event on a weekend, there's a big lead up to it; it sucks up a lot of my time. I have a family, a husband, kids. I like to rest. I like to travel. I like to live. So I feel that there has to be a cap on Nathalie as an event planner. I do not want to work every weekend as a planner.

I've tried to have my assistant take the lead on an event, but inevitably I get sucked back into it in a significant way so I spend a lot of time thinking about ways that I can impact scale up my current business and that has led to my next idea—a dinner party rental service.

One of the things I know is that when I bring people together, beautiful things happen. Because of the environment we create and because of the little details that we think of, new opportunities pop up. And I thought, *How could I do that en masse without necessarily having to be the planner who's working 24/7?*

There used to be a time when people actually had dinner parties and came together and connected with each other in their homes, so I came up with a business model, which is essentially a do-it-yourself dinner-on-demand service, but highly curated and very, very beautiful.

I thought about this for two years and I was really, really, really, *really* scared. I mean, Martha Stewart can do something like this; she owns every vertical to make this possible. But me? *Oh you can't do this Nat. You're not even a businessperson, really. You're just an event planner.*

I agonized over all the reasons my idea wouldn't work, and then one day, I presented a proposal to one of my clients and he told me he didn't really want to spend as much as I was charging for his party. When I chatted with him about his event, I found out that he advises startups and corporations and does a little bit of angel investing as well.

I told him about my idea and he said, "You've got to go for this, Nathalie." He agreed to help me in exchange for a reduced rate for planning his party. I mean, this is a man who charges thirty–forty-thousand a month to each of his clients.

Then I read an article in the newspaper about a business accelerator that said, "Seeking women business entrepreneurs with prototypes and ideas." I had to Google "What is a prototype?" because I didn't even understand the term, but I figured, "Wait a minute. Maybe I can apply to this accelerator. Maybe this is the fire I need to get this going."

I ended up joining the accelerator program. It was phenomenal. There were 20 other women there; it was a very highly selective process. I came in second place, which was a dream come true.

I would sit in class and they're talking about net profit. They're talking about operational protocols. And I knew none of these terms. I had been a lawyer and I ran a business but I knew no business lingo. I was very, very insecure and extremely intimidated, but I saw what I wanted to build and I knew what I had to do to get there.

I'm among brilliant women. They're teaching me and I'm soaking it in. I rose so quickly in that accelerator that FedEx actually sponsored me. They looked at several of the business models and they chose mine. They said, "You know what? We're going to sponsor your seat." And they donated $25,000 for this lab and they paired me with a mentor. She's a senior executive at FedEx and to this day she and I talk every two weeks.

It has been a great service to me to be able to speak with people who have experience, who challenge me, who I learn from. I fail all the time and no one kicks me or reprimands me. Everyone just gives me advice or encouragement, which is what I need. I have learned how important it is to have an advisory board, whether it's personal or professional.

When I finished the accelerator, I applied for *The Miami Herald* Business Plan Challenge. My company won that, and I landed on the cover of the business section. People love the idea of an experience that brings people together. There's definitely a need for connection. We're wired for connection, so I knew that I was on to something.

So now I'm building my new concept and running my event planning business. I won't ever stop being a planner. My idea is to do maybe three really big events a year, to still be the expert while I continue to scale this dinner-party-in-a-box process.

While I was in the accelerator program, one of my friends asked me to be Principal-for-a-Day at a local high school. I specifically asked to go to a school where the population is Haitian because I want them to see me. I want them to understand that I was just like they are and that anything is possible for them. All they need is access.

So I went to shadow the principal at Edison Senior High School. It's a great school and I loved taking to the students. And then, coincidentally, the day after I took a tour of the school, I had a meeting with a client of mine who was opening up a new restaurant.

In one of our meetings he asked, "What can we do in the community?" I knew they were redesigning their space and getting rid of all of their old furniture and appliances so I said, "Well, there's a school where I was Principal-for-a-Day. Let me ask them if they need anything."

It turned out they have a culinary program, but they didn't have any supplies or equipment at all, so I made an introduction and my client supplied the school with all of their restaurant equipment.

My client had brought a two-star Michelin chef over from Italy to work in his new restaurant. After we installed the equipment, we scheduled a master class where the chef could go talk to the school's top students. In that moment, when that two-star Michelin chef said to the kids, "Work hard and maybe one day I'll be eating at *your* restaurant," I knew that I had changed someone's life. When I saw how engaged the students were, it was just remarkable. All I had to do was make that connection. It was the exact "access" I had told the kids about. The same access my mentors had given me. And now I was able to give it to someone else.

That's where I am now. Even in my startup company I'm making a lot of pivots, because that's the most important part of starting up a new business—responding to the market, fine tuning the product, making adjustments, doing whatever it takes until you figure it all out.

And now I'm probably going to have to pivot again because of Coronavirus—who knows how it's going to affect the catering business? One of the things I learned is to be nimble, to try not to take anything too personal, and just to move and go, move and go, move and go—never stop. I think when anyone takes those steps, they'll end up where they need to go. Sometimes you'll think you know the path, but other times things will push you one way or another.

Look at my path: law school, federal clerkship, law firm, another law firm, event planning company, startup company. I just go with it.

Move and go. Move and go.

Rick Beato, YouTuber, Musician, Music Producer

I was watching a YouTube video of Eric Clapton, George Harrison, Tom Petty, Neil Young, and more superstars playing The Byrds' version of Bob Dylan's "My Back Pages." Near the end of the song I reached behind me to grab a guitar and see if I could play along. While my back was turned I didn't notice YouTube advance the selection to "What Makes This Song Great? THE POLICE — Every Little Thing She Does is Magic," by Rick Beato.

In the video, a white-haired guy who looked to be about my age dissected the Police song with such insight and deep musical knowledge that I was completely captivated. After watching more and more of his videos — and spending the better part of a day traveling down Rick Beato's YouTube rabbit hole — I sent him an email and asked if I could interview him for *Is That All There Is?*

Rick Beato

I went to college as a music education major undergrad but I didn't have any idea what I wanted to do next. And when you don't know what you want to do with your life, you go to grad school. So that's what I did.

I knew I definitely didn't want to teach high school or anything like that, so I decided to get my master's degree in jazz guitar and then I could figure out what I would want to do from there. But after two-and-a-half years at the New England Conservatory in Boston, I still didn't know what to do with my life. I decided to go back to Ithaca, New York, where I had gone for undergrad and still had a lot of friends.

I moved in with a couple of buddies who were also musicians. I was just going to stay for a couple of weeks and chill on their couch and hang out, but while I was there I booked a gig with Steve, my old guitar teacher. After the gig, he said, "Man, that sounded great. Listen, we opened up a position in the jazz department for next year for a second teacher to teach alongside me. I want you to come and teach improv, conduct one of the big bands, teach theory, all that stuff. You don't have to let me know now, but the job is yours if you want it. Let me know in a couple of weeks."

So I talked to my friends, I talked to my family, and I was like, "I got nothing else cooking, I'll take the gig." So I ended up staying in Ithaca and I got my college teaching gig.

Now, I had just graduated from there a couple years before, so here I am walking into the faculty lounge with all the teachers who had been my professors. It was weird and I liked it. It was a great job—a really great job and Ithaca is a beautiful town to live in.

I wrote my *Beato Book* when I was in my second year as a professor. There were no textbooks for teaching what I was teaching— music theory, improvisation, guitar, or whatever because I didn't just teach guitar; I taught improv to all different instrumentalists. I had to write a book that would talk about principles and things that were my own concepts because I had concepts that weren't in any books.

I spent about ten months or so writing this book, and I wrote it by hand. I sold it to my students. I sold it for $30 a copy. I had it Xeroxed and bound and that was my textbook. The last one I sold was in 1991 or so, and it's sad, I just had it sitting in a box for 25 years.

But I liked teaching and living in Ithaca so much that even when a buddy asked me to play on a demo, I was like, "I don't really play rock anymore." As I said, I was happy doing what I was doing.

My buddy was pretty adamant, "Come on, just play on it." So I took my guitars to the studio and played on this demo. The songs weren't even done but he went ahead and had a little party and played the demo for everyone and it sounded great. A couple of weeks later, he called me up and said, "The vice-president of Elektra Records just called me. I sent him the tape and he says, 'You have hit songs.' He wants to sign us to a development deal."

I said, "What do you mean *us?*"

"Well, I told him that you were in the band and told him that it's you and me; we're the band. He's going to give us money to cut a real demo."

"How much money?"

He said "$5,000."

Now back in the '80s, they paid college professors nothing really—$20,000, $22,000 a year or something like that—so $5,000 was a lot of money. He said, "I think we can do the recording for about $500 and we can split the rest of the money for ourselves."

I couldn't say no.

We ended up doing that deal and we started writing songs together, and he taught me how to write songs. Nothing ever came of that demo, but a couple of years later, we were playing a gig in New York and this guy comes up and gives me his card.

"My name's John Titta. I run Polygram Publishing. I'm going to send you a publishing deal. You guys have hit songs."

And we're like, "Yeah, sure, sure." We didn't believe any of it because we had heard all this before.

But we talked to our manager, we called our lawyer, and they said, "Yeah, this guy's totally legit," so we signed a publishing deal with Polygram in 1992 and I took a leave of absence from teaching to work on the new album.

By then I'd been teaching it for five years and I was getting a little bored with it. I was about to turn 30 and I thought, "If there's ever a chance to do this, to try and make it in a band, this is the time."

So I quit my teaching gig and what happens? The band breaks up six months later, of course!

Now it's 1994, and I've got no money. I wind up moving to New York city and moving in with a buddy of mine. I auditioned for five different bands and I got offers to join all five of them. I picked one of the bands because they were going to England and I got to go with them and play bass on their recording. The project got canceled the third day we were there, but I was paid my $5,000, and I figured it was enough to travel around Europe. I traveled around for about five weeks. I had a return ticket scheduled for five weeks later and I traveled around spending the money and going to see all these different music scenes that were happening.

At the time, England had bands like Portishead and a lot of great bands coming up. I was really into the scene that was going on there at the time. I traveled to Amsterdam. I went to Wales. I just went to different towns and checked out the music scenes for a few days at a time until it was time to fly back to the states.

Once I got back to the US, I started moving around. I went to Chicago for about a month or so; I checked out the music scene there. Then I went to Denver. I lived there for three months and checked out the music scene there. I went back to New York for a bit and then I went down to Nashville and I stayed for a couple of months. Then I was on my way to Austin, Texas and I stopped to have lunch with my old college roommate in Atlanta. He got me a gig playing in a cover band the first night I was there, and he and another friend came up with a scheme to get me to stay. I moved to Atlanta in 1994 and I tried to start a band there.

After I put the band together we went to New York and had a whole bunch of labels come out to see us. I thought we were ready but we had a disastrous gig in front of about ten labels and didn't get an offer from any of them. We decided to come back to Atlanta and make a record on our own, which took about a year.

While I was trying to make it with the band I also taught in a music store here in Atlanta. I taught private guitar, about 50 students a week, teaching all different-aged kids, beginners, everyone. Some kids I taught for five years or so, the startups, beginners who went on to become professional players.

But man I was humping—really humping. I was trading art for money and that's a very hard gig. And it was worse because I'd already been a college professor for five years. To go back to teaching at a music store for less money because I was trying to make it in the band was tough—really demoralizing.

On my birthday I called my brother, John, who's four years younger than me. He's a guitar player too, but he doesn't do it for a living. I said, "John, should I just hang it up now? I just turned 36 years old and I'm nowhere. This is a joke."

He said, "Just give it one more year."

Well, about three months later, we got signed to a record deal. The studio gave us a producer but he turned out to be a drunk, just getting hammered every day, and before long he disappeared from the studio.

I didn't know anything about production, so me and the singer were doing most of the recording ourselves. The label had already spent $430,000 on this record, and one day they came in to check our progress and caught the producer drunk in the studio and fired him. Right before we were ready to release the album a big merger happened and our label got bought out and we got dropped. I couldn't believe it.

Because our producer was a drunk, *I'd* been the one producing the album. I didn't really know what I was doing so I would just read magazines and ask questions to people about recording. Basically, I taught myself how to record on my own, and I did my first project as an engineer, mixer, and producer in 2000. Before I knew what was happening, I was a producer and I was in demand. In fact, between 2000 and 2016, I had a couple of platinum records and a few gold records to my name.

But it wasn't always easy. In fact, in 2009 after the economy crashed, it became quite difficult because there just weren't any label gigs anymore. Rock and roll was no longer in vogue and I just got so burned out. There was no talent, nothing interesting, no new ideas, just people doing the same kind of music all the time.

In the meantime, I'd gotten married and had my first two kids in 2007 and 2009. I remember saying to my wife, "I can't do this when I'm 60 years old. I mean, I just can't do it."

She says, "What are you going to do?"

"I don't know. I could go back to teaching. I have no idea, but I can't do this kind of work anymore; I hate it. I can't produce these kinds of bands; they're terrible. I mean, one out of every 30 bands is great, that's it. The rest of them? They just want me to tell them how good they are. I just can't do it. I mean, is that all there is?"

My son Dylan has insane perfect pitch, and I had taught him music theory and everything. I took a video of him calling out obscure chords I'd play on the piano and I posted it on my Facebook page and it just took off with millions and millions of views. We ended up doing about four videos over the course of the year. It seemed so unreal that we had 80 million views on social media. 80 million!

I realized how powerful social media was so I started doing some stuff on Facebook but that really didn't go anywhere. Sometime in 2016 my intern, Rhett, came in and said, "You should try YouTube."

I was skeptical. "There're no white-haired guys on YouTube."

But he was like, "No, no, no; I'm serious."

"What would I do?"

He says, "Music theory, music production, talking about song-writing, talking about film scoring, whatever."

I said, "I don't know how to use a camera."

He goes, "I'll bring my camera tomorrow and I'll help you shoot your channel trailer."

I didn't even know what that was.

"It's what you do to announce what your channel is about. First time somebody comes to your channel, they see your trailer."

So the next day he brought his camera and his laptop, and we shot the channel trailer. He edited it right there in the studio and we put it up.

At the time all I had on my YouTube channel were videos of

my kids for my brothers and sisters and my mom because it's too hard to email videos.

Rhett said, "Take down all the videos of your kids and we'll post music stuff."

About a week later I started making my own videos and editing them myself at night while I was producing. Within the first year I had made about 340 videos and got 100,000 subscribers.

As I started making these videos, I realized that I could make videos about anything I want — any subject, any topic, anything in music. I called my channel "Everything Music" because I talked about film scoring, jazz improvisation, and famous albums and ear training, film scoring, playing different instruments, music history from Bach to Beethoven, the history of the guitar, the history of the bass, whatever, all different types of things. I figured if it interested me it would interest others.

It was so satisfying to do this because it was the first time that I wasn't working for somebody. I was actually doing something creative on my own, essentially being an artist, but I wasn't a part of a band. It was like being a solo artist, I guess. It was all about creativity every day, just coming up with ideas and making them real. I mean, I'm thinking about a video for today. I haven't decided what I'm going to do, but I just made an Instagram post. I'm going to make a video on *some* topic. I already have a couple of ideas, but I'm going to make something and put something out today.

I was 54 when I started my channel. I didn't think anyone would watch an old guy my age with white hair, but I've found that being older, I have certain credibility because I have a lot of experience. I mean, I basically lived through the entire history of rock music. If you think of the Beatles starting in 1962, I mean I was too young for Elvis, the beginning of Elvis, and I missed Chuck Berry. Basically, I missed the beginning of rock and roll, but from 1962, I heard it all.

When I talk about famous records or whatever, they're all things that I experienced firsthand, and you can't do that if you're 29 years old. You're just looking back. You don't have 58 years to reflect on how the music industry has changed or how people were influenced by other people or hearing new artists and seeing if they're drawing on new things or if they're regurgitating old things. It's great to have perspective and young people appreciate me having the experience. It's actually turned out to be an asset, whereas I thought there was going to be ageism. Believe it or not, my biggest demographics are young people.

When I started the channel, I had a guy reach out to me who had about 40,000 subscribers when I probably had about 3,000 or 4,000. Dotan had a channel called "Piano Around the World."

He had some viral videos on YouTube, and I had had viral videos on Facebook with my son, but Facebook didn't pay anything. I asked him, "You have these videos, do you make a living on YouTube?"

He said, "Oh, no. You can't make a living on YouTube."

I said, "Well, how much do those videos pay you?"

"Well, a video with a million views pays $1,250."

"That's it?"

He said, "Yeah, you can't make a living on YouTube."

But the music theory book that I wrote back when I was a college professor in Ithaca—my *Beato Book*—plus tee shirts and mugs and things like that that I sell through my Beato club are how I've been able to make a living and do this. That's what allowed me to quit my production job because I just needed to make enough money so I didn't have to do that anymore.

And it's funny because that book sat in boxes for 25 years after I left Ithaca. Who knew how important it would become all these years later? I never planned that. Truth is, I never planned any of this. I was just trying to move forward. If someone had asked, "Rick, do you see your journey as 'I did this, then I did this, then I did this,' or was it just the way things happened? You didn't have any great plan, did you?"

I'd have to say, "No, there was no plan. We create the plan afterward when we look back at it, and that's why kids look at us and think, 'You were a fully formed human being. Surely you had this idea.' But, "No, no, no; not really."

But there some takeaways—some learning—some things I opened my eyes to and thought, *You know what? I've got to keep tabs on this.*

There are some things I always knew about myself that helped me to be successful in pretty much all my different endeavors, from college professor to music producer, to YouTuber.

I can outwork any 20-year-old. I'm just unbelievably driven.

I set goals for myself and I have to achieve them, whatever they may be; I'm a finisher. That's the big thing. I told you I'm going to release a video today. I don't know what it'll be about. I don't have an idea for it yet, but I will create an idea, film it, and put it out today—something. It's a challenge and it's fun. It's like figuring out a puzzle. I'm not obsessed with money, I'm not obsessed with subscribers, anything like that—none of that stuff, really. I don't really care about stuff like that. I'm obsessed with getting things done.

I wish more people were interested in music as not just listeners, but as players, like they were when I was growing up. I wish that playing music was more a part of our culture, worldwide. That has nothing to do with the United States. When we were growing up, 30%–40% of people learned an instrument. They played in the school band, the school orchestra, they took guitar lessons, piano lessons, violin lessons. It was common. It doesn't matter where you are, either. I mean, the only places that it's common now are in Asia.

My wife grew up in Korea and she's half-Korean. When she was growing up, everybody took piano lessons or violin, and my kids go to a language immersion school and they learn Mandarin. When my son took piano lessons, 80% of the people in the piano studio here in Atlanta were Asian.

That used to be an important part of our culture. I know that a lot of people don't have the disposable income to go take lessons. I've been so fortunate to have a world-class education on multiple instruments in multiple genres of music. The way I can give back is by creating a channel with free lessons on everything I've ever learned.

It's like Khan Academy. A lot of schools use Khan Academy as an addition to whatever their curriculum is to augment it because there's lessons on everything. It's very well organized— K-through-12 or K-through-college education, even preschool-through-college. That's for free on YouTube or through Khan Academy.

I always thought that was brilliant. I love the story of a hedge fund guy who has a Harvard MBA who started making videos for his niece or nephew who was having problems with algebra. He made these tutorials that he sent over YouTube, but other people started watching them, and then it became this huge thing. Then the Bill and Melinda Gates Foundation invested in it, Google invested in it, and I thought that was such a great idea.

There should be a Khan Academy for music, so I thought that can be what I do. That was the beginning of my channel. I was thinking about that—that everybody should be as lucky as I am.

When I was a kid, this guy who lived two blocks away from me owned a music store, and he was a phenomenal guitar player. I used to mow his lawn and he got me to come take lessons in his store. He was a jazz guitar player, and there was this whole community of great players in Rochester, New York. All the teachers there were amazing. I mean, I just randomly went and mowed his yard, and things like that just happened that changed my life when I was a teenager. I took all these different educational opportunities I've had, all the experience I've had working with the best recording engineers and mixers; I took all this knowledge and just put it out there on YouTube, on my channel for free.

I could have mowed the lawn on the other side of the street and never met this guy. Who's to say? It's both the opportunities you're presented with and what you do with those opportunities that really make you who you are.

Rashmi Airan,
Speaker and Consultant

I get lots of great things from my running group besides a group of dedicated people who hold me accountable to drag myself out of bed at o'dark thirty in the morning and get my sweaty miles in.

One of the best things is the new runners I meet. When I first ran with Rashmi Airan, she told me she was interested in transitioning from her former career as a lawyer into the speaking business, and she asked if I could give her some advice.

We got together for breakfast after a run a few days later. When I suggested she attend an out-of-town convention of the National Speakers Association she told me that she was on probation and wasn't allowed to travel. My confused look invited Rashmi to tell me the rest of her story, and when I heard what she'd been through, I realized that Rashmi had a lot more to teach me (and you) than I had to teach her.

Rashmi Airan

My dad was motivated by his father to reach for the stars. He had always wanted to be a lawyer but for a number of reasons he earned a master's degree in public health and then a PhD in environmental engineering. He was running his own engineering consulting practice and he ran into some trouble; he was asked for a bribe by a local politician.

I can remember sitting in the car with my dad when I was a little girl. I was probably five or six years old and he was explaining this to me and I remember asking him "What is a lawyer? What does a lawyer do?"

To make a long story short, my dad ended up reporting the bribe to the State Attorney's office. He wound up working with the DA and was wired with a listening device. The politician was arrested and went to jail, and that experience incentivized my father to go to law school and start practicing. I remember my dad telling me, "Rashmi, you'll be a really good lawyer one day. You love to argue. You're very analytical."

That stuck with me.

I did debate all through high school. Even today when my kids ask me, "Mommy, what was your sport in high school?" I answer, "Ha. I was the biggest nerd. I was a debate person. I spent every weekend in debate tournaments. I didn't ever touch a ball."

When it came time to figure out what I was going to do after college, it was a foregone conclusion. I applied to law school, and I never allowed myself to even consider the possibility of not going to law school.

After I sent off my law school applications, some of my friends were in New York working in investment banking. I got this bright notion that I would drop my résumé off at their companies, maybe do really well in the interviews, and get a couple of trips to New York to see my friends. I'd interview with these firms and maybe even get a job before law school. I ended up getting a few job offers in management consulting and investment banking in New York. I took a job at Morgan Stanley in New York. Luckily Columbia Law School agreed to give me a two-year deferral so I could work on Wall Street for a few years, which they agreed would be a great experience for me.

Of course, even my successes in finance didn't dissuade me from being a lawyer. After a couple of years on Wall Street I went to Columbia and ultimately graduated top of my class. I practiced law in San Francisco for a year and then went back home. I worked for a mid-sized litigation boutique and then I worked for the government. I was a county attorney for a couple of years until I left to start my own practice in real estate law.

Even though I was a good attorney, I didn't really love it. But I thought, *This is what I'm supposed to be doing. This is it, man. This is what I trained for. This is what I'm meant to do.* I thought I was living my destiny. It was 2007 and I was married to a firefighter and we had two children. My kids were two and three years old, and I was the major breadwinner.

One day I was introduced to a local real estate developer. I had run into an attorney I'd met when I was working for the county, and she called me a day or two later and said, "Hey Rashmi, would you like to meet a real estate developer who's been looking for a new attorney to work with him? Would you be interested?"

I jumped at this opportunity. I was a solo practitioner and I had a small practice and I had been pounding the pavement trying to grow my business. If I could get a big developer as a client, well gosh, that would mean more business, and that would mean financial stability. That would mean more time with my kids. That was what went through my head.

Maybe two days later I went to meet with this developer. What was odd was that the developer himself, the principal guy, sat in a side office and never came into the main conference room to meet with me. Instead, his two right-hand guys met with me. They explained what they were doing, which would now be described as creating buyer incentives to purchase their units.

They would tell the potential buyer, "If you buy this condo unit, we will give you a two-year rental guarantee. My management company will manage it for you. It'll be disclosed on the settlement statement and you won't have to worry about a mortgage payment for at least two years."

I thought, "My God, that's kind of creative, but okay. You're disclosing it on the settlement statement. All right. Let me see if I can do this." And in the moment, all I could think of was, *I want to try to get this done. I want to win this client.*

I went into a different side office right there and called my underwriting counsel. I began to describe this scenario, and I said, "I'm sitting with a developer, and I really want to work with him. He's doing these third-party disbursements on the settlement statement. Can I do that?"

Of course, hindsight is 20/20. Now I recognize that I intentionally left out some very important facts — specifically, that the buyer was getting a benefit. But I had convinced myself that all that mattered was the escrow in and out from my account, and as long as I was describing and illustrating exactly what was supposed to happen from the settlement statement, and what I describe is exactly what actually happens from my account, then that's all that matters and it's fine."

I won the business and within two weeks I had my first closing request and it was like a steamroller. There was so much going on that I never made the time to do my due diligence. I didn't look into the people I was now in bed with. I didn't ask for a second opinion. I didn't go and ask for help. I'd been surrounded by attorneys all my life, and I could easily have gone to any number of mentors, colleagues, friends, even my parents, who were both attorneys by this time. But I never stopped to ask for help or to ask for another opinion.

What I recognize now was that I didn't ask because I didn't want to know the answer. I was just so focused on getting the client and then making the client happy and keeping the client that I sort of made my decisions in a silo. I just kept going and going and barreling down and producing.

And so the steamroller took over. I did about a hundred closings in Palm Beach and another hundred in Tampa over the course of 15 months. By then I was burnt out so I stopped doing transactional work altogether. I joined my father's practice and worked with him doing defaults.

Fast forward two years later and the FBI knocked on my door. It had been four years since I first met the developer. The FBI agents came in and showed me their badges, and it didn't even dawn on me that I could have said, "I will come back and meet with you with my attorney." Kind of stupidly, I didn't know any better. I thought, *My God. If I don't talk to the FBI, they're definitely going to think I did something wrong, and so I need to talk to them.* And I had convinced myself that I hadn't done anything wrong. Instead,

I thought, *I just need to be an open book, and I'll cooperate, because that's the right thing to do.*

So I sat with them for four hours while they grilled me. They showed me pictures and emails, and I answered their questions definitively, as if I actually even remembered exactly what had happened four years earlier. Of course, there's no way I could have remembered precisely who I had met, what email I may or may not have seen, whatever.

After they left, two years went by and I pretty much forgot that I'd ever met with the FBI. But then one day I received a grand jury subpoena for documents.

At the time, I was still operating under this pretense that I hadn't done anything wrong so I submitted all the documents they asked for, which were all my closing files for this developer.

Three months later, my attorney, who was like a mentor, a father figure to me, called me into his office and told me to sit down. He said, "Rashmi, you're a target of an FBI investigation."

I started shaking uncontrollably. I'm on the other side of it now and I'm at peace, but back then I was literally shaking hysterically. This was my whole life. This was everything I had worked for, and all I could think about was, *I've disgraced my family and my parents and my kids, and my life is over. My entire community is going to shun me.*

To his credit the prosecutor kept trying to get me to come in and talk to him, and I kept saying, "Look. I don't know anything. What am I going to say? There's nothing to say. I didn't do anything wrong."

But I had. And in April 2014, I was indicted for one count of conspiracy to commit bank fraud and 23 counts of bank fraud, which are basically the 23 real estate closings that they attached to the complaint.

For four months I barreled down and focused on my case. I printed out all the discovery, which totaled 200,000 pages of documents and another 15,000 emails. I was on a mission. I was convinced that I would prove my innocence and find the smoking gun. I was going to go through every single piece of evidence and find all the facts that would exonerate me.

And I did that. Every single day I would take my kids to camp, and then I would go through the discovery. I would take out good and bad pieces of evidence and periodically meet with my attorney. My trial attorney was a friend of mine, because my first attorney said I was going to need him as a character witness at the trial. Within four months this attorney, David, called me and said, "Rashmi, let's have a meeting with your parents. Why don't you come in with them?" It was August 2014, and a trial was set for December. My parents and I walked in thinking,

"Okay, we're going to talk trial prep and strategy and exhibits and expert witnesses and all the stuff you talk about when you're getting ready for trial."

Instead, he and his partner ran us through an entire presentation of the trial. He said, "Rashmi, this is what you're charged with. This is what the government's going to use to prove their case. This is what we're going to use to defend your case, and here's how the government's going to rebut."

Then he said, "If you go to trial, you are going to lose. Before the jury hears your case, they're going to get a whole host of jury instructions, but let's just discuss the two that are relevant to you. The first is conspiracy, and the conspiracy jury instructions says something to the effect of, 'If the defendant knew even one detail out of 500 million, you, the jury, have to convict.'"

He looked right me and said, "Rashmi, you're my client and you're a good attorney. If you want to go to trial, we'll go to trial, but I'm telling you right now, you will lose. Your name is on every letter, every check, every email, every document. Do you really think a jury is going to believe you didn't know what was going on? Because here's the thing: You did know. At least you knew the details. You knew that there was a rental guarantee and you knew that there were all sorts of other things happening outside of your closings."

During my research of the discovery, I had found that there were many, many other aspects of my client's scheme that I hadn't known about at the time. I only discovered them when I started looking through the documents, but none of that mattered. If I had known even one thing, that would be enough to indict me and to convict me.

Then he told me about the second jury instruction, which is willful blindness. My attorney lowered his voice and said, "You can't put your head in the sand. You can't turn a blind eye, because not knowing what you did is wrong is still doing something wrong." He said, "As an attorney, you had a fiduciary duty to ask more questions. You could have asked more questions but you didn't. I understand that you didn't go into this planning to commit a crime. But you did know enough that you should have known it was a crime and you've got to own up to it. I understand that you want to go in there and fight, and I respect that, but I'm telling you right now, if you do that you are going to lose. And then you're looking at spending 20 years in prison. Your children will be adults by the time you get out."

The next thing I did was the hardest thing I've ever done, and it was also one of the most pivotal moments in my life. I took off my fighting hat and owned up to what I had done, and I recognized that for the rest of my life I would be a convicted felon.

I pled guilty a few months later.

Before I was sentenced, I made a conscious decision that I was going to call everybody in my life and tell them what had happened. It was really important for me to call people—my mentors, colleagues, friends, people I knew in the community, everybody. I didn't know if the US Attorney's Office was going to issue a press release so it was really important to me that I told everyone myself. I didn't want anybody who knew me to read about it in the newspaper first.

One-by-one I picked up the phone and called people and told them the story just like I'm telling you. I was absolutely sure I would be shunned. I thought everyone was going to disown me, nobody was going to stand by me, nobody would support me, but the gift I got out of this was the recognition that people are very forgiving. I really believe that because I took ownership of my bad decisions, people stood with me and said, "We still love you unconditionally and believe in you and stand by you." Out of that I got a lot of community support and the judge received more than 200 letters on my behalf. And everyone was there for my sentencing hearing, which was pretty amazing.

I was sentenced to a year-and-a-day in prison. The hardest part was telling my children the truth and letting them ask the very real questions that any 9 and 10-year-old would ask their mom before she goes away.

I ended up spending about six months behind bars.

I had a couple of jobs when I was in prison. I started out working in the commissary warehouse, which was where all the huge pallets would get delivered every day. There were five different prisons on that one campus and the contents of those pallets needed to be divided up. And we women did that job because we were the only ones who were allowed to work in the entire complex.

When the trucks unloaded, I would receive the pallets, log them in, and then take them apart. I didn't know how to operate a forklift, but I could separate the contents and then deliver them to the various other prisons in a golf cart accompanied by one of the guards. I did that for a couple of weeks, and then my next job was as the trash girl. That meant that every night just before recall—which is the time when you have to be back in your housing unit—it was my job to go to the bottom of the two residential buildings and get these ginormous blue rolling garbage bins. I would have to take one and roll it over to the other side of the building, grab the second one, and then roll them both to the very back of the compound.

It was pretty scary, because it was dark and really desolate. There was nobody there although sometimes there were these enormous rats. I'd have to open the door to the huge trash compactor and then, one by one, take the bags out of the bins and put them into the trash compactor and shove them down to the bottom. Thankfully, I had gloves because the bags always busted open and all this gross garbage spewed out. And I did that assignment rain, shine, cold or not. That was my job. I had to do it every night for three months. It was disgusting.

There's a part of the prison that's set up for inmates who want to take classes and maybe pursue their GREs or maybe they just want to learn. I knew the program needed teachers, so I hand-wrote a resume and submitted it. And after I had been on garbage duty for about two-and-a-half months one of the inmate teachers was released from prison, and a position opened up and I got the job.

I taught a math class in English at 10:30 in the morning and then I taught the same class in Spanish at two o'clock in the afternoon. There were grown women there who had never learned how to add fractions; they didn't even know what fractions were. Just before I was incarcerated, my kids were in the third and fourth grades and I had taught them their fractions. I used the pizza and pizza slices analogy and I used the same stories to teach the other inmates how to add and subtract fractions and mixed numbers and so on.

There were a couple of women who wanted to study for their GREs. One woman in particular was super-young. She lived down the hall in my housing unit. She came to my cell on the weekends and asked me to help her to prepare, which I did. I sat with her and helped her get ready for the test.

When she passed and received her GRE, she came to tell me and asked, "Okay, so what can I get you from commissary?" Because pretty much everybody in prison had a hustle where they are doing something so they can get paid by commissary, because, unfortunately, they don't have the ability to get any money from the outside. I was truly blessed that my parents always put money in my commissary account, but a lot of women don't have that luxury, and so people ran all kinds of side-hustles so they could afford their little luxuries. She thought I had been helping her because I wanted something, too.

She came to me and asked, "How much can I pay you for tutoring?"

I was surprised and said, "Huh? Nothing. I did this for you. I don't need anything. Just enjoy." And she couldn't believe it. No one had ever done anything like that for her before.

When I decided I was going to plead guilty, I went through what I would call a spiritual transformation. When I was initially indicted, I was full of bitterness and anger about a lot of things, not the least of which was, *Why isn't the developer being indicted? Why isn't the woman who introduced me to the developer, the woman who made the most money, the one who sort of planned this whole thing, why isn't she going to jail? How about everyone else?*

I was so angry. I kept asking, "Why aren't the other 500 attorneys who are basically doing the same thing getting caught? Why am I the only one getting indicted?" All these things were floating around in my head and I was so consumed with anger and negative energy. I ultimately got some great advice from my uncle, and he led me to a place where I understood that while I didn't know why this was happening *to* me, I was going to believe that it was happening *for* me. I came to a place of forgiveness. I learned I had to forgive myself and then forgive everybody else in the process—everybody who wasn't going through what I was going through.

You know what? Their karma will come to them in whatever way that is meant for them, but it doesn't affect my path or my life. This is obviously my life path; this is what I'm supposed to go through. The peace I came to was very profound and very important for me, because when I was in prison I was able to make it as positive an experience as I could.

That meant I had a routine. I'd get up every day, I'd work out, I'd go for a run. I had a job to do and books to read and I tutored the other inmates and tried to make the most of the time there and learn as much as I could while I was away. That included reflecting on what I'd been through to try to figure out what the hell had happened that I had allowed myself to go so off my path.

Because many of my friends, including my own attorney, had seen me go through this transformation, they began to encourage me to start speaking and sharing my story. That's where my new life started. The first talk I did was at my alma mater, Columbia Law School, and then word spread. I found my message when I prepared my TEDx talk, and it's evolved since then.

I don't know if you've been in a federal courtroom, but when I was there for my sentencing, there were these very, very tall, huge, high-ceilinged rooms. Outside of the courtroom there were two rooms on opposite sides of a hallway. The defense is usually housed on one side and the plaintiff is on the other side. Before the hearing started, all my friends and family were piling in, and they were trying to say hi to me and wish me luck.

I was in the room with my attorneys and in walked my prosecutor, Joe Capone. He popped in, and he gave me this huge bear hug. He kissed me on the cheek and he said, "You're going to do okay today, Rashmi. Just have faith and be strong in there," and he walked out.

David, my defense attorney, was in shock. "In a million years, in my entire professional life, not one of my clients has ever had the prosecutor come in and wish them luck. Only you, Rashmi. Only you."

And now I'm doing presentations with Joe. After 30 years he retired from the federal government and last month we did our first presentation together. We titled it *From Target to Teammate:*

The Journey from Adversaries to Allies, and we got this incredible, overwhelming response.

It's really interesting how my perception of Joe changed along the way. As you would imagine, I hated him at the beginning, but now I have the utmost respect for him. We have developed a beautiful one-of-a-kind relationship. One of the things I've learned about myself I learned from Joe. Listen to what he told our last audience:

"What I've noticed about Rashmi is that she's always all-in. No matter what she's doing, she's all-in. When she was a little kid and all through her school years, she would go to school and she was always all-in. You can see that from her grades, from her awards, from where she went to school. She was just always excelling, because she was always all-in.

"The same can be said when she met the client who ultimately caused her downfall. She met the client and she wanted to get the client, keep the client. She was all-in, which meant she put blinders on and didn't allow herself to see the red flags that were there, because she was so all-in and focused on getting the job done for the client. Then, once she realized what she had done and took responsibility for it, and decided to plea and help the government and own her bad decision, she was all-in again. She did everything she could to help us and to review documents for us. She went the extra mile, more so than we would have ever expected her to do, spending hundreds of hours for us and with us, preparing for trial and getting ready to testify.

"Now, you see her out of prison, and again, she's all-in. She's completely reinvented her life and started this whole new career. She's all-in, trying to help people through her story."

It's a really interesting analysis of me, especially because it came from my prosecutor. It's quite valid. I feel really blessed that I have him as a colleague now. I was just invited to speak at an event, and I got him a speaking engagement with me in September, so he's going to get paid to speak with me, which is wonderful. No one's ever seen anything like it.

After I speak to an audience about what I've been through and what I've learned, people always ask, "If you could go back and change what happened, would you? Would you go back and change what you did and change your experience?"

My honest answer is complicated. Of course, I wish I could go back and make better decisions and not have gone through this and not have hurt my family or the victims. In my own odd way I think that I contributed to the financial crisis of 2008, so yeah, I wish I could go back and make better decisions. But I will say that having gone through the experience of going to prison, of losing everything—including my bar license, my money, my marriage—has transformed me in a way I never could have expected.

I believe I had to lose my freedom to gain complete freedom, and today I have this gift of living in complete transparency and vulnerability all the time. I don't have to pretend to be anything I'm not. I don't have to pretend that I have great things or nice things, because I don't, because I've lost all my money and I lost my marriage.

My sentence was one-year-and-one-day of incarceration, 200 hours of community service, three years of supervised release, and a multimillion-dollar restitution judgment. I've done my time and my community service and I'm working on the restitution. I am required to pay 10% of my gross income every month. I actually go to the bank and get a money order and send it to the clerk of courts. Then those funds get divvied up between my three victims: Bank of America, Chase, and Wells Fargo. Those three banks get money from me every month.

I don't think there's any realistic rhyme or reason to how the courts came up with the number I owe. I think they took all the mortgages I had ever closed on for this developer, added them up, put a penalty on them, added interest, and came up with an exorbitant amount. It was 200 closings and whatever else, so I'll never pay it all off. I'll never own an asset again. I can never have a mortgage. I can never take out a loan. I'm pretty strapped and that's a huge blow.

I can't vote and I can't even restore my right to vote until I satisfy all the terms of my judgment. I also can't apply to the bar until all the terms of my judgment have been satisfied. I can't apply to the bar again because I have not restored my rights, and I can't restore my rights because I have such a large judgement owed to Bank of America, Chase, and Wells Fargo. It's kind of crazy if you think about it logically. I can't pay off my penalty if I can't work, and I can't work if I can't restore my license, and I can't restore my license if I can't pay off my penalty.

I also lost my marriage. Truth be told, it had already started to fall apart before the case started. My husband had already moved out and by the time the grand jury subpoenaed me, we were already in therapy. We were trying to reconcile and working on getting back together, but when the grand jury subpoena came in 2013, all bets were off. I was freaking out and so scared that sadly I had no bandwidth for him. All I could do was try to take care of my kids and myself—physically, mentally, and emotionally. Whatever strength I had left went to work on my case.

Unfortunately, there was nothing left for him. To his credit, he stuck by me and was there when I needed him. He wasn't living with me, so it's not like I had somebody cuddling me and holding me every night and telling me, "You're going to be okay, Rashmi," but I think that has made me a lot stronger as a woman and as a person in general.

When you're in prison, you have a lot of time to think and reflect and own your issues, so when I came out I told him, "Look. Let's reestablish our relationship. And we both tried; we really did. But there was a lot of miscommunication and things that just went wrong in our marriage.

I said, "Let's reestablish integrity in our marriage. Let's really try. let's go to therapy. Let's make this work." But we couldn't make it work so we had to move on. We got divorced in 2017. It's funny, because now he's done a lot of work on himself and I've done a lot of work on myself, and we're the best of friends. He's over here all the time with the kids and me. We have dinners and meals and we go to our kids' games together. We travel together for our kids' tournaments and we stay in the same hotel room. We have a very healthy, modern family relationship, and we co-parent very well which has been great for our kids.

This has all been a liberating transformation and I am happier today than I ever thought I could be again. Now I get to meet new people every week and talk to new people and inspire people through my story. I actually feel like I'm making more impact in helping people now than I ever could have as an attorney.

I look back. When I was a little girl and my dad said, "You'll be a great attorney," I wanted to make him so proud of me. That was so much of what led me to go to law school. I'm thankful that I have the education, but I don't think I was really meant to be an attorney. I think there are a lot of other things I would have been good at. Having gone through this really led me to figure out how to be a better mom. I used to think I had to be perfect all the time but now I tell my kids, "My goal is to be the perfect imperfect mom for you guys." Now that I've gone off-path and recognized it and come to terms with it I realized that, "Hey, I'm just a human being, and that's okay."

I don't want my children to feel that same pressure that I felt. My son is very much a mini-me, and he puts a lot of pressure on himself. I've learned that I have to reign myself in because I do have high expectations for him, because I know what he's capable of. But as a mom, my biggest thing is always teaching him and his sister: "Do the right thing. Be accountable. Take ownership for anything that happens. You're going to have to pay consequences, but you'll learn from it. Then, hopefully you'll make better decisions next time."

We have to expect our children to make mistakes, and we should expect them to and want them to fail so they can learn from the experience. It's funny, June 16th, 2015, the day I got sentenced, was the day my life changed. I understand that any other person who hasn't been through all this would probably say, "That was my most glaring day of failure because that was the day I was sentenced to prison." Yet I look back on that day and I think, *What a day of success!* because there were 200 people in that room and they stood up for me unconditionally.

My definition of success truly shifted that day. I used to think that success was getting good grades and making money and going to the best schools and winning all the awards and all the things I worked so hard to do a as a kid and a teenager, but now I realize I'm successful every day by inspiring people and touching other people's lives. And to me, that is really an incredible recognition of what I see as my purpose and my mission.

Michael Grimme,
Gulfstream Jet Pilot

Michael and I met in a business group and quickly became friends. Before long we were looking for ways to do business together. One day Michael told me he needed to fly his plane from Park City to Fort Lauderdale and invited me to take the cross-country trip with him. Somewhere over Albuquerque, Michael started telling me about his life journey and I started taking notes. Michael's interview grew from that first conversation.

Michael Grimme

As a kid I was always intrigued by boats and planes and particularly by the sense of adventure and travel that came with them. My brothers and I started buying small boats with money saved from our paper routes and with no-interest loans from our dad that we made payments on weekly.

When it was time to go to college I went to The University of Delaware and I got a Mechanical and Aerospace Engineering degree. Why? I don't know. I guess it was because my father was an engineer. It just seemed like a good idea at the time. I thought maybe I'd build boats or build planes one day, although my dad would tell me that I would not build an entire plane; I'd probably just be assigned to a team designing a door or something. Clearly I was pretty naïve. So I went to engineering school and struggled but eventually I got through it and graduated with a degree, surprising everyone by getting it done in four years!

When I went looking for a job, I was fortunate that after interviewing with countless companies, I got a job working for an oil company, even though I knew absolutely nothing about oil.

Truth is, up until then my only real college summer work experience was my dream job of lifeguarding at the beach in Wildwood Crest, New Jersey. I didn't realize it at the time but that job gave me incredible socializing and networking skills that helped me tremendously later … but it would have been far easier to get a permanent job if I had listened to my dad and went after internships instead during college summers.

When I look back on my overall experience, I'd been working since I started a paper route when I was 11 years old. And without knowing it, very early on, I had learned accounts payable, accounts receivable, customer service, and accountability, which are so important in life. I didn't know what I was learning, but I was already learning those skills at 11 years old.

I also learned that once you have a customer you can sell them more stuff, and that it's easier to keep a customer than to get a new one. Once I was delivering their newspapers, I would cut their lawns, rake their leaves, shovel their snow, clean their gutters. Whatever they needed, I did it. So I always had a few extra dollars in my pocket because of that.

I became a hustler — an opportunistic hustler.

You see, I grew up in the Philadelphia area and played outdoor hockey. I wanted to go to Flyers games. I didn't have much money but I did have enough to share season tickets with my brothers because of the paper route money and all these other odd jobs we did.

But that wasn't enough for the expensive food and drinks at the games, so we ended up scalping — buying and selling tickets in front of The Spectrum. The simple rule was that when the game started, you didn't want to have any tickets left in your hand. That was the key. I learned the basics of trading at the age of 14. And as I get older and look back, it's dawned on me that all of these things maybe made me a little different and set me on some of the different paths that I'm still following today.

After getting the job with the oil company — Sunoco — I made a gutsy move. Even though I was lucky to have secured such a great job, I asked them if they would mind if I started in September instead of May because I wanted to backpack through Europe with my brother. Surprisingly they said, "Sure, you can do that."

My brother Mark and I went to Europe for six weeks. I think I took the last $400 I had. We slept in parks, in hostels, on trains, and in train stations, anything we could do to keep our costs down, but we were all over the place. We traveled all over England. We were up in Sweden. We were down in Greece and everywhere in between.

That trip across Europe completely changed my life.

When I came back, I started working in an oil refinery. My life was belching steam and gases with my shoes covered in tar and me thinking that my life was over. I mean, after having sipped coffee on the Champs de Elysée, climbing the Matterhorn, and hanging out on nude beaches in Corfu, Greece, this new reality was a big adjustment. All I could think of was getting back overseas, but as much as I wanted that, I didn't have any idea of how I was going to do it.

I started poking around Sunoco, reading their internal help wanted ads, and asking about the different jobs and the different departments, all with an ear for hearing how I could get back overseas. And I learned that in an oil company the only jobs where you are able to travel internationally are the ones where you're the guy buying the crude oil. So I started researching that job. What were the requirements? What did you need to get it?

Turns out you needed an MBA, so I got one. It took me 18 months at night, all while I was working full-time during the day. I was in classes four nights a week and studying every other night and every weekend.

At that time Sunoco was paying for 90% of books and tuition as long as I maintained a C average or above. Shockingly I got mostly As and realized I had more of a business mind than an engineering mind, but the combination became very powerful for me.

The job I wanted also required experience in barges and transportation and pipelines so I took all the positions that would earn me those experiences. The job I wanted required that I understand operational planning and economics so I took those jobs, too.

Yes, it was a long route, but by the time I was 29, not only did I become a crude oil trader for Sunoco, but quickly after that I was picked off by a Wall Street firm to trade for them. The job was for Phibro Energy, then a division of Salomon Brothers, which is now part CitiGroup. They paid me double what I was being paid at the oil company, plus they promised me a big bonus if I did a good job and met their trading goals.

I dove in headfirst, worked 7am to 7pm in the trading room, went into New York City at night to schmooze with the trading partners (including singing karaoke with Japanese trading partners till 2 am in piano bars), and took calls from the other Phibro trading offices around the world throughout the night.

It was a lot, but it all paid off. By the end of the first year I made ten times what I made working for the oil company the previous year. Sure you could say I was lucky, but it was actually the nine years of acquiring all of those skills I needed at Sunoco so that when I got that job, not only was I qualified for it, but I could excel at it.

What I learned was that to be successful, you have to come up with the long-term goal, develop a checklist to reach that goal. You must fanatically follow that checklist like a racehorse wearing blinders, always keeping your long-term goal in mind.

Within two years I was living in Zug, Switzerland, then London, England, and traveling all around the globe on a daily basis doing oil deals. I ended up living overseas for eight years, but I always knew that it all came from that trip backpacking through Europe, which completely changed my view and my aspirations and gave me a goal I could stick with through thick and thin.

Looking back, I realize that I developed my life in stages, with long-term goals for each. This started with the Before-Kids stage.

The Before-Kids Stage

I was a bachelor for most of this time. In this stage of my life, I'm responsible only to myself and I can do whatever I want. I can try to make as much money as I want. I can be selfish, if you want to call it that, and focus solely on achieving my goals. As long as I'm not hurting anyone, that's all right.

I was lucky enough to marry my wife, Pam, just before I joined Phibro. She understood my goals, supported me 100%, and allowed me to make the commitment to the trading company. Pam knew it would not be forever and that the position could hopefully provide us with financial security.

I was solely focused on my business and my career. I was trading day-in and day-out for seven years. It was all-consuming, 24/7/365, every minute of every day. That's what success required and that's what I was willing to do.

But eventually children came into the picture … and I got a real life. Our first daughter, Ashley, was born in Stanford, Connecticut. Our son, Michael, was born in Switzerland. Then two more girls, Chelsea and Amanda, were born in England. And all of a sudden, I'm a married family man with four babies at home but I'm still traveling the globe. I was 100% focused on matching wits with some of the most intelligent and aggressive traders in the world, and it took every bit of my energy to do it. But I started thinking, *Wait a second. Who is potentially being hurt by my focus and my schedule?*

You see, I saw traders getting into drugs, getting into heavy alcohol use. I saw them burning through marriages, losing their relationships with their kids—and I didn't want that for me.

I had grown up with that song, "The Cat's in the Cradle"—you know, that old Harry Chapin song—about a father who didn't spend time with his kid. And then the kid grew up and had no time for his father.

I didn't want that.

I had grown up in a household where both my parents were around and very supportive and I'm sure that that played a big part in my life, so I made the decision that this situation wasn't for me anymore. I'd made enough money. I was never going to starve. I was 38 years old and managing a football field-size trading room with people from 17 different countries working there, all with their own definitions of business ethics. I decided that I wanted to do something else with my life.

I was now in the Family Guy stage.

The Family Guy Stage

What did being a Family Guy mean? I stopped trading … completely. I knew that to be successful in oil trading required fanatical focus 24/7, something I was no longer willing to do. I moved back to the States. I moved to Florida both for quality of life and the tax benefits. It's something I always wanted to do, live in warm weather near the ocean.

After looking around, writing down my personal goals, writing down my business goals, trying to come up with that next play for that stage of my life, I realized that my priority was having my own business so I could have control of my own schedule. I wanted that because I didn't want to miss school plays, ballet recitals, soccer practice, or football practice.

Up until the time I was 12 or 13 years old, my grandparents owned these little mom-and-pop motels on the Jersey Shore. I can't say I grew up in that business, but Nana and Pop-Pop were spending time with their grandkids while running a motel business during the summer. We often had odd jobs there filling the soda machines, sweeping sand off the decks, pulling weeds, helping the maids, etc. I became extremely close to Nana and Pop-Pop during those days, and that kind of life made sense to me and who I was at that stage. I came up with this crazy idea: What if we could run a hotel business in Fort Lauderdale and I could be around my kids while they're growing up?

And that's just what my wife and I did.

We ended up owning 125 rooms and 33 boat slips spread over about different eight properties, all little mom-and-pop motels around Fort Lauderdale, all on the water. And I owe that to my Nana also because I remember her always telling me, "They don't make any more waterfront."

Of course, when the preteen me would try to offer her suggestions on her business she would also say, "If you are so smart, why
aren't you rich?"

All of her comments stuck with me.

My wife and I bought these properties one-by-one and ran them
very hands-on. These were all old, beat up Spring Break properties or extended-stay-type properties where retirees would spend
their winter months back in the 1950s. We converted them into
upscale boutique hotel properties.

Eventually my kids were involved as well, and we were all
together while we built a kind of a waterfront land bank play.
I had strong appreciation from the properties along with some
income, although most of the income that came in went right
back out the other way to run the business and invest in improvements. But I did have this underlying asset that was appreciating—
waterfront property in South Florida.

I got lucky when I moved to Fort Lauderdale because I saw
the area with fresh eyes. After moving from London, real estate
in South Florida looked cheap to me. The city was in transition
from being the Spring Break Capital of the world (that ended in
1986) to becoming the Venice of America and the yachting capital of the world.

Other local people didn't see it that way because they were used
to what Fort Lauderdale real estate values used to be and thought

the city was already overpriced. Many of the locals thought I was crazy buying these properties.

So it turned out that I picked the right time to be buying, and then, years later when I was selling our hotels and properties, everybody else was telling me, "Don't sell. Don't sell. Prices are only going to go higher."

But because I could lean on my trading background, I knew better. I knew that while pigs get fat, hogs get slaughtered. I knew that nothing goes up forever. Instead, I saw an opportunity to get out and it was at just the right time. We also had been through the scare of 9/11. After the planes exploded into the World Trade Center all of our properties were completely empty overnight. We were highly leveraged and we knew we were vulnerable. Had the economy not rebounded quickly we would have been in deep trouble with our multiple bank loans.

While we had the hotel business, other opportunities and necessities came our way. We got into the web business, primarily to help us market our small properties but we did outside work as well to help cover the overhead. We got into the furniture liquidation business, buying obsolete assets from high-end hotels to supply our own properties and eventually also to refurbish and sell to other properties nationally and internationally. Once again, I found myself drawing on my trading and international experiences.

It was a busy, busy time for us, but I always had time for my kids. And when we sold the hotels, I was flush with cash for the first time in a long time and we were in a great place.

I had always wanted to go to Africa. Our kids were at the right age to really enjoy it, so my wife and I took our family there. My son Michael and I stayed an extra week and climbed Mt. Kilimanjaro. He's my number two child and was 17 at the time.

Exactly one month later I lost Michael in a car accident. It was the most devastating thing that ever happened to me in my life and was just as devastating to my wife and daughters.

The cause of the car wreck had nothing to do with him. It wasn't his fault. It wasn't my fault. It was just a tragedy and it completely changed our lives.

Today, when people tell me they're going to keep working and they're going to do whatever it takes to make a lot of money, and then they're going to spend time with their kids, I always tell them my story about losing my son. I have to tell them, no matter how hard it is, because you never know what's going to happen tomorrow. And you only get one opportunity to raise your kids.

After that experience, we had a total "family meltdown.. My wife had a meltdown. My children were melting down. I was melting down. And then, right after that, the economy melted down and crashed. It was 2006, 2007, 2008. We had the company and

I had about 60 full- and part-time employees. It was the most horrible experience one could ever imagine.

I got counseling. I tried to stay positive. I tried to be "the strong one" as the head of the family … doing the best I could while internally I was falling apart. I tried to keep the focus on my wife and my daughters and get everybody through it. My girls had trouble at school and trouble dealing with all the questions from others and their friends and teachers trying to say "the right thing" which often came out wrong. They all had their own challenges. They all suffered in their own way. Nobody escaped the tragedy.

About four years ago, 12 years after the tragedy, I finally realized that all my kids are in a great place. They're all out of the house with their own careers and their own lives and their own relationships and maybe it was time for me to look at a new path—a new stage—something different for Pam and me.

At that first stage, which was *Before-lKids,* I could do whatever I wanted. Then during the *Family Guy* stage, I had to make the adjustments to control my time and be physically there for my family. Now I was in the *After-Kids* stage.

The After-Kids Stage

With my kids out of the house, it was time to develop a plan for the next stage of our lives. It was very challenging for me because at that time several family members were very involved in our liquidation business. We had a lot of money tied up in that company and no one was happy. To make things worse, our margins were shrinking very quickly but our bank loans were not. It was a very stressful time.

I had to step back and look at the situation like it was an engineering challenge. There is a well-known saying in engineering, "Define the problem and the solution is easy." I just needed to better define the problem.

I was fortunate to be in a Vistage group, which is a group of businesspeople who get together once a month and help each other with personal, business, and health issues, whatever their issues happen to be. This gave me a safe place where I could vent and tell them my issues and they would give me suggestions on what to do based on their own experiences.

With their input and my own soul searching, I finally realized I needed to come up with a dramatic change in plan that would be in the best interest of everyone. So I did what I always do— I started writing everything down, first defining what the problems are and then what the potential solutions could be.

Once everything's on paper, I try to look at my writing as if I was an outside consultant looking at it and not the person going through it. I say: "What makes sense here? What can be done?"

I sometimes tell other people, in similar situations, that you need to do a SWOT analysis on yourself—take an inventory. What are your strengths? What are your weaknesses? Where are your opportunities with those strengths and what are the threats with what you're looking at doing?

I did the same thing for myself. It was clear that my wife Pam preferred to spend more time at our home in Utah, and also wanted the flexibility to spend more time with her aging mother in New Jersey and I also wanted the flexibility to spend more time with my aging parents, also in New Jersey.

That meant getting out of the liquidation business and its 24/7 operation, selling off the associated real estate, and getting into something that would give us far more mobility and free time. I also wanted to be excited about whatever path I chose and have a new challenge and focus.

One thing rose to the top and that was that I am a pilot.

I learned to fly because when I was a trader I needed a mental escape from the 24/7/365 focus of the job. And when I was flying I wouldn't think about trading. I *couldn't* think about trading. Flying allowed me to escape. If I was sitting on a beach, I would be thinking about trading. If I was having drinks with friends or having dinner, I would be thinking about trading. I was always thinking about trading. But when I was flying, I was not thinking about trading. I was thinking about how I was going to stay alive. So flying was a really good way to clear my head. I used my small planes for business and I used them for family trips and for pleasure, but mostly I just used them to make everything else go away—and I just continued flying.

So when I tried to decide what to do next, I thought, "What if I could fly? And what if I could fly professionally?" Which was something I had always wanted to do. I had always looked up at jet pilots and thought that would be kind of a cool thing to do. And I really wanted the opportunity to go back overseas because I had loved it so much, but during the *Family Guy* stage I didn't like the impact it was having on my family; I didn't like being in a career where I was away all the time.

But now that wasn't a concern so I started looking at *Well, what if I flew long-range jets? And better yet, what if I could fly Gulfstream jets?* Then I would get the opportunity to fly, to go to different places. So I'd have my passion—my hobby—and also get the international aspect. But more importantly, it was also another great challenge for me.

I started looking into it and I got a lot of comments from seasoned pilots. They would tell me that my chances of becoming a Gulfstream pilot were about the same as my chances to become an astronaut. What they meant was it's not going to happen for me because I don't have the experience. But at the same time, while they were teasing me with that, they said, "Okay, let's, let's look at this. Let's look at your résumé and see what you've got."

And they looked at my résumé, which was full of all my business achievements—the jobs I'd held, the companies I'd owned, the awards I'd won—and they looked at all those achievements and awards and experience and said, "Yeah, sorry. Strip it all out. No one cares." Lucky for me, I could just laugh with them and strip it all out so I edited my three-page résumé down to three quarters of a page.

Now I had a pilot's resume, but they still told me that I'd never be a Gulfstream pilot.

What my pilot friends didn't know is that I have a lot of marketing experience from having owned businesses. Marketing is the key to sales and I know how to find leads and close deals. The first thing I did was get a database of all the Gulfstream operators. And I'd reach out to them. After all, what did I have to lose? I got all their email address, prepared my letter, and pushed the "SEND" button just to see what would happen. And within 30 minutes I had two companies call me with interest. Within a couple of days I was being interviewed. And a couple of days after that, I had a job as a Gulfstream pilot.

What did I learn? Sometimes you just gotta go with your gut, believe in what you believe in, and believe in yourself.

Sure you should listen to what more seasoned people have to say, but always be thinking about what they could be missing with the advice they're giving you because they don't know you as well as you know yourself.

The big charter company couldn't figure out why I would want to take a job making less money than I've made since I was 29 years old, but when I explained what I was trying to accomplish, they understood. As the owner saw it, here's a guy with a really strong, proven business background. It would be good to have someone like that on the road because he can see things from a business perspective that our other pilots may not recognize and maybe he could contribute in that way. And from the moment I joined the company, my goal was to provide as much information from a business perspective as I could and be completely open-minded to let them teach me the aviation side because they were way ahead of where I was.

I'm still doing that today and I think I've contributed a lot to the company at the same time that the company's contributed a lot to me. So I was able to make a dramatic change to being a pilot, being on the road, which I love.

My wife doesn't mind the traveling because I work a schedule of 17 days on call and then 15 days off. I have plenty of time at home. And when I'm off, I'm off, both physically and mentally, which I never was with my own business or when I was trading.

My wife and eldest daughter manage our vacation rental properties. We still get to enjoy them because we've carved out owner's
suites for ourselves. And the best part is we don't need a crystal
ball to know when our kids (and hopefully grandkids) want to
visit. We can just block dates when they are coming without drastically effecting our income or long-term appreciation.

The business is great. My relationship with my wife is great. My
relationship with my kids is great. My life is great and I'm really
happy. It all works.

But that happy ending is not the end of the story. Because I'm
coming up on age 65, which for most charter pilots—especially
if you're flying international—means your days are numbered.
Why? Because at 65 you can't be a charter pilot in Europe. So once
again, I'm now doing an assessment of my strengths, my weaknesses, my threats, and my opportunities, my little SWOT analysis so I can decide what I want to do with my life from 65 to 75.

The After-65 Stage

Ages 65–75: This is a foggy crystal ball timeframe for me, but
one thing I've learned is to seek out mentors. I tell this to young
people every day of the week: Seek out mentors. Don't seek out
your boss, but your boss's boss's boss, somebody who's been there,
done that—somebody who can show you their roadmap, share

some of their mistakes, and perhaps help you crystallize your own roadmap. Because once you know where you're going, you'll get there. And you'll get there faster than you ever thought you would.

But you have to have that roadmap because otherwise you're just zig-zagging. You're wasting your time and energy and as you get older time becomes a precious commodity. You could also be wasting money or throwing away relationships while you're chasing these rainbows, instead of taking the time to think about where you want to go.

One of my Vistage friends used to say, "I like to fix my mistakes right here," and he would be pointing at the eraser on his pencil. His thought was that it is so important to write out your plan and make a budget and do your projections before moving forward with that plan.

So now I constantly seek out older friends I can talk to—guys in their seventies, eighties, nineties—people I admire—people who seem to have the right balance of family, business and outside interests—people loved by their families and respected in the community. I'll buy them breakfast and I'll ask them questions and then I'll just sip my coffee and shut up and listen. And that's the cheapest learning I could possibly do.

I recommend you do this right away no matter what you're dealing with. Just make sure you pick the right people. You want mentors who are willing to tell you what they did right, and more importantly, what they did wrong. You want to know what they wouldn't do again because that knowledge is so powerful. It can help you so much and give you a much better quality of life than if you think you know it all already.

And maybe you read a book here and a book there and you pick up a few more things that you need to know. The key is that you always want to be learning. You always want to be learning from others, always seeking out mentors and listening to what they're saying.

The kind of mentor you want to find depends on two things: First, what stage of your life you're in, and second, what you want.

At this stage of my life, coming up on 65, the number one thing I want is for my family to be happy. I want to be physically healthy and have a high quality of life for as long as possible. And I want to pay it forward, to give back to the community.

My wife and I have given away a lot of scholarships in our deceased son's name, and now our main focus is a business ethics program. Business ethics are really important to me because we lost our son due to a lack of business ethics by others. So that has become a passion. We have established a curriculum in perpetuity at Broward College for the automotive, aviation, and marine mechanics programs, and our intention is to grow that over time.

I think you have to look for opportunities in life. You have to look at the constantly changing landscape. When there's a change or a setback, how do you make the best of it? Don't be Johnny Raincloud. Go figure it out. Because when you identify the problem, the solution is out there.

Nelson Hincapie,
CEO, Voices for Children

It was at one of my Strategic Forum meetings that I heard Nelson Hincapie talk about his journey and explain how his life experience had led him to where he is today. I believe his story will touch yu just as it touched me.

Nelson Hincapie

I was born in Bogota, Colombia, to an upper-middle-class family. Both sets of my grandparents and my mother and my father were from the same town in Caldas, the country's coffee-growing region. They all came very from humble beginnings; my father was one of only two children and then his only brother died when my dad was four years old. But my mother was one of eight children. She has since passed away but I still have seven living uncles and aunts.

My parents had sort of an arranged marriage. My mother's parents knew my father well from the town. They knew where he had grown up. They knew where he had graduated from both high school and college, so they considered him a very suitable partner for my mom.

My grandparents invited my dad to visit them often and made a point of making my mother like him. Eventually my parents did what was expected of them and got married, but I don't think that my mother was ever in love with my dad. My mother was quite a beautiful woman and my father was very attracted to her. I don't know if he knew that she didn't love him as much as he would've wanted her to, but they got married regardless. Their wedding was on her birthday and I think that says a lot about him. He thought he was her gift is how I see it.

I was born in 1973. From very early on what I remember about my parents was a lot of drinking and a lot of fighting. I remember being in kindergarten and being afraid that my parents were going to kill each other. It caused me a lot of fear, a lot of pain, and a lot of sadness, which eventually turned into anger. When my parents would lock themselves in their room and yell at each other our nanny would try to protect us. She'd take us into another room and lock the door. I'd kick her and throw things at her to get out of the room. Then I would stomp around the house, breaking windows and china and anything I could find just to try and get my parents' attention.

I don't remember seeing my parents ever display affection to one another. By the time I was eight, they were fighting constantly and being at home was unbearable for me. By second grade, I was acting out and getting in trouble in school My parents were called into my class because I wasn't listening, wasn't paying attention. I was aloof and distracted.

How did my father try to solve the problem? He bought me a guitar. Of course I didn't go to guitar classes and I certainly didn't have the discipline to practice. There were no suggestions as to what I was supposed to do with the guitar. I guess it was supposed to be an outlet or a coping mechanism, but it didn't work.

When I was in third grade my mother shook my sister and I awake around midnight and hurried us out of the house and into a taxi. It was dark outside and she was wearing sunglasses because she had a swollen black eye.

We went to my grandmother's house with my dad following us in his car. We ran into the house, and I was crying and didn't know what was happening. I remember my grandmother yelling at my father, cursing at him.

The next thing I remember is being at party where there was drinking and a lot of strange adults I didn't know. I was locked in a room but I was able to break out of that room by kicking my uncle, who had been blocking the door. When I ran out of the room I saw my mom making out with some guy and a lot of other stuff that children should not be exposed to.

Before long, my mom figured she couldn't live in Colombia anymore so we moved to the States. My uncle had sent one of my aunts to Houston to get away from her boyfriend and to study English, so my mom decided to move there. My sister and I lived with my dad for two years back in Colombia while my mom started her new life in Texas.

Of course I didn't understand why my mom had abandoned us. My dad tried the best that he could, but that didn't mean very much. I remember when I turned 11 I planned my birthday party myself. I invited a teacher and four classmates to the house and made instant tomato soup from a package and opened a bag of chips. I don't think there was even a cake.

That's probably the last memory I have of Colombia because shortly after that my mom came back and took us with her to Houston. I didn't speak a word of English and I didn't want to go, but dad insisted that we should live with our mom, so we did. We moved to Houston and I was enrolled in elementary school. Being the new kid and not understanding English made everything very difficult. I got into trouble and I got into a lot of fights. I was sent to the principal's office a few times. They used to paddle you in Texas and I got paddled a lot. I was bullied and made fun of because I didn't understand English. That hurt and the insults added to my anger.

After a year or so we moved again so my mom could be nearer to her new boyfriend, and I was enrolled at a new school for fourth grade. My teacher was Mrs. Johnson and she was one of the best human beings I'd ever met. Mrs. Johnson was the first person who made a profound difference in my life. She was loving, caring, compassionate, and she liked me. She saw something in me. She would send my mom notes that I was a great kid, that I was very intelligent. It was the first time in my life that I ever felt that somebody thought I was somebody.

I remember being in her classroom and watching the space shuttle Challenger lift off. When we saw it explode, Mrs. Johnson immediately turned the TV off. That was the first time I ever saw an adult cry. I have that memory engraved in my heart. Mrs. Johnson didn't say much. She wasn't weeping, but she did shed tears. Thinking back, that set the tone for what my life would be later on in life. I'd feel pain and then accept it. I was getting good at knowing my own pain.

When I was 10 or 11 years old I was hanging out with another kid at the park on a Saturday. This fifth-grader named Tom came over and said, "Hey, do you guys want to get high?" Neither of us thought about it twice, so the first time I got high, I was in fourth grade. Nothing actually happened, but I think that set the stage for what was to come.

Starting in sixth grade, I went to Pershing Middle School in Houston. My English teacher there, Mr. Reeves, was a very cool guy. He was one of the best-liked teachers and he liked me. He thought I was intelligent and he earned my trust.

One day he saw me walking home and asked me if I needed a ride. I hopped in his car and went with him. On the way he pulled into a big parking lot and asked me if I wanted to learn how to drive.

We swapped seats and he let me drive his car. I was 12 years old and had this teacher showing me how to drive. How cool was that? Mr. Reeves told me that it was a secret, that I couldn't tell anybody because I wasn't supposed to be driving until I was 16. But he wanted to teach me and he trusted me so I kept that secret. Of course, that was how he was able to abuse me later on because he kept me hostage by keeping that secret. He was able to see if I would tell anybody or if I could be counted on not to tell.

A few days later he invited me to his house to play video games, but instead of video games, he put on a porn movie and we watched it together. Then he molested me. When I left, I felt ashamed and I obviously did not tell anybody. But right after that I started skipping school and I started doing drugs. I tripped on acid for the first time when I was 12 and I started hanging out with kids who were just as broken as I was.

At 12 it seemed to me like I had done things that a lot of older kids do. I had already smoked weed in fifth grade. I had skipped class. I had drunk beer. I had done different drugs. I had already done what I thought were a lot of bad things. The worst part was I blamed myself for allowing this abuse to happen because I thought I was a bad kid.

By that time things in Colombia had gotten very difficult. My grandfather's ranches were being threatened by the guerillas so he wanted to move the rest of the family to the States. He bought a small hotel in Miami Beach and asked my mother if she would manage the place. So halfway through seventh grade we moved to Florida.

Even though I was doing all those drugs back in Houston, I was always very athletic. I had joined the track team and the swimming team and the cross-country team so I was pretty active. I guess when you're 13 years old it takes a lot of drinking and drugging for it to really take an effect on you.

But my new middle school didn't have a swimming pool and they didn't have track. They didn't have any athletic stuff for me to do so I immediately started hanging out with the wrong kids and getting high and skipping school.

At this point my mother had her own void that she needed to fill, so she would date any guy who would look at her the right way and say the right things to her. This time she was dating a Canadian guy and going back and forth to visit him in Canada. That meant that my sister and I were by ourselves a lot of the time. Yes, my aunt was living in the hotel, too, so my mom figured we weren't technically alone, but in reality we had no adult supervision and I took advantage of that situation until my mom finally said that she couldn't deal with me anymore.

Her solution? Send me back to Colombia to live with my dad.

When I started school back in Colombia I was seen as this cool American kid. I had a skateboard. I had weird hair. And I could speak both Spanish and English.

From the first day I started getting high and I joined the basketball team and I had an incredible time. I hadn't been good enough to play basketball on the team in Houston but I was good enough to become an instant celebrity at my boarding school in Colombia.

I had gone from being a nothing in the states to being on top of the world back in South America. The bad news was that there was drinking, partying, and a lot of drug use at the school. By the time my dad figured out what was going on, I was already doing cocaine and smoking weed, tripping on acid. I tried something called *basuco,* which is what crack is called in Colombia. It was horrible because I did things to get high that I would never do if I were sober.

One time I stood on a street corner and let a guy grope me for $20 just so I could get high. I was picked up by the police. I stole counterfeit US dollars from people I knew. I started stealing drugs from people who were sending drugs to the U.S. I got into a fight with a drug dealer. I stole my dad's car and totaled it. Worse, he was working for the Colombian government at the time, and they had given him a car that only he or his driver could use. Since I had destroyed it, he was at risk of losing his job.

Deep in my core, I didn't want to be that rebellious and bad kid. I knew that I had it in me to be a good person, but I had no control over what would happen when I started drinking or using drugs. After that crash, my dad couldn't deal with me either so he sent me back to the States. Suddenly I was 18 years old and back in the U.S. where the drinking and partying continued as if I had never left. In all the time I'd been away, it seemed that nothing had changed.

When my mom first moved to Houston, my grandmother, the one who had cursed my dad all those years ago, was a very religious, deeply devout Catholic. She used to pray and count her rosary every night. When I cried about missing my mom, my grandmother told me that if I prayed with enough faith I would have the family that I wanted. So right before my mom left for Houston, I used to get up early in the morning so I could walk to a church close to the house and pray that I would have that family. But it seemed like God was either too busy for me or he just didn't exist. I believed it was all a figment of my grandmother's imagination. That's when I stopped believing in the God that my grandmother had taught me about.

Once I got back to the U.S. my mom kept saying, "You need to do something with your life." So I enrolled at Johnson & Wales University because I just wanted to get her off my back, and I thought cooking was pretty cool. I thought being a chef would be the perfect career for me because you work at night and you could drink in the kitchen.

While I was there I had a friend who got in trouble and was being deported. He drove a Corvette and he gave it to me for safekeeping before he left. The day I got the Vette, I went to a party and got ripped. I was at a friend's house, drinking, smoking, and doing everything else. I was so wasted that I didn't remember to put the car's lights on.

I was driving in the dark and got pulled over by the police. I was drinking a beer and I got so scared when I saw the flashing blue lights in the rearview mirror that I spilled the beer all over myself. Of course the policeman knew I was wasted. "Have you been drinking? he asked.

"Just a little" I said.

He arrested me.

My drinking and drugging were out of control, and my mother didn't know what to do with me, but she knew that I'd be safe in jail so she left me there for a couple of days.

While I was behind bars, I promised I would never drink again and my life would turn over. Unfortunately, those promises didn't last. By that summer I was already drinking again and getting into all kinds of trouble. It continued until my mom simply told me, "You either go into treatment or I'll kick you out of the house."

I was almost 21 and I had nothing to my name—no job, no money, simply nothing. Treatment was the only option.

I was shipped off to a treatment facility in Mississippi. I was there for three months. I was part of a sexual addiction treatment program because I had a lot of issues with women and sexuality because of the abuse I had suffered.

I did well in the program. I did so well that after three months I was given permission to go home for a weekend visit. The visit went well and I felt good. I had gone three months and hadn't touched a drug or a drink. So I was on the train back to Mississippi, and this guy sitting across from me asks, "Hey, do you smoke?" I said, "No, no, no. I don't smoke." He said, "Do you mind if I smoke, and can you just look out for me?" I said, "Sure."

But as soon as I smelled that dope, it was like I was roped back in. I said to him, "Let me take a hit of that." I got high and immediately I felt such shame. I realized I had thrown away three months of hard work in a second, but I decided not to tell anybody. After all, it was just weed. It wasn't a drink; it wasn't coke. I was still technically sober. I didn't tell anybody and now I had a new secret to deal with.

Back at the treatment facility there was a whole community of sober people who were supporting each other. When I returned I never told anybody about what I had done on the train. I got a job and started working, but I always kept that secret within me until I couldn't live with it anymore. I felt like such an imposter. Here I was saying that I was sober, but I knew in my heart that I had already used, that I had gone back to smoking again.

On Valentine's Day of '97, I got arrested again. This time for reckless driving and having an open container in the car. I got out of jail after a few days but I didn't stay out of trouble for long.

I was going to a party in a friend's van. We had a considerable amount of weed and other drugs in the van with us. For some reason I decided that it would be funny if I mooned the people in the car next to us. Turns out the car was full of undercover FBI agents, and they pulled us over to give us a scare. Fortunately, they never searched the car. The guy that was driving wasn't drunk yet and they let us go. But everybody was pissed at me.

We got to the party and I got high and drunk. Too high to know better, my friend and I climbed up to the roof of the building. When we got there my friend and I looked at each other and said, "There's nothing else for us to do. Let's just jump and end it."

We walked up to the ledge and got ready to jump off, but before we did it, he looked at me and he said, "Wait. We need to let people know how the world wronged us and why we're jumping; let's write a manifesto." So he convinced me not to jump. Instead, I went home and checked into South Miami Hospital for treatment.

When I got there the director didn't care how many drugs I used. He didn't care about anything I had done. He just asked, "What's your story?" Up until that point, my excuse was only, "I'm from Colombia. I moved here. My parents got divorced." The story was never really the story that I'm telling you now. The story was always a superficial story that really didn't come from the heart. What it did was help me evade as much pain as possible.

For the first time I had this guy who was asking me and prodding me to go in deeper and look at my real story. I slowly started seeing that even though my parents had done the best they could with the resources that they had, it was certainly not enough. Not to blame them, they did the best that they could, but the best they could do was simply terrible for me.

A month into that treatment, I heard somebody share their own story and share their own pain and discuss what they were doing when they were 12 years old. I related so much to that story that I felt that guy's pain and I couldn't stop crying. For the first time in my life, I was sober, and I was feeling pain, and it hurt. It hurt a lot. I couldn't stop sobbing and I couldn't stop shaking.

That was the turning moment for me.

There was a guy at treatment who was loud and obnoxious and I hated him. I always complained to my sponsor about this guy. Finally I said, "What should I do about him? Should I fight him?"

My sponsor said, "You need to do something nice for him. You need to do something nice for him and do it with love."

I was like, "What? I can't do that. I can't do anything." But because I had gone to culinary school, I knew how to cook. I knew he had lived in Mexico and he loved Mexican food. So I invited him for breakfast, and I made *huevos rancheros*.

That act of listening to somebody with more experience and then doing something for somebody I didn't like really opened the door to who I am today. That gift of breakfast started a friendship that has lasted 23 years now.

Once I got out of treatment, I went back to community college. I went to the Honors College and got great grades. I became president of the Honors Society. I won an internship to work at a psychiatric hospital in Bedford, Massachusetts.

I was able to shadow the director of that center, Dr. Dolly Sadow, who is an amazing clinician. I was under her wing for about six months. During sessions, she would ask me how I was doing.

During my internship I made a connection with a veteran who no one had been able to connect with. All it took was sitting on a street corner in Boston and smoking a cigarette with him. After that day, he'd ask where I was. It was a surprise to everyone in the program because nobody had been able to build rapport with this guy. They were all psychologists, psychiatrists, PhDs, and they hadn't been able to connect with him. Yet this kid, who was not even a graduate student, had been able to make a connection. Dr. Sadow told me that the most important thing was the ability to connect with people because that's when transformations happen. She told me that she didn't know if I would ever be a great therapist but she knew that I would be a great healer.

After I finished the internship, I came back home and started working on the Universal Pre-K Amendment in Florida. I visited almost every county collecting petitions so that every four-year-old in the state of Florida could go to Pre-K for free. When that passed, the mayor offered me a job in his office as his protocol coordinator. And when he decided to run for the U.S. Senate, he asked me if I would go and manage his campaign in Orlando, Tampa, and Daytona.

Around the same time, my cousin had a friend from Colombia who was coming to live with her for about six months. She said, "Hey, if you want to take her out for ice cream or just to show her around, it'd be nice." And now, after 16 years and four kids and a dog and a house and a beautiful life, we're still together.

After I finished community college, I won a presidential scholarship and went on to college. During my first semester my cousin Alex was diagnosed with osteosarcoma. When he got sick I'd finish class and jump in my car and shoot across the state to Naples to spend time with him. I also became his family's translator because they didn't speak English well. Being with my cousin and my uncle and aunt became more important to me than going to school.

Because I was taking care of my cousin, I spent six months totally neglecting my classes. I was able to spend the last six months of his life with him, and I was there when he passed away. After so many years of disappointing my family I was finally able to be there when they needed me. Yes, I lost my scholarship, and yes, I had flunked out of school again, but I didn't care. My heart was full because I had done what I needed to do, which was to be there when it mattered.

Soon after my wife and I got married, I started working for the new mayor, but before very long we had a child and I needed to make more money. I went to work for an organization that works with children who are in foster care. Although I had worked on the Universal Pre-K amendment, I'd never really been exposed to the world of foster care.

My office was upstairs from the shelter where they used to bring kids when they had been removed from their homes. I met a ten-year-old named Israel. He was incredibly smart but he was a little troublemaker. Israel would sneak upstairs and break into all of the offices and take gum or take things like pens and stuff.

I would bring him to my office and just let him hang out with me. Although my job was development and raising money, I knew I could make an impact on this kid's life. Unfortunately, management didn't see it that way. To them my job was simply to raise money; I was not a therapist or a psychologist or a counselor. My job was to raise money so I shouldn't be wasting time with talking to the kids or spending so much time with them.

When I learned about Guardians Ad Litem, I left that place and joined Voices for Children. I was told all I was supposed to do was raise money there too, even though that wasn't really what I wanted to do.

Yes, raising money was important, but I wanted to see how we could transform these kids' lives. I knew from my involvement with Israel that we had the ability to impact kids in a very profound way if we simply took the time to listen to them, ask the right questions, have compassion, love them, and not judge them.

When I started at Voices for Children I was working for a divisive board; everyone was pulling in different directions. Eventually we developed a cohesive group and they saw that even though our mission was to raise money for the Guardians Ad Litem program, we had a lot more leverage. We could do a lot more than just simply raise money. Thanks to this new understanding of child welfare, we started a number of very successful programs that changed the way the overall system works.

About five years ago the director of one of those programs we had started was making a presentation at a regional summit in Orlando. When I walked in the room she recognized me. She stopped her presentation and said, "Oh, my God, one of our founders and one of the reasons why we're all here today just walked in the room. Please give him a round of applause." Everyone stood and clapped. That was nice.

Afterward, a young woman approached me and said, "Thank you so much for everything you've done. I appreciate it."

I told her I wanted to learn more about her program. "Why don't we get together for lunch, and you can tell me your story?"

We got together the next day and I told her my journey. It was very close to this story that I'm telling you, minus the sexual abuse, but definitely the drugs, and definitely my mom leaving me and all of that.

Then she told me her story, which was about her being a teen prostitute. Despite what I'd been through I couldn't believe what I had just heard. "But what do you mean?" I asked.

"Yeah," she said. "I was part of a house and I used to dance at clubs. I had a pimp and I had to work every night."

I couldn't believe what I was hearing. How could this be going on and nobody was stopping the guy who did this. I started to mentor this young woman, and she became a friend and really an expert in what human trafficking is, what it involves, the damage that it causes, how it begins, who is at risk.

Because of my relationship with her, I learned about the world of human trafficking and I got Voices for Children involved. Today I mentor about 12 young women who have been victims of human trafficking. And that guy, her trafficker, is in jail. Even better, the young woman whom I still mentor is about to finish law school and will soon be an attorney.

Last year she called me and said, "Listen, don't take this the wrong way. I appreciate everything you've done for me. I appreciate that you're my mentor. But you're too pushy when it comes to having us prosecute our traffickers. Frankly, you haven't even gone after the teacher who abused you so what right do you have to tell us that we should do that?"

A couple of days later, my 12-year-old daughter was diagnosed with appendicitis. Her mom and I were with her in her hospital room when the nurse walked in.

"Listen, I have to ask you some personal questions" she said. "Do you want your parents to stay in the room or do you want them to leave?"

My daughter stared at her for a minute and said, "I don't want my parents to leave my sight."

So the nurse started going down her checklist, asking questions like: "Do you smoke? Do you vape? Do you drink? Do you do drugs? Are you sexually active? Do you like boys or girls?"

My daughter hesitated for a minute and then answered slowly. "I don't like any of those ... I don't like anything."

She was looking at this woman like she's crazy and I could almost hear what my little girl was thinking: What kind of questions are these? I'm just 12 years old.

And all of a sudden, I realized that I had been the exact same age when that man took advantage of me. He had carefully groomed me because I was a child. Regardless of how big I thought I was in my mind, regardless of how badass I thought I was, there was nothing that that child could've done to protect himself against this abuser, the pedophile who had violated my trust.

As soon as my daughter got out of the hospital, I made the call to the Houston police department, and I reported the abuse that had occurred 30-plus years before. Now I understood what this young woman meant when she said I was too pushy because that call to report my abuse was the most difficult call I've ever made in my life. But it peeled a layer of shame off of me.

When I was at the treatment center and I spoke about my sexuality and my abuse and what I had done to get high, one of the therapists said to me, "Listen, you don't become Chinese just because you eat Chinese rice." And that comment opened up a whole new world of possibilities. I've forgiven myself and I've forgiven my abuser. That doesn't mean I've forgotten; I still want him to be brought to justice so he can't hurt any other children.

Since I called the police department to report my abuser, I have begun to own my story in a complete way without worrying what people are going to think of me and without feeling like I'm going to be judged. I know I have a beautiful family. I know that what happened to me doesn't define me.

A lot of things have happened in the last ten years of my life, physical, emotional, and mental. But I think the biggest change has been the spiritual growth that I have experienced. That has been thanks to my wife who has been the key to everything good that has happened in my life.

When you train for a marathon, you can see your development, you can see yourself getting fitter, you can see your times getting faster. You can measure your pace. You can see the improvement.

When you're studying for a test, you can gauge how advanced you are by the scores you get.

But an improving spirit is very difficult to measure. How can you tell how you're advancing other than how you react to everything that happens outside of you? Do you surrender? Do you fight? Do you have faith? Do you need to control everything?

Finally I can say that I've returned. I am the prodigal son. I've come back to the church, to the loving arms of our creator. I know that I am the beloved son of God, and I know that I was loved with an infinite love even before I was created. I see this in my faith. I see this in everybody that I work with. Yes, it's important to be educated and yes, it's important to be healthy. But in the end we are all called upon to be children of God. Spiritual growth has become the center point of my life and it's what I want the young men and women I work with to know and develop so they can set themselves free too.

Terry Bell,

Former Creative Director,

Vickers & Benson

I met Terry Bell at an advertising event in Taos, New Mexico and we quickly became friends.

Years later, my wife and I were house hunting. We had found a home we loved but it was a bit beyond our budget. We were driving from the house to grab a bite to eat and we were debating whether or not we should stretch and buy the home. That's when my phone rang. It was Terry and he said, "Are you sitting down? You won't believe the choice my doctor just gave me. I don't know what to do."

After listening to Terry's story and doing my best to be helpful, I hung up the phone, wiped my eyes, and said to my wife, "What are we waiting for? Let's buy the house today."

Terry Bell

My high school was probably responsible for me getting into the advertising business.

Why?

Because I was absolutely miserable there. High school in Canada was usually four years long—from grade nine through grade 13—a lengthy period. John Roberts was the premiere where I lived in Ontario, and the joke was that I was on Roberts' 10-year plan because I kept repeating every grade at school.

I failed grade nine, I went on to grade ten. I failed grade ten. I went to summer school in grade ten, made up the difference, and then quit altogether during first semester in grade 11 because I just couldn't handle it anymore. So now I have a great tenth grade education and I'm living at home. My relationships at home were somewhat tense because my parents and I didn't see eye-to-eye on my freedoms and personal liberties.

I realized that I had to get out but in my mind, I had no way of escaping. That finally changed when a neighbor who was in the advertising business said to me, "Hey, you like to write, right? I've seen some of the stuff you've written. Why don't you apply at the advertising agency I work at? Maybe you could get in there as a junior writer."

Of course, when you're unemployed and you like to write and you want to escape from home, that just sounds like a whole lot of wonderful.

So I put together a résumé that talked about how I had worked in a shoe store and how I made ice cubes in an ice factory, and I thought, *Okay, I've got to add something more than that to impress them,* so I started quoting Plato and Cicero and got all philosophical, and I went and I met the vice-president of an advertising agency called Vickers and Benson. We talked and he looked at my résumé and he smiled warmly and he said, "Okay, I'll talk to the creative director and I'll see if there are any openings. I'll get back to you."

And he did. He called me back and said, "You know what? There's absolutely zero opportunity for you as a junior writer here right now, but there is an opening in the mail room if you want it."

And I said, "Yes, I do. I do want to take that."

And that was the beginning of my career in advertising. I got into the mail room, I did something that nobody else in that job did, which was to put on a decent suit and show up on time. I pushed the mail cart around and I got to meet everybody in the agency because I would walk into their office with a stack of stuff and put it in their boxes and along the way we'd talk. And then the opportunity came up for somebody in the broadcast production department, running a projector and splicing tape and splicing film together, and they said, "Would you like to do that job?" And I said, "Yes, absolutely."

Working in the broadcast production department, I got to meet creators from outside of the agency, people who were writing jingles and doing music, and one of those people said, "Why don't you come over and represent me?" And I thought, "That could be fun."

So I went there, and I became an agent for a very, very successful jingle writer in Toronto named Terry Bush and my salary increased considerably. My job was to go around to other advertising agencies and sell his work as a composer. Doing so I met a lot of agency creative people and I was offered jobs at various agencies. I accepted one and then another and before long I had worked at probably three different agencies, and by the time I was about 25 I was offered the opportunity to return to Vickers and Benson, as a writer and then as an associate creative director.

If it all seems kind of random, it's because it was. I didn't have any thoughts about how long I might be there. For me the interesting part was the chance to create and write. And then, as so often happens within the ad business, you realize that the quality of your work is often client-dependent, meaning what you work on determines the quality of the work that you do and the quality of the client you get determines the work that you do. And

I think most people in the creative business who are successful manage that, which is to say that if you can't work on good business that's going to help build your portfolio at one agency, you leave and go somewhere where you can.

So I went through that process repeatedly. I would join an agency and I would do the best I could on whatever business I was assigned and then I'd realize that maybe that wasn't going to expand my portfolio in a way that I wanted it to, and I would leave that position and look for another job somewhere else. And that's interesting for me because I think there's this sort of thought process that says I've done this for a while, maybe a long while, and now I need to do something else. So that represents the pivot point, and I think that's a creative person's job. After all, not everybody gets to sign with the Yankees and spend their whole career there; you have to make moves to enhance your opportunities.

In my case I worked at Vickers and Benson. I left and then returned and then I left again and I probably worked at another nine or ten agencies in between, including three stints at McLaren Advertising.

When I was at McLaren, I was involved in one of the most newsworthy things to happen in Canadian advertising at that time. One day I received a call from *The Globe and Mail,* which is Canada's national newspaper. They asked me if I would comment on the latest Canadian Airlines commercial that featured the chairman of the board of Canadian Airlines. I told them that I'd be happy to but I'd have to run it by my president to make sure he's on side with me talking to the press. And so I did that. I checked in with him and I invited him to the interview lunch, and he said, "Oh no, there's no reason I should go to that lunch. You'll do a great job."

So I did the interview and I told them that the commercial was terrible and why I thought it was terrible. You see, the chairman of the board of Canadian Airlines never once looked into the camera, which meant he never once looked into the viewer's eyes, which was pretty darned boring.

The day after that went to press, I got called into the office at McLaren and immediately fired for cause. The reason I was fired was because, unbeknownst to me, McLaren's Calgary office had the tiniest bit of Canadian Airlines business, and when the chairman of Canadian Airlines saw the article in the national paper, he called up the president of McLaren Advertising and told him "Get rid of that guy."

And they did. Nobody was more shocked than me.

A day or two after being canned, I was at breakfast and flipping through *The Globe and Mail*, the paper that had run the article, and on the front page of the business section was a headline that said, "Ad man loses job for speaking his mind." And I go, "Damn, that guy sounds just like me. Wait a minute … that guy is me!"

Marketing Magazine, which was the Canadian equivalent of *Advertising Age,* picked up the story and they were absolutely bombarded with mail, all of it in my favor. So they took a poll and asked a dozen Canadian ad executives whether I should have been fired or not. In typical Canadian fashion, four people said yes, four people no, and four people said they didn't know. Then *Marketing Magazine* asked some of the biggest advertising brains around the world to comment.

They ran a story titled, "International ad community unanimously backs Bell." The director at Saatchi and Saatchi, who I love, said, "Not having an opinion should be a fireable offense." And that pretty well summed it up for me. So even though I was now unemployed, I had a big door opened for my third time around at Vickers and Benson. That's when a man by the name of John Hayter, who was in the process of buying the agency got ahold of me and said, "You know what? I love gutsy work and I would really like to talk to you about coming to join us."

We had that meeting and he said, "What would you be looking for?" And I said, "Well, you know I have another job on the table at the moment, and they're offering me a lot of money, but my concern is that I don't ever want to be in a position again where I'm that easy to get rid of—I'm not willing to be an employee anymore." Hayter came back a couple weeks later and said, "We'd like to have you be a partner in our company." And that's when my third and final journey at Vickers and Benson began.

At the very beginning, when I was working in the mail room at Vickers and Benson, I married a girl I had gone to school with. That lasted for about five years, until one day we looked at each other and said, "What the hell did we do, getting married at 21 years of age? That was kind of silly. Let's not do this anymore." And then on my return trip for the third time to Vickers and Benson, I was married again. But not long after that we split.

My third time there I met a woman named Victoria who was a junior account person. I had more or less promised myself that I would never be involved with anybody who worked where I did, but love has a way of altering the course of just about everything.

Victoria and I snuck around with the idea that absolutely nobody was going to know about this. And it was maybe six months into that sneaking around that somebody said, "Oh my god, we saw you like, six months ago on the street holding hands and making out. We've known about you two forever." So clearly, the jig was up. Victoria was an account executive at that time, and she realized that her future at Vickers and Benson was not going to work out terribly well. She believed, and rightly so I think, that anything good that would happen to her would be seen as a result of her connection to me. And that wouldn't necessarily be true, but she believed that would be the perception so she left.

At this point, life was good. Life was very good and Victoria and I decided to get married. One of the things that we talked about was not to have kids. Let's not talk about having kids until we've been married for a couple years, and then we can do that, but let's just suck up some oxygen on our own for a while. So that's what we affectionately refer to as the Häagen-Dazs years, where all of life was just a big party, just a wonderful, easy party—no kids, no responsibilities, no nothing. And the business was doing extremely well. I was fulfilling my own personal goals, which were winning best TV Commercial three times in Canada, cleaning up at the award festivals, doing all sorts of cool, good stuff, and just generally loving what I was doing.

And then babies came into our life and I became a first-time father at the age of 52, much later than most people. And so now there were my twin babies and a woman I adore and life was moving along at a really, really rapid pace within advertising. There are a lot of pressures within the business and the subject comes up in the office that given our ages maybe we should consider what's going to happen as we move on. Maybe my partners and I should start to think about selling the business.

The general consensus was that we should actually get busy on this, because the process could take some time. And at that time, my partner, John would have been about 59 years old, and

Jim would have been a little closer in age to me, so he would have been somewhere around 54. We figured we'd put it out there and see how it went.

That became the most pressure-filled time of my career in advertising and probably the least fun. Just prior to doing that, John, who was president of the company, said, "You know what? I really don't want to do this job anymore. Let's go hire somebody to be president." And I said, "I'll do that job. I'll be the president." There's a great example of being careful about what you ask for in life, because you're just liable to get it.

So I was president of an advertising agency for a couple of years, and it was just a terrible decision on my part, because it pulled me away from absolutely everything that I loved to do. When you're the president of an advertising agency, you spend a lot of time putting out other people's fires and a lot less time actually doing the work. I think that probably was the beginning of my pivot out of the business. I started thinking that maybe there should be life after advertising, particularly probably because of my two babies.

It took close to three years to sell the business. And that's because there were several suitors and we spent a fair amount of time with each of them, trying to figure out their level of sincerity, and then what they envisioned would be a good deal and whether or not we thought it was a good fit, and how might it be structured and yada yada yada yada.

I think we made a smart decision when we decided to find somebody to broker our business. We chose a venture capital company that had experience in that area and we told them, "We would like our conversations with our suitors to be about the business and how to grow the business and the quality of work. We'll leave all the financial stuff to you guys so we don't actually have to sit across the table with our suitors and talk about money." And that was a hugely smart decision because it kept us focused on what we actually did best.

So we went through a number of suitors. We had the largest Canadian agency wanting to talk about buying us and they wanted us to talk about going public and structuring a share deal with us. But I don't think we ever found the love we wanted there. And then we had a deal that was cut, a done deal in our minds, with a terrific U.S. agency out of Boston called Arnold Advertising. We signed on the dotted line and the deal was going back to Boston for them to sign. But on Monday we got a call saying, "The deal is off because the chairman of Arnold just bought the Washington Redskins."

I think he paid 780 million dollars or something like that and the board said, "That's it. There's no more buying anything else for a while, because that's big." We were a little heartbroken about that because we thought this was going to be the deal we wanted and we liked Arnold a whole bunch.

Oddly enough, about a year later we got a call from a company in Paris, France called Havas Communications. They said, "We're about to buy an agency in the United States by the name of Arnold Advertising. And Arnold told us that we should be talking to you, too. They have a big love affair with you guys and they think that you and they would be absolutely simpatico, so we're talking to you, too." We met with the people from Havas and we closed the deal with them pretty quickly and we became V&B Arnold Worldwide.

My partners and I all had three-year agreements to stay and build the business. I think we did a terrific job. We brought in the right management group so we could exit and not damage the company. I put creative directors in place and I put myself in the position where I was the agency Yoda. I sat in my corner office and once, twice, maybe three times on a busy day, somebody would come into my office and say, "We got a problem here. What would you do?" And I would give them that knowing Yoda look and say, "Well, if it were me, maybe I'd do this…" and they'd say, "Oh, that' just fantastic. Thank you." And they would leave, and that was my day.

After two years of that, I went to my partner John and said, "I don't think I can do this anymore. I've got to get out.

And he said, "Well, it's funny that you're saying that now, because I just heard from the people at Arnold and they want you to sign on for another three years. They just think it would be a really cool thing and of course there's good money in it."

And I said, "Well, it would be a really good thing for *them* perhaps, but I'm going to put a gun to my head if I have to do this Yoda act any longer." You've got to go to them and say, "Is there a problem with Terry leaving early?"

And I remember the question my partner asked me next, which is probably a key question to the issue of pivoting. John said to me, "Holy moly, you really want out. Do you have enough?"

And I went, "Do I have enough what?"

He goes, "Are you going to have enough to live on? Do you have enough going forward? What are you going to do?"

And I could see a sense of almost panic in his question, and I said, "Well, I've given it some thought and I think the answer is yes, I do, but now that you're mentioning it, I'm not really sure." And ultimately I decided that I think I did; I think I had enough.

And that allowed me to say, "Yeah, I'm going to leave this business; I'm going to see what happens next." So I did.

Before I exited, my former art director Larry Gordon and I started a very small freelance company called Big Lovin'. The business card we designed from Big Lovin' showed two absolutely gorgeous women in bathing suits, identical twins, and they each weighed about 300 pounds. Our whole idea was that two minds are better than one, and we went out as a little freelance opera-tion to other agencies in town.

We quickly got picked up by a friend of mine who said, "Now you got to come work with my agency on a freelance basis. We went and did that and it lasted for about a month-and-a-half, until I told him, "I'm sorry, but I'm not having fun and I don't want to do this anymore." And I left and that was it. I never looked back. I never went back into advertising.

I think there's a really critical point that people have when they think about pivoting. A friend of mine was a lieutenant colonel in the Air Force and he retired about five years ago. He had done his time and he was thinking, *Oh god, I'm thinking maybe I should get out but what am I going to do with myself?* You could hear all that angst going on.

Since I had done it, I said to him, "You know, there are a lot of those questions that you cannot be expected to answer now, and that's because you've never had time away from the thing that you're now contemplating leaving."

There are people who have clear and decided ideas of what they're going to do when they leave and that makes it easier, and there are people who say, "Oh, I've got to get out of here, but I have no idea what I'm going to do."

That's absolutely reasonable because what people need is time away to let things steep, to let things brew, to let things boil away and allow them to see their life in a completely different way again, and that's just not possible without leaving whatever you've been doing.

And I remember my friend Jack, who was the lieutenant colonel, said to me, "Well, you've got to throw me a line here. What is the single best thing about retirement?"

And I said, "The single best thing about retirement, and truly the most meaningful for me, is dominion over your days. You are not at the beck and call of anybody other than yourself."

He carried that forward and now, five years later, he tells me, "You were absolutely right; that's the best part." So much so that it's worth it even if you have to reduce your financial expectations and your style of life to maintain that autonomy over your days. I think that is clearly the best part of it.

After exiting my agency I was absolutely weary and fatigued. It was like, *Oh my God! Enough already!* But flash back to the fact that I became a first-time father at 52. There were also two really important factors in my decision, and they go by the names of Chloe and Spencer.

I had not only left the business, I now had three-year-old twins and they represented a whole new world for me. Now I could actually be a father the way I never knew a father to be and I don't think any of my friends knew, either, and that was that I was generally available to my children all the time. That was a whole level of newness and excitement.

I remember saying to people, "Wow, this opportunity exists," and they said, "Oh my God! Really? Those little kids are going to drive you nuts." And because Victoria was about to retire, too, another thing I heard was, "You've now got two retired people living under the same roof with two little kids. Aren't you absolutely going to go insane? How are you going to do that? Even when the kids start school, how are you going to do it, living under the same roof all this time with your partner?"

Victoria and I had been absolutely outstanding at giving one another space, which we understood became our way to make it all work, just granting each other all sorts of room to move around, and that made it easy for us to do this together.

One of the great gifts we give ourselves is when we decide to grow up and do what works for us right now. We can take something that doesn't work anymore and say, "I don't have to be that way." That's the part I hope never changes—this desire to constantly expand.

I left advertising because I knew it didn't match up with my concept of life; it didn't jive with my soul, and that struck me as a hugely important reason to look for an exit, right? We were at a point where a lot of our angst and frustration in life happens when we do something that doesn't line up with who we are.

I think there are people who will make their pivots for exactly that same motivation, and the reason that happens is because we grow. Hopefully we all grow along the way, and things aren't necessarily the same at year-20 in a career that they were at year-two in a career or year-five in a career or year-10 in a career. Don't you think? I think there must be times where a surgeon is doing their 170th heart operation and they think, *Oh, God. How much longer am I going to be doing this?* I think we reach a point where it dawns on you that you are just mailing it in, right?

You realize that on the worst day you are ever going to have, on your absolutely worst day as a creative guy you're ever going to have, you still are not going to produce a piece of shit. It's just not going to happen—because you're a professional. That day is gone. That is, on all your worst days from now on, you will be better than good. You'll be better than just good. And you'd think that that's a good thing. But instead you say, "Oh, God. Where's the learning curve? Where's this going? What's the point? What am I doing?"

At a certain point in time you say, "Okay, the reason I'm doing this is because I'm making a piss pot full of money and that's just enough reason to do it." And sure, that's admirable and fine, but you can also reach a point where you say, "I'm tired of doing this. I just don't want to do this anymore. I don't care how much they're paying me."

After I had been out a bit we decided there was no reason we had to stay in this big city anymore. We could go anywhere we wanted. And what Victoria and I thought was, *Wouldn't it be better to raise our kids in an environment where they can do something as simple as walk to school from a very early age?* Because back in Toronto, nobody let their kids walk to school downtown anymore just because of the anxiety people had of things going wrong in a big city.

So when we decided to come out here to Halifax, that was part of the plan. It's a tenth—oh my God—it's like a twentieth the size of Toronto, and our kids started walking to school when they were five—four-and-a-half or five, and it was a totally different experience for us to be able to raise them in an environment like this.

I started meeting people who had connections with people in the advertising business, and they said, "I could set you up. Do you want to meet people here? Because they'd be happy to have you. You're this big-hitter from the big city. You're well-known; you've got a great reputation. Would you want to do that?"

And I'd reached a point in my life where I said, "No, I don't want to do that. I don't ever want to go back to the way things were at that point in my life." And they'd ask, "Well, what is it you're actually going to do?" And I kept saying, "Well, I don't really know, but I trust that I'm going to be happy, whatever that thing is going to be."

And people say to me today, "Well, what did you do today? Or what do you do with yourself?" And I swear to God, I'm not really sure how to answer that, because I think whatever answer I'm going to give is going to be incredibly unsatisfactory to them in some shape or form. They will not understand it. In fact, I have a dear friend who says to me, "If I lived your life, it would kill me. I'd die."

There's such emphasis put on "Who you are is what you do," but I don't relate to that much anymore. I don't think in those terms. There's a wonderful Buddhist expression, which is, "Nothing to do; nowhere to be." And I relate to that more than anything. Nothing to do; nowhere to be. That's where I am. I've been retired 15 or 16 years now. I can't possibly imagine another life that isn't giving me these choices that I have.

A few years into retirement and having my twins and moving to Halifax, I was diagnosed with bladder cancer. The doctors said, "It looks kind of aggressive. Here are the paths that are open to you: We can put you through a more traditional thing where we give you a concoction which is a virus that we'll inject into your bladder, and that will either kill your cancer cells or it won't. That's one option."

"The other option is we get really dramatic and we rip out your bladder and we rip out your prostate glands and seminal glands and pelvic lymph nodes and we throw them all away and we make you a new bladder from your upper intestine and we connect all the parts together and with any luck you'll be able to have this new bladder that allows you to pee again and there won't be any more cancer in there."

It's an intense surgery and the recovery time can be a year or more. Even then the thing may not work. You might never get an erection again; you may never be able to stand up to take a leak again. You may have to use a catheter for the rest of your life.

So all of those things were on the table, but going through the process I never said, "Woe is me. Wow! Life! Oh my God! I retired with this idea of having this great life and now my life sucks." That never crossed my mind because by the time that happened, I'm 58 years of age; I've had this incredible life. I have twins who are six years of age. I have a wife who I adore. I'm just going and going. My life sparkles. Period. It doesn't matter whether I'm sick. It still sparkles. And if I'm sick, what a better time to have life sparkle?

So pessimism was never a factor. I never changed my view of what I was going through. And then, a few years later I had a heart attack. Three weeks ago I was in the hospital again for two nights because I had another cardiac event. That turned out not to be a heart attack, but now they're saying, "You might have unstable angina." And I said, "Oh, okay. Let's do something with that if we can." But the constant remains the same, which is I have a fucking awesome life, and neither of those things make it really any less awesome. There are all sorts of people who are in a zillion times more difficult shape than I am, in every facet of their life.

I've even struggled with trying to figure out where my medical adventures fit into the story that I'm telling you, because it really hasn't put a dent in my journey so far. I'm still planning on going to the American Southwest in September and putting several thousand miles on a scooter, and I plan on riding motorcycles again this summer, and Victoria and I plan on booking more trips, and I have a really good friend who has a house in the Florida Keys that I plan on visiting with my honey and hanging with him and his honey. Does any of that make sense?

Listen, I'm not without a whole lot of empathy for people who are diagnosed with cancer or whatever and are going through all the anxiety of *What's going to happen?* Who are they going to be after the surgery? One of the things I hear that people ask is "Why me?" And I never have grasped that concept because I ask, "Why *not* me?" Because at the same time I'm suffering from it, there are only about another 40–50 million people out there who are suffering, who are being diagnosed with something awful. So it really is not about us ever. It's never about the individual; it just happens. It's a random act.

Not to mention that when I looked at my bank balance after they transferred the money from the sale of the agency, I didn't ask, "Why me?" I said, "Cool." But it's the same thing. It's just two sides of the same coin. And you may have figured this out about me by now, but I am a huge believer in good fortune. There are people who are clearly on the side of "There is no such thing as luck; you make your own luck," but I'm not one of those people. I believe that I am hugely fortunate. Another word that might be used is hugely blessed by the Universe, that I'm held in a great state of grace by the Universe. I believe that profoundly, and so I have nothing to whine about because I feel my life has been so incredibly fortunate.

12

Boiling it All Down

That's quite a collection of powerful stories and valuable experiences to learn and grow from. Here's a quick summary of the central themes, lessons, and ideas from each of our new life guides:

Robert's Rules of Order (Robert Mazzucchelli)

1. Transition into something you're really passionate about.
2. It all starts with really knowing yourself. You need to know:
    a. What you're good at.
    b. How much risk you're willing to accept.
    c. What you don't want to do.

3. Know how to manage stress. Robert exercises every day regardless of how long he works.

4. Learn to love the problems. The way you manage them emotionally, physically, and intellectually will determine whether you succeed or not.

5. Remember that you can't cross a wide chasm with two small jumps.

Susan Says (Susan Ford Collins)

1. Most people don't know what success is for them.

2. The right answers are not going to get you where you want to go.

3. Allow chance and serendipity to appear in your life.

4. Love the obstacles.

5. Be open to guidance from the Universe.

6. Lean in and trust the process.

Chris' Craft (Christopher Crowley)

1. Do something you really want to do to use your gifts at the highest level.

2. Repotting yourself can be a true joy.
3. Everything goes to hell unless you do stuff. And that starts with regular exercise.
4. Sing a song you believe in.
5. All of life is a series of breaks and beatings, breaks and beatings. If you don't like today's beating, wait for tomorrow's break.
6. Energy is the key to life.
7. You oughta live more than one life.

Werner's Ways (Seth Werner)

1. Stick with what you know.
2. If you want people to follow you, get them to like you and want to be around you.
3. Always conduct yourself with the highest integrity and honesty.
4. How you do anything is how you do everything.
5. Buy your straw hats in the fall.
6. Wear a tie.

Gayle's Guideposts (Gayle Carson)

1. Be persistent and dedicated. The most important thing you can do is to show up.
2. Follow your heart. Find good mentors but trust yourself too. Do not listen to other people telling you what you can't do.
3. Don't worry about the ones who say "no."
4. Concentrate on the ones who say "yes."
5. Dance every chance you get.

Fraser's Phrases (Alex Fraser)

1. Failure is the key to success.
2. Find good mentors.
3. Your best year can follow your worst. But your worst year can also follow your best.
4. Exploit your natural talents and assets.
5. Your best efforts might not be enough. Always be ready to pivot.

Ed's Edge (Edward Wasserman)

1. Your ability to reach out to your personal network is one of your most valuable assets.
2. You must be a good steward of your contacts and networks.
3. Don't expect that things are going to turn out the way you expect they will.
4. Jump in and learn by doing.
5. Decide what your priorities are. It won't necessarily make things easier, but it may keep you from being regretful.
6. Remember that your experiences and accomplishments may help you in ways you can't imagine yet.

Ian's Issues (Ian Wolfe)

1. It's important to have a vision or moral purpose.
2. Being uncomfortable is the only way to push yourself harder and further.
3. Most people are just trying to survive. Respect and empathy are the ways to build relationships.
4. The only path forward is forward.
5. Never quit.

Nathalie's Notions (Nathalie Cadet-James)

1. Be nimble.
2. Try not to take anything too personally.
3. Move and go, move and go, move and go.
4. Have an advisory board for personal and professional.
5. Access is the key.

Rick's Picks (Rick Beato)

1. Be obsessed with getting things done.
2. Don't worry about having a plan. You can create the plan afterwards when you look back at what happened.
3. Don't forget that the things you've done in the past can help create your present and your future.
4. Keep an eye on what's going on. You never know when opportunity will present itself.
5. It's the opportunities you're presented with and what you do with those opportunities that makes you the person you are.

Rashmi's Rationales (Rashmi Airan)

1. Own your own story.
2. Losing your freedom buys you complete freedom.
3. Sometimes your greatest failures will turn out to be your biggest success.
4. Sometimes the hardest thing you'll ever do can lead to the most pivotal moments of your life.
5. The people who love you are very forgiving of your humanity.

Grimme's Fairy Tales (Michael Grimme)

1. Create a vision of your perfect life for that stage of your life, come up with the checklist to get there, fanatically follow the checklist, and always keep the goal in mind.
2. You only get one opportunity to raise your kids.
3. Write everything down, first defining what the problems are and then what the potential solutions can be.
4. Sometimes you just have to go with your gut, believe in what you believe in, and believe in yourself.

5. Seek out mentors.

6. Listen to what more seasoned people have to say, but always be thinking about what they could be missing with the advice they're giving you because they don't know you as well as you know yourself.

7. Have a roadmap. Because once you know where you're going, you'll get there. And you'll get there faster than you ever thought you would.

8. Always be learning.

9. Once you identify the problem, the solution is out there.

Hincapie's Hints (Nelson Hincapie)

1. Healing begins with respect.

2. Tell your story. And let people tell you their stories too.

3. We have the ability to impact if we simply listen, ask the right questions, have compassion, show love, and don't judge.

4. You don't become Chinese just because you eat Chinese rice.

5. Forgive yourself.

Bell's Bellwether (Terry Bell)

1. Never stop learning.
2. It's not personal.
3. Never ask, "Why me?" Why NOT you?
4. The most meaningful part is dominion over your days.
5. Nothing to do, nowhere to be.
6. Angst and frustration happens when we do things that don't line up with who we are.
7. Sometimes you just need time to let things steep.

13

Looking Forward

Robert Cumberford, Design Editor, *Automobile Magazine,*
May 1999, Saint-Genies, France, wrote about the original Volvo
V8 1800:

> We designers are farsighted people. That's our job. We
> are supposed to see things before others do and act on
> our visions. Sometimes those actions give splendid results,
> sometimes they're just too far in advance of practical
> realities.

If Cumberford is right, then it's not enough to simply look back
at what others have done. We also need to look forward, hoping
for a glimpse at what's coming next. True, we can't see around

corners and we can't see too far ahead, but it can still pay enormous dividends to try. Because otherwise we're just wandering aimlessly, without any clear path in mind.

Besides needing to be farsighted, thinking people also need to be creative in the way we process information. We need to behave like sponges. We must constantly absorb input from all sources—art, literature, music, conversations, news, philosophy, travel, wherever—the same way that a sponge can soak up random hues on a watercolorist's palette.

Then, when it's time to solve our problem, we can reach deep inside and squeeze the sponge and a new color will squish out. It is made up of all the input we've absorbed, but it doesn't look anything like the colors that came before.

Others might look at the result and ask, "Wow, how did you ever think of that?" or say "Big deal; I could have thought of that." But either way, if we've done our job correctly, our result is a new and creative solution to the problem at hand.

What's the Big Deal About Creativity?

A few years ago, I visited Graceland, Elvis Presley's home in Memphis. After oohing and ahhing in the Jungle Room and checking out Elvis' cars and airplanes, we walked through the museum.

Behind the glass was a huge collection of Elvis memorabilia: guitars, motorcycles, posters, and mannequins dressed in his various stage and movie costumes — a highway patrolman outfit, army fatigues, a cowboy getup, a construction worker's jeans and blue denim shirt, the suede breeches and vest of a native American chieftain, a biker's black leather jacket and chaps, and more.

And that's when it hit me! The six guys in the disco band The Village People must have been wandering through Elvis' Graceland museum when they got the idea for their distinctive look. Elvis had assembled all the costumes for them. All they had to do was put them on and start their story telling.

Their looks weren't new. The Village People just put them together in new ways.

Everyone makes such a big deal about creativity. But maybe it's just this simple.

Steve Jobs Got It Right

Deepak Chopra said, "The domain of awareness (is) where we experience values like ... intuition, creativity, insight and focused attention."

Charles Mingus said, "Making the simple, awesomely simple: That's creativity."

And Donatella Versace said, "Creativity comes from a conflict of ideas."

But Steve Jobs said simply, "Creativity is just connecting things."

Based on this simplified understanding of creativity, couldn't you have thought of some of our most recent phenoms?

Facebook?

Facebook is just the online version of those slam books we all passed around in junior high school. We'd fold back the pages and scribble in who we liked, whom we wanted to kiss, and who our friends were. The only thing missing was the Internet. And emojis.

How about eBay?

Its founders took the concept of the flea market or the bazaar, the world's oldest business (okay, the world's second oldest business) and combined it with the power of the Internet.

And Google? The original company was just a digital version of Mrs. Kradish, my elementary school librarian, who knew where absolutely everything was kept on every shelf in the library.

Your Digital Story is Like Mustgo Stew

Maybe I'm thinking too big. Maybe the idea of creating the next Facebook, eBay, or Google is too daunting. In that case, what will you combine in your life that can change the outcome just enough that people will take notice? Like the "Mustgo" stew that my friend Pamela makes from whatever's been sitting in her refrigerator for too long, combining old ingredients in new ways can create wonderful new inventions and appealing new flavors that people haven't enjoyed before.

Good ideas are just like the stuff sitting in your fridge. We've all got them, but few of us have the time, vision, resources, or plain old gumption to mix them in new ways and see them through to fruition. And all too often, even though the great idea is kicking us in the shins, we don't look down long enough to see it.

It's certainly not as obvious as "I saw a bird and invented the airplane," but inspirations and ideas do come from everywhere. Reading Chris Crowley's self-help bestseller, *Younger Next Year* inspired an advertising campaign that improved sales for a Florida retirement community by 62% and created a whole new business for me as well as the idea for a new television reality show, not to mention a rich payout for Crowley. And then, all these years later, Crowley's bestseller—and the relationship it fostered between me and Chris—led to the interview that became an important part of the book you're reading now.

What Do Our Uncommon Life Guides
Have in Common?

Cumberford continued: "A creative person's essence is to take what is common and make it new and to take what is new and make it common." The designer invites us to take what we've learned in the interviews and put those best practices to work for us.

So what were the common themes that reoccurred in the various interviews we've read?

It's Not *What* You Know; it's Not *Who* You Know;
it's Who Knows *You*

Almost everyone you've read about talked about how important their network of contacts was to their journey:

Ed Wasserman said he believed that his network was his most important asset. He talked about running into a friend in Kinshasa and later being recommended for a job by someone he had stayed in touch with. In fact, most all of Dr. Wasserman's moves, to the *Sentinel,* to Casper Wyoming, to *The Miami Herald,* to Steve Brill's company, and to the ethics chair position at William and Lee University all came from the recommendations of people Wasserman knew.

Remember when Alex Fraser said, "...One day a good customer of mine telephoned and said that someone he knew who owned a local bank wanted to talk to me"? That was an example of Alex's investment in his contact list paying dividends for him.

Seth Werner talked about, "...calling a guy I went to school with..."

Ian Wolfe became a climbing guide because of a guy he'd paddled with on the canoe kayak team in high school.

And Chris Crowley had "... the great good fortune to have someone I knew introduce me to Dr. Harry Lodge, one of the smartest guys I've ever met...."

It's interesting that some of our guides, such as Wasserman, actively point out how important their networks are. Others, like sergeant Wolfe casually referred to how their networks pointed them to opportunities. But regardless of the value given to their databases, most of our guides used their networks to help them find their way on their journeys to the next stages in their lives.

Que Será Será, Whatever Will Be Will Be

Another theme that reoccurred time after time was the importance of serendipity.

Susan Ford Collins explained how her pivot happened when she "... bumped—literally—into Buckminster Fuller."

Nathalie Cadet-James found that the person she was planning an event for was also the exact perfect person she needed to advise her on starting her new business.

And Rashmi Airan is actually doing presentations called *From Target to Teammate: The Journey from Adversaries to Allies* with the very same man who prosecuted her fraud case.

Just like the importance of contacts, some of our guides think serendipity is planned or preordained.

Others think it's coincidental.

Susan Ford Collins talked about the Universe providing and guiding your path with "little explosions."

Ed Wasserman talked about how his PhD from the London School of Economics seemed like a waste of time. It didn't show its value until nearly 25 years later when he credited the degree with landing him the Knight Ethics Chair at William and Mary College in Virginia:

> ... that PhD probably gave me a big leg up over other people that might have grabbed that job at Washington and Lee... When I look at the quality of people who don't have a prayer getting a job where I work now, and I look at just how strong their resumes are as journalists, and

how difficult it is to get jobs in academia, well, I got really lucky. And so what I thought was a kind of a career-mutilating choice that I'd made in my mid-20s, where I could have put those five years into my career instead of studying for my PhD, turned out to be a real lifesaver.

Keep on Keepin' On...

Gayle Carson's life is a constant story of not quitting regardless of what anyone said. Remember that when she wanted to work in a radio station, she sat in their reception area until something happened. "I was in the lobby one day and the general manager came out and said, "You're here every day. Who are you?"

I said, "I'm here to get a job."

And he said, "Well, we don't hire anybody like you."

I said, "I know you don't, but I will sit here every single day until you do."

Of course, Carson did keep going back and she got hired.

Not one of the journeys you tagged along on was free of failure or heartbreak. Each one of our guides lived lives just as full of ups and downs as yours and mine. We've seen the same litany of the Nine Ds—Divorce, Downsizing, Disease, Disability, Disasters, Debt, Death, Disillusionment, and Disappointment—repeated over and over in a most demoralizing fashion. But we've also seen those problems dealt with and discarded, allowing our travelers to continue on their journeys with their heads held high and the promise of a brighter future calling them forward.

Ian Wolfe had such a hard time as a freshman at MIT that he simply walked away and spent the next two years climbing mountains in Nevada and Vancouver. It wasn't until he went returned to the school and struggled through three more years that he started getting As and Bs in his senior year.

Alex Fraser told us that playing basketball trained him "to understand that failure is a big part of all the good that happens."

Rashmi Airan learned that what she thought was her greatest failure actually led her to what she now considers her greatest success.

And Seth Werner saw failure as one of an entrepreneur's key motivating drivers, pushing them relentlessly towards success.

And in his writings, Ian Brown "considered the inevitability of failure as a potential benefit."

Nathalie Cadet-James simply said, "Move and go, move and go, move and go."

Ian Wolfe put it this way: "It's about putting one foot in front of the other and never allowing yourself to stop no matter what. If you know that you have no other alternative but forward, when you realize that success is your only option, there's no decision to make—you just keep going. No matter what. Never quit."

Do What Matters to You

Besides the idea that failure is often defined by one's inability to accomplish what they set out to do, we've seen struggles with another kind of failure. That is, the inability to measure up to the potential one believes they had been given. Clearly a life measured by FOMO (the Fear Of Missing Out) is not an easy one.

Author Ian Brown again:

> My guilt is the seeping sense that I missed something, that I haven't lived up to my promise. It's a form of regret that seems to surround everyone to some extent, for all the popular wisdom about not having any.[20]

Berkley dean Ed Wasserman talked about having "some disappointment that I didn't do more or matter more ... I do feel like I've been blessed with a lot of capacity that I haven't used to my satisfaction." But he also realizes that he made the right decisions because of what else mattered to him: "... when it comes to my wife and children, I realize how blessed I've been. I'm happy to have given up what I gave up raising my family. I don't regret any of this."

When asked about meeting one's potential, I think our puckish author, Chris Crowley, put it best, "... that, by the way, is my notion of the secret of life—using your best gifts at the high end of life. I think that's the great secret to happiness."

Don't Go it Alone

Time after time we've heard about the power and significance of mentors.

Alex Fraser told us that he was "… fortunate to have good men in (his) life like (his) dad and Coach Ham."

Nathalie Cadet-James believes that it was a "great service to me to be able to speak with people who have experience, who challenge me, who I learn from. Everyone just gives me advice or encouragement, which is what I need. I have learned how important it is to have an advisory board, whether it's personal or professional."

Thanks to winning an important case, the US Attorney for the Southern District of New York, S. Hazard Gillespie took Chris Crowley under his wing. As Crowley says, "We never really became friends, Gillespie and me. But the great blessing of my career was that he became my mentor. He took me on and just marched me along."

But it's not just a matter of finding mentors; being a mentor is important too.

Nelson Hincapie mentors 12 young women who have all been victims of human trafficking. Cadet-James mentors Haitian students in an inner city high school. And Rashmi Airan even found a young woman to mentor when they were serving their prison sentences together.

It Ain't Over 'til It's Over...

Regardless of the ages of the folks you've heard from, there's one consistent theme they all ascribe to — they're still in the game and still playing to win.

Seth Werner is still making new contacts, still looking for new deals, still defining what success means to him.

Gayle Carson is recording podcasts and creating an online radio network for women over 50. The 82-year-old says that her audience loves me because "... what they do know is that I'm going to keep going for as long as I can. Maybe even a little longer."

Susan Ford Collins, "... just keep(s) learning and researching and discovering and exploring."

Alex Fraser is working on a succession plan for his credit card processing company so he can spend more time on his plans to invest in inner city real estate. According to Fraser, gentrification has been too hard on the people who have lived in their neighborhoods for decades. Fraser believes it's time to try "gentlefication."

Turning 65 and changing his life yet again, Michael Grimme says, "The key is that you always want to be learning. You always want to be learning from others, always seeking out mentors and listening to what they're saying."

In spite of everything he's achieved, Ed Wasserman is transitioning out of his dean's position at Berkley because, "After all these years, I'm still trying to find my voice and make a difference."

And even though serial-pivoter Ian Wolfe earned his MBA from Harvard before he left the army, he is now looking for his next adventure. Wolfe's only advice is the same thing he tells anyone who asks him how to become a Green Beret:

"Never quit."

Always Look on The Bright Side of Life

Despite a medical diagnosis that could have been a potential death sentence, Terry Bell was very clear that he never stopped and wondered, "Why me?" Instead, he asked, "Why not me?" because he understood that his good and bad luck were just different sides of the same coin.

Nelson Hincapie endured almost unimaginable treatment and yet was able to reimagine his life and dedicate himself to helping others. Rashmi Airan lost almost everything she had worked for and held dear. Yet she was able to find happiness tutoring her fellow inmates in prison and feels lucky to be pursuing her potential—all in spite of the details of her sentencing which she points out means that "I'll never own an asset again. I can never have a mortgage. I can never take out a loan. I'm pretty strapped, and that's a huge blow.

And Now for Something Completely Different

At the end of his masterpiece, *The Sun Also Rises*,[21] Ernest Hemingway expressed his dystopic belief that the concept of human beings changing for the better is an unattainable myth. To prove his hypothesis, Hemingway filled almost the 250 pages of his novel with continuous violence and substance abuse. And at the end, his cast of characters wind up precisely where they began – no better off for the horrors they'd been through. And perhaps you're thinking that that should come as no surprise. After all, Hemingway lived a life fraught with the same alcohol abuse, episodic warfare, and blood sports that he wrote about so passionately, ultimately dying a terribly violent death from a self-administered shotgun blast.

Not only can't I write like Hemingway, I also can't agree with his theory. Because as we've seen, lots of people have lived lives full of all sorts of experiences – good and bad – and still used what they've gained and what they've lost to work their way towards fulfillment.

You can too.

While every story we've heard was different, each followed an oddly predictably similar path. Each person talked about starting, struggling, surviving, striving, and finally succeeding. But what I found most interesting was that at some point, our guides were able to eliminate the struggling and surviving phases from their pivots. They'd start, strive, and then achieve success. And even when they weren't successful with their new direction, they'd use that experience to move them along to yet another transformation which could help them get where they wanted to go.

At the same time, we've also seen where our guides did accomplish what they set out to do and still transitioned into something new. For example, staff sergeant Ian Wolfe did the unimaginably hard work it took to become a Green Beret, did work he was proud of, and still decided that he needed to transition because he couldn't affect the changes he wanted within the military's bureaucratic confines. What's more, he learned how great it felt "to be able to do some good in the world without having to carry a gun."

What seemed to change for Wolfe and our other storytellers was that at some point between their earlier forays and their later successes, they decided to follow their own advice and create their own definitions of success. And with that change in mind, they were able to move effectively forward.

Your journey will be different because you are different—different goals, different challenges, different strengths, different weaknesses—and why would you want it any other way?

The beginning of the rest of your life starts the minute you put down this book and head out on your new journey, one very intentional step at a time.

I hope that you have found the inspiration to make change happen and craft your own, personal answer to that oh-so-important question: *Is that all there is?*

Acknowledgements

This book never would have been completed without a lot of help from a lot of very special people.

Of course, I'm indebted to my panel of experts. Their willingness to be open, transparent, vulnerable, and trusting was both an inspiration and an enormous help to me learning about how life pivots happen. A big thank you to Rashmi Airan, Rick Beato, Terry Bell, Nathalie Cadet-James, Gayle Carson, Susan Ford Collins, Chris Crowley, Alex Fraser, Michael Grimme, Nelson Hincapie, Robert Mazzucchelli, Ed Wasserman, Seth Werner, and Ian Wolfe.

Dave Bricker was responsible for both riding herd on my ramblings and editing my thoughts into a cohesive story. And if that wasn't enough, he generously designed the page layouts and applied his masterful typesetting skills to make my words as legible as possible.

Designer Carlos Segura took me at my word when I told him that I wanted a cover that was every bit as thoughtful and challenging as the lives lived by my subjects. He created an innovative piece of art that describes all ±400 pages of the book in just five letters.

Susan Ford Collins, Ana Polyakova, and Caroline de Posada each read chapters as I completed them. Their consistent energy and kind words helped me stay focused, motivated, and excited about this project.

Will and Phoebe Ezell took the concept of the book and interpreted it into workshops, websites, strategic roundtables, and other marketing materials. When the message of *Is That All There Is?* ultimately helps people around the world, it will because of Will and Phoebe's good work.

Books & Books owner Mitchell Kaplan has been a huge source of knowledge and information for me ever since my first book was published in 1999. His experience and advice have made every step of this project easier.

Authors Ross Bernstein, Barry Banther, and Bob Burg and publisher Clint Greenleaf all reminded me of what matters most and helped me keep my feet on the ground while I was reaching for the stars.

Publishing agent John Rudolph at Dystel Goderich & Bourret worked mightily to find the perfect publisher for ITATI? And in a surprising turn of events, each publisher's representative who turned the book down actually gifted me with good constructive criticism all of which served to make the final product even better.

Thank you all.

Notes

1   Ford Collins, Susan (2003) The Joy of Success, Greenleaf Book Press, Austin, TX.

2   This Boy's Life (1993) Knickerbocker Films, Warner Bros

.3   McKenzie, Gordon. (1996). Orbiting the Giant Hairball, The Stinehour Press, Lunenburg, VT.

4   Rumi, Coleman Barks (Translator) (2004). First published 1273.Essential Rumi, HarperOne, New York, NY.

5   Dr. Louise Aronson, *Elderhood,*

6   Epstein, Joseph, The Way We Age Now, The Wall Street Journal Saturday/Sunday, January 18-19, 2020

7   Weiss, Alan (2017) Threescore and More, Bibliomotion, New York, NY

8   BBC. http://news.bbc.co.uk/2/hi/south_asia/8421867.stm

9   "The Virtuous Midlife Crisis," *The Wall Street Journal* by Andrea Petersen Jan. 12, 2020

10 Christoff, Nicholas, (2019) https://www.nytimes.com/2019/12/28/opinion/ sunday/2019-best-year-poverty.html, The New York Times. Dec. 28, 2019

11 Yuval, N. H. (2011) Sapiens, https://www.amazon.com/Sapiens-Brief-History-Humankind/dp/B0741F3M7C/

12 Yuval, N. H. (2015) Homo Deus, https://www.amazon.com/Homo-Deus-Brief-History-Tomorrow/dp/B01MYZ4OUW/ref=sr_1_2?crid=3DB12XFS3S81C&keywords=homo+deus&qid=1572374159&s=books&sprefix=homo+deus%2Caps%2C154&sr=1-2t urkelschapsi-20

13 Haley, Brett; Basch, Marc (2015) *I'll See You in My Dreams.*

14 Sumner, Gordon (1985) *Consider Me Gone,* The Dream of the Blue Turtles

15 Brown, Ian (2015) *60,* Penguin Random House

16 Brown, Ian (2015) *60,* Penguin Random House

17 Taylor, James (2020) Break Shot, My First 21 years, Audible

18 Amabile, T., Kramer, S. (2011), The Progress Principle: Using Small Wins to Ignite Joy, Engagement, and Creativity at Work, Harvard Business Review Press, Boston, MA.

19 Andrews, Andy (April 6, 2012) The Traveler's Gift, Thomas Nelson Publishing

20 Brown, Ian (2015) *60,* Penguin Random House

21 Hemingway, Ernest (1926) The Sun Also Rises

Index

CPSIA information can be obtained
at www.ICGtesting.com
Printed in the USA
BVHW080023240821
614878BV00006B/23/J